WOMEN OF POWER
IN
ANGLO-SAXON
ENGLAND

WOMEN OF POWER
IN
ANGLO-SAXON
ENGLAND

ANNIE WHITEHEAD

PEN & SWORD
HISTORY

AN IMPRINT OF PEN & SWORD BOOKS LTD.
YORKSHIRE – PHILADELPHIA

First published in Great Britain in 2020
Reprinted in paperback format in 2021
by Pen and Sword History
An imprint of
Pen & Sword Books Ltd
Yorkshire - Philadelphia

ISBN 978 1 39900 053 6

A CIP catalogue record for this book is available from the British Library

Typeset in Times New Roman 11.5/14 by
SJmagic DESIGN SERVICES, India.

Printed and bound in the UK
by CPI Group (UK) Ltd, Croydon, CR0 4YY

Pen & Sword Books Limited incorporates the imprints of Archaeology, Atlas,
Aviation, Battleground, Digital, Discovery, Family History, Fiction, History,
Local, Local History, Maritime, Military, Military Classics, Politics, Select,
Transport, True Crime, Air World, Claymore Press, Frontline Publishing, Leo
Cooper, Remember When, Seaforth Publishing, The Praetorian Press, Wharncliffe
Books, Wharncliffe Local History, Wharncliffe Transport, Wharncliffe True
Crime and White Owl.

For a complete list of Pen & Sword titles please contact
PEN & SWORD BOOKS LTD
47 Church Street, Barnsley, South Yorkshire, S70 2AS, England
E-mail: enquiries@pen-and-sword.co.uk
Website: www.pen-and-sword.co.uk

or

PEN AND SWORD BOOKS
1950 Lawrence Rd, Havertown, PA 19083, USA
E-mail: uspen-and-sword@casematepublishers.com
Website: www.penandswordbooks.com

Contents

Acknowledgements vi

Introduction viii

Part I   Pioneers: Abbesses and Peace-weavers
                 in Northumbria 1

Part II   The Saintly Royal Family of Kent 31

Part III   Murder in Mercia and Powerful Royal Daughters 44

Part IV   Serial Monogamy: Wessex Wives and Whores? 70

Part V   Dowager Queens and Mothers-in-Law:
                 Wessex in the Eleventh Century 96

Part VI   On Foreign Soil: Travel, Widowhood and
                 Living in Shadow 126

                 Fair, but not Weak 154

Appendix   The Saints' Cults 159

Notes 166

Bibliography 199

Index 210

Acknowledgements

Writing a book is a solitary experience, but there comes a point when no author can 'go it alone'. I've always been interested in the Anglo-Saxons, and readers of my novels have commented that the female characters are often the strongest. From the persuasive, forceful and sometimes downright uncompromising women of the seventh century, to Æthelflæd Lady of the Mercians and Queen Ælfthryth, all have been subjects of my fiction. As I've begun to write more nonfiction, I've been keen to highlight the lives and careers – almost forgotten and scarcely written – of the other queens, princesses, dowagers, abbesses and 'evil' women of the pre-Conquest period. My first nod of gratitude must therefore go to Claire Hopkins, who listened to my ideas and commissioned the book.

Many people have provided practical help and I would like to thank Lin and David White of Coinlea Services for producing the family trees from my sketches. I'm also grateful to Dr Cathy Guthrie, Hon. Secretary, Tourism Management Institute and Julie Edwards, Senior Tourism Officer at Thanet District Council for their assistance regarding the history of Minster-in-Thanet and to Sister Aelred of the community of Minster Abbey for providing the beautiful photos of the Anglo-Saxon fabric of the building. Mention must also be made of the people who kindly supplied additional images for me to use. Thank you to David Satterthwaite, David Webster, Mia Pelletier, Canon Dagmar Winter, Rector of Hexham Abbey and Esther Russell, Hexham Abbey Parish Administrator, and to Gary Marshall from All About Edinburgh for the image of St Margaret's statue, shown on the front cover.

Thanks as always must go to Ann Williams, whose inspirational teaching when I was her undergraduate student gave me the 'bug' and who has continued to offer advice and information ever since. I should particularly like to express my gratitude to Ann for graciously allowing me access to two of her papers pre-publication and for sending me a copy of a third, published, paper. Vanessa King has been endlessly patient with me as I sought to pick her brains, and Marie Hilder has also been a source of information and inspiration. I'm grateful to both for their insights.

There are still times during the writing of a book when the author feels isolated. At those moments my Pen & Sword 'stable-mates', Sharon Bennett Connolly and Helen Hollick, have always been at the end of, if not a phone, then an email or message. I thank them for their support and friendship.

Introduction

The *Anglo-Saxon Chronicle*, commissioned by Alfred the Great in the ninth century, tells the story, year by year, of the major events in English history. Yet up to the year 1000 there are fewer than twenty occasions where a woman is mentioned by name. Two queens who came to prominence after that time are mentioned more, but before that we are given only the odd cursory reference. Those two queens, Emma and Edith, both had their lives documented in more depth, but in works which were commissioned by, and thus heavily biased in favour of, the queens themselves. In both cases – the *Encomium Emmæ Reginæ* and the *Life* of King Edward the Confessor – there was a specific political purpose behind the writing, and the queens are portrayed in a flattering light. Other information about royal women comes to us from the hagiographies, or *Lives*, of the female saints, but in many cases these were written by, or for, the religious communities which claimed possession of the relics of those saints and so again, were biased towards those houses and against rival claimants. (Arguments about the possession of relics becomes somewhat of a recurring theme during this period.)

Luckily, we have other records besides the *Anglo-Saxon Chronicle* and the *Lives*, but even in these, some women 'talk' to us more than others, depending on the sources and their reason for having been written. We only know about these women because someone had a particular motive for writing about them and we are often only presented with one side of the story. In the earlier period we hear far more about the women of the Church, simply because this is what interested the earliest writers, for example the 'venerable' Bede. We have wild tales – even about those revered as pious nuns – of escape from hot ovens and down sewers, of women bringing animals and even themselves back to life, all of which seem fantastic but were told to serve a purpose.

The woman who escaped down a sewer was protecting her chastity and one who came back to life after being killed was demonstrating her sanctity whilst also solving a murder case. Even the darker tales – three-in-a-bed romps and the murder of innocent children – were told to fit a particular narrative and in amongst the escapology, the saintly virgins and the murderous termagants, we have royal consorts who exerted great influence, not necessarily as queens, but through their children. Despite the rights and privileges and their protection – in theory – by the laws of the land, noblewomen were still prized, whilst not necessarily being valued and there is more than one story of abduction. The bloodline of royal women was something they conferred upon their offspring and it helped to strengthen claims of their husbands and sons.

Often, in fact, we find that women are only referred to in terms of being someone's wife or daughter and perhaps we should not be surprised to find an 'anti-feminist' tone in the religious writings of the early medieval period. However, in the very earliest years of the Christian conversion, the abbesses held a great deal of authority without the Church seeming to mind, and in the later period to be a royal mother was to be the power behind the throne.

Historian Doris Mary Stenton said that, 'The evidence which has survived from Anglo-Saxon England indicates that women were then more nearly the equal companions of their husbands and brothers than at any other period before the modern age.'[1] We should note the words 'more nearly', but women could certainly hold land, inherit it, and bequeath it. They could not be forced into marriage or into a nunnery and were protected by law, as early as the seventh century. The laws of King Æthelberht of Kent, dated around 602, forbid the taking by a man of a widow and prescribe penalties for carrying off a maiden by force. By the time of King Cnut's reign in the eleventh century the laws made it clear that 'a widow is never to be consecrated as a nun too hastily' and that 'neither a widow nor a maiden is ever to be forced to marry a man whom she herself dislikes, nor to be given for money, unless he chooses to give anything of his own freewill.'

A document dated somewhere between 975 and 1030, concerning the betrothal of a woman, or general rules for such an occasion, stated that if a man wished to betroth a maiden or widow, he could only do so if it pleased her and her kinsmen and she had to accept her suitor before the betrothal could proceed. Furthermore, the bridegroom had to declare what he would grant her in return for her acceptance of his suit. Whatever she was granted was guaranteed and was hers to keep if they had a child together. It seems like quite a civilised arrangement, affording her some small amount of financial security.

A marriage agreement from a similar time confirmed that the groom gave his bride some land to give and to grant to 'whomsoever she pleased during her lifetime or after her death', so it was clearly hers to bequeath and deal with as she wished. Another agreement from Kent, from the very early part of the eleventh century, explains that, when a man named Godwine wooed Brihtric's daughter, 'He gave her a pound's weight of gold in return for her acceptance of his suit, and he granted her the land at Street with everything that belongs to it, and 150 acres at Burmarsh and in addition 30 oxen, and 20 cows, and 10 horses and 10 slaves.' It makes clear that, 'Every trustworthy man in Kent and Sussex, is aware of these terms.' It should perhaps be pointed out, however, that the document does not furnish us with the woman's name. Yet, according to law, if a man died intestate, his property was to be, 'very justly divided among the wife, the children and the close kinsmen, each in the proportion that belongs to them.'

A woman was not a man's property. It has been argued that while an example of a marriage contract states, '*cyning sceal mid ceaþe cwene bebicgan*' (a king shall buy a queen with property), there is much evidence that the bridegroom paid the *morgengifu* (morning gift, or bride-gift) to the woman, and that it was not a payment to her father.[2]

Excavation at a cemetery in Lincolnshire recently revealed women to have been buried 'richly-dressed' and laid out surrounded by amber necklaces, glass beads, clasps made of ivory and buckles made of silver. These graves have been dated to around the late fifth to mid-sixth centuries and clearly show that even in the earliest period of settlement, women were highly regarded in society.[3]

So it is perhaps surprising that we do not hear more about the individual women in the documentary sources. But can we find out? Is the information there?

I have studied, read and written about Anglo-Saxon England for many years and have always been aware of the powerful women who walked and worked alongside the key male characters of the period. I have also noticed that the chroniclers were not afraid to mention them, but only in passing, or when their stories, such as that of Æthelflæd, Lady of the Mercians, stood out. It may come as a surprise that women had many legal rights in Anglo-Saxon England and that women were revered and respected. They were important, they played a prominent role in politics and their marriages were not only highly symbolic but also of huge political and strategic significance. Yes, the chroniclers mentioned them, but not as if they were anything unusual, or a phenomenon that needed to be remarked upon. Sometimes the references are written almost incidentally, the role the women played recognised but not analysed.

While the earlier sources found little to remark upon, the later chroniclers waxed lyrical, in many cases going off on flights of fancy, leaving us to try to sift the truth from the hyperbole. In contrast to the succinct and, frankly, sparse entries in the *Anglo-Saxon Chronicle* (*ASC*), we have many more flowery histories from the later, Anglo-Norman, chroniclers, who give us tales of homicidal queens scheming murder and practising witchcraft, often with no attempt at analysis. The history of the abbey of Ely, known as the *Liber Eliensis* (*LE*), for example, will happily tell tales of tenth-century Queen Ælfthryth's pious works whilst also accusing her of devil worship and murder.

Christine Fell agreed with Doris Mary Stenton that Anglo-Saxon women had far more liberties and legal standing than post-Conquest women. But this book's purpose is not to compare pre- and post-Conquest, nor is it to explore the role and lot of women generally. Too many excellent works have already done that, Christine Fell's being one of them. So this book will set out to examine the lives of the individual women of power within a chronological framework, and in a way that has so often been done for the Anglo-Saxon men but not, to my knowledge, for their wives, sisters, mothers and daughters.

Although the title hints at the lives of women in England, this book contains the stories of some women whose influence lay elsewhere but who had Anglo-Saxon heritage. Two notable examples are St Margaret, queen of Scotland, and Balthild, the English slave-woman who became a queen in a foreign land.

Often we hear about even the most powerful women only in relation to their men, unless the women were later venerated as saints. Every now and then there is a small statement loaded with significance: Æthelburh destroying Taunton, Seaxburh ruling for a year, Bebba having a fortress named after her; tantalising glimpses but often no more than that.[4] Of so-called 'warrior women', there are hints in the sources, but far fewer than might be supposed, particularly for perhaps the most famous of them, Æthelflæd, Lady of the Mercians. The paradox of her story will be examined.

These women did not often have direct power, but they had status and influence, even if we do not know precisely what that status was: 'The Church lacked any definition of the role of queens.'[5] We have women who are called queen but have little to do with rule, and a woman who ruled yet was never called queen.

The title of queen, and the role thereof, changed over time and sometimes those who had the title wielded less power than those who were never officially styled *regina*. Queens were mentioned in poetry as being ring-givers. In the poem *Widsið*, a queen Ealhild is described as a 'gold-wearing queen distributing gifts.' A ninth-century queen of Mercia gave a gold ring as a reward and, as we shall see, the ring survives to this day.

Whilst there are many laws protecting the rights of women and widows, including ones prohibiting their being married off against their will, it is doubtful that those royal women given in marriage to cement alliances had very much choice in the matter.[6] Additionally it is arguable how successful these 'peace-weavers' were. It was not always a happy story for these women; some of them endured heartache, but a notable few were able to turn life to their advantage. Queen Eanflæd in the seventh century was one such lady who, whilst suffering personal loss, still had a successful career as mentor and influencer, running her own successful household.

Marriages were often dissolved and of the royal marriages we hear about, many ended because one or other (sometimes both) of the partners chose the religious life. In later centuries, there is a hint that these decisions were not always entirely voluntary. But as will be shown, it is a myth that a cloistered life was one shut away from the world and something to be avoided if possible; certainly those royal women who pursued that life or were given over to it still often had high status and an active role in politics.

Many of the women in this book fall into specific categories – queens, saints, murderers, regents – but several also fall into more than one of those groups. The book is therefore set out chronologically, apart from the last section. This is not an attempt to study the development generally of Christianity, the nature of queenship, or the role of women in wider society, but to give details and analysis of what we know about specific women, although there will be some general comment. It is hoped that the chronological approach will also give a better overall history of the Anglo-Saxon period. For all but the last section, there is a 'family' tree, with the women marked in bold, and those men who were kings of England, or of English kingdoms, marked in italics.

We will meet royal and high-ranking abbesses who also had secular influence, becoming involved in politics, being sought out for their wisdom and advice and, in one case, using wiles to trick a king out of land in order that she might build a minster on it. The stories which grew up around such royal female saints show how important they and their minsters were to their families, and to the political landscape generally.

It is perhaps useful to outline the development of the monastic institutions. In the earliest of the periods referred to, the abbeys were double houses, where both men and women lived. Double houses included Hartlepool, Whitby, Coldingham, Barking, Ely, Bardney, Wimborne, Winchcombe, Thanet and Wenlock (sometimes Much Wenlock). We know that Wenlock was a double house because of a letter describing a vision of one of the monks there during the tenure of a ruling abbess.[7] Contact between the two sexes in the double monasteries probably varied widely. We know, for example, that the two houses at Wimborne in Dorset were separated by high walls, while at Coldingham, as we shall discover, conditions were relaxed to the point where it created scandal. We can glean a little of the set-up of Whitby Abbey from a story in the *Life* of St Cuthbert. Cuthbert is feasting with the abbess at a 'possession' of her minster when he sees a vision of one of her community being carried up to heaven. The abbess sends a messenger to her 'bigger minster' to ascertain who has died and discovers that it is one of the brethren in the shepherds' dwellings. It would seem that while Whitby was the centre, it had outlying areas which might equate to the later granges.[8] It appears that there was also a cell of Whitby at Hackness, which will be discussed in the appendix. It is probable that in fact the earlier princess-abbesses all ruled double houses, rather than all-female communities.

The abbesses began to lose something of their power and status with the decline of the double houses. The last specific reference to such an establishment was in a letter of 796[9] and monasteries gradually began to be ruled by priests. Possibly it was the priests attached to the monasteries who had greater direct roles in pastoral care. The abbesses acquired lands so that they might drive their sheep there, but this is not to say that they went out personally with their flocks. Hild of Whitby famously encouraged the talents of the poet Cædmon, who looked after the monastery's sheep. The rulers of the abbeys probably arranged for the provision of the pastoral care rather than undertaking it themselves, and perhaps it was the local priests who went out into the community and became indispensable rather than the aristocratic and courtly abbesses of the double houses. Those houses were probably well into decline before the arrival of the Vikings[10] but there can be no doubt that much was lost during that period, not only in terms of records and treasures, but also of life and limb. There is an anachronistic story of one of our featured ladies mutilating herself in order to save her nuns from Viking attackers, but we do not have enough evidence to say how many religious women were physically attacked. What must be true though is that many secular, married women were widowed during this period and found their way to the nunneries.

Endowing minsters was a popular move by kings who could almost become monks by proxy, installing their female relatives. There is of course a sense in which these female members of the royal family could only fulfil their usefulness in one of two ways: either by producing royal children or running abbeys. To do the latter did not mean to hide, or be shut away, from the world. These women were landladies, they had political power, and they governed large communities and vast estates. Networks of royal minsters made for lucrative income for the royal coffers, as well as providing, in many cases, royal family saints. Some abbesses held life-leases on formerly independent minsters, and two Mercian women, one a queen and one a princess, controlled minsters which brought them into conflict with the archdiocese of Canterbury. It may be assumed, too, that some of these women chose the religious life over marriage, and we will see examples of women exercising choice about their marital status.

After the double houses declined, and particularly after the monastic reform of the tenth century, we hear much less about the abbesses. The royal women granted land to monasteries already in existence, apart from a few notable exceptions – Queen Ælfthryth, for example, founded one allegedly to expiate a murder – but the influential women of the later period lived their lives at court, rather than in monasteries, unless they retired to one. The abbesses did not participate in political life in the way that their seventh-century counterparts had done.

We get occasional glimpses of how these religious women lived and their world was perhaps not as austere as one might imagine. We have a description of a church which is lit up by the light of the sun shining through the windows, has gold-embroidered altar-cloths, and golden chalices. Excavations of monastic sites have uncovered opulent dress-pins, showing that the women's clothing was reasonably elegant. Indeed, one abbess and later saint, who will be introduced in Part IV, was accused of dressing too ornately. Other finds have included pottery and glass, which is to be expected, but also items which offer glimpses of more personal habits, for example tweezers. Also revealed were many items relating to writing activities, hinting at a high level of literacy.[11]

Women – religious and secular – were noted for, and sometimes defined by, their embroidery skills; some stunning examples have survived and King Alfred the Great's will even differentiated between those on the 'spindle side' and those on the 'spear side', but as will be shown in Part VI, no distinction was made when it came to beneficiaries of wills. Both men and women alike could inherit land and wealth.

For those who did not take the religious life, we might wonder whether any of the marriages were love matches. Despite the law codes proscribing forced marriage, for the royal women the choice was perhaps much more restrictive. Were the kings routinely faithful? Evidence suggests that one seventh-century king, Oswiu of Northumbria, was not and there are hints that even the pious Alfred the Great might have had an illegitimate son, born after Alfred was married, but it seems that there was more serial monogamy than anything else, unless of course such extra-marital affairs were not routinely recorded.

Sometimes it requires painstaking research to establish the parentage of the featured women. It is important, because these women remained part of their families even when they married elsewhere, travelling with their own retinue from their homelands. Two royal women of Kent, mother and daughter Æthelburh and Eanflæd, took their own Kentish priests with them when they travelled to Northumbria to marry. Married women seem to have kept their identity as members of their own family group; bloodlines were important as we shall see in Part I where a kidnap sparked a feud, in Part III where men resorted to murder to secure access to the bloodline of royal women, and in Part V where women became powerful because of their kin, especially Cnut's first wife, Ælfgifu of Northampton. They could be despised, too, because they were 'foreigners', as was the case with Eadburh, daughter of Offa of Mercia but wife of a king of Wessex, and Osthryth of Northumbria, killed by the noblemen of her husband's Mercian court.

This examination of the women of power begins in seventh-century Northumbria, the northern-most of all the Anglo-Saxon kingdoms.

The last of the ladies in this section came from East Anglia, and her family had connections to the kingdom of Kent, which is where we will travel to in Part II. These Kentish ladies established connections in the midland kingdom of Mercia, and Part III explores the lives of the abbesses, queens and infamous women of that realm in the eighth and ninth centuries, ending with Mercia's most recognised lady, Æthelflæd. From there, we will follow her family into the West Saxon kingdom of Wessex, discovering the generations of tenth- and eleventh-century influential queen mothers, learning about yet more scandal and murder, before Part VI looks at the women who were, in the main, not attached to any of these families yet still wielded power.

Our story starts though, with a princess whose name is barely mentioned in the chronicles, but whose blood was rich enough to start a war.

Anglo-Saxon England.

Part I

Pioneers: Abbesses and Peace-weavers in Northumbria

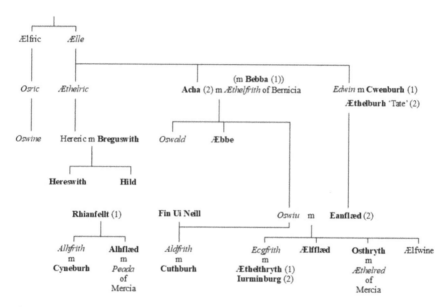

The Royal Houses of Northumbria.

The earliest of our women of power is someone of whom we know virtually nothing, but what happened to her had wide-reaching repercussions, the incident setting off a chain of events which linked all the women in this first group. Acha of Deira had something special: the blood that ran through her veins.

In the early seventh century, the Anglo-Saxon kingdoms were still forming and expanding, sometimes sitting alongside British kingdoms, sometimes absorbing them by aggression or agreement. There were seven main kingdoms, generally referred to as the Heptarchy. The most northerly was Northumbria, which was originally two kingdoms: Deira, which centred around the city we now call York, and Bernicia to the north, centred around Bamburgh. The kingdom of the West Saxons, later to become known as Wessex, was in the southwest. To the east lay the kingdom of the East Angles, and there were also minor kingdoms of the East Saxons and the South Saxons, and the kingdom of Kent. Occupying the land between north and south were the Mercians.

We know a great deal about Northumbria and Kent in this period particularly, because Kent is where the English conversion to Christianity really began, and because Northumbria is where Bede lived, and where he wrote his ecclesiastical history of the English people, the *Historia Ecclesiastica* (*HE*), with a heavy focus – some would say bias – on Northumbria.

Northumbria was sometimes ruled as one kingdom, but the separate realms of Deira and Bernicia never truly lost their identity, even up to the eleventh century when they remained separated because Bernicia was not conquered or settled by the Danes and remained more 'English' than its slightly more southern counterpart. There was a great deal of intermarriage between the ruling families of the two kingdoms, and the story begins with the king of Bernicia, whose name was Æthelfrith. He was an aggressor who, in 604, having fought and defeated various British kings, turned his attention to Deira.

The founder of the Deiran line was Ælle, about whom very little is known[1] and it is likely that at the time of the Bernician attack, it was Ælle's son who was king of Deira. Since we hear no more about him, it is also likely that this son of Ælle perished in that attack. His brother and sister, however, survived. The brother, Edwin, was, along with his nephew and his cousin, driven into exile. The sister, Acha, is the first of our important royal women, though her lot was not a happy one.

It seems that Acha's status as a princess of the rival house was important. So much so that Æthelfrith, having killed one of her brothers and driven the other into exile, then married Acha. Nothing is stated in the surviving chronicles about the details of the marriage, but it seems unlikely that this was any kind of negotiated, much less consensual, arrangement. Given the circumstances, it is hard not to conclude that Acha was taken as a bride against her will.

Acha was a princess of a royal house, and as such her blood would enrich the claims and royal credentials of her children by Æthelfrith. He had been married before, to a woman named Bebba. She, too, must have been an important woman, for we learn from Bede that Bamburgh, the mighty fortress and centre of Bernician power, was named after her. Sadly, this is the only certain fact we have about her.[2] She and Æthelfrith might have had at least one child, a son who would, in his day, become king of Bernicia, albeit for a short time. Bede tells us that this son, Eanfrith, was the eldest son of Æthelfrith[3] and the fact that he only ever claimed Bernicia and not Deira, indicates that he was a son of his father's first wife, Bebba.

But the immediate tale of Northumbria concerns Acha and her exiled brother Edwin. Bede mentions Acha only when referring to her as the mother of King, later Saint, Oswald[4] and the *ASC* does not mention her at all. From Bede's information though, we might hazard a guess regarding her birthdate. According to Bede,[5] Oswald was 37 when he died which would tally with a marriage date for his mother of 604 or perhaps 605. Bede tells us that her brother, Edwin, was 47 when he died in 633, which would put his birthdate at around 586. Presumably Acha was unmarried when she became – willingly or unwillingly – the bride of Æthelfrith of Bernicia, so if Edwin was only around 18 when he was forced into exile, it is possible that Acha was even younger, perhaps only 16.[6]

The *ASC* entry for 617 tells us that Æthelfrith's sons were Eanfrith, Oswald, Oswiu, and four others. We know that Oswald was Acha's son, so if these are listed in birth order, then it suggests that all but Eanfrith were sons of Acha's. There was at least one daughter, Æbbe, of whom more later, though Æbbe's parentage has been the subject of debate by historians and it is possible that a question mark hangs over the parentage of Oswiu too (discussed below). If Acha really was being kept against her will, it must have been a pitiful existence which saw her giving birth to possibly seven or more of her abductor's children.

We do not know what happened to Acha, although if these children were all hers then she must have survived for at least a decade after her marriage. The entry in the *ASC* naming all of his sons records the occasion of Æthelfrith's death, in 617, at the hands of Rædwald, king of East Anglia – of Sutton Hoo fame – in alliance with Edwin, the exiled brother of Acha.

When Æthelfrith attacked Deira, Edwin, his cousin and his nephew went into exile. His cousin's place of refuge is not known to us, but sanctuary seems to have been offered to Edwin's nephew in the British kingdom of Elmet, in the modern-day area of Leeds[7] while Edwin at first found shelter in the midland kingdom of Mercia, where he married the daughter of the Mercian king.[8] At some point, probably a decade or so later, Edwin made his way to East Anglia and there he forged his alliance with Rædwald. After his victory over Æthelfrith in 617 he became king of both the Northumbrian kingdoms. We are not told whether there was any reunion between brother and sister but we do know that Æthelfrith's sons, including those by Acha, went into exile in various British and Pictish kingdoms. Did Acha stay in Bernicia awaiting her brother's return? Or did she accompany her sons into exile? Edwin wanted his kingdom back, and that would have been his main motivation, but it is hard to dismiss the idea that he would also seek vengeance for his sister's abduction. Sadly, her only significance to the chroniclers is her bloodline and we do not know how or where she ended her days.

Edwin's reign was documented by Bede, with detailed reference to the king's conversion to Christianity. It would be another generation before conversion took place amongst the Mercian royal family, so it is safe to assume that Edwin's Mercian wife was a pagan. We do not know if she travelled with him to East Anglia when he left Mercia, nor if she went with him to Northumbria, although it seems as if her sons did – or joined their father at some point – for they were reported as fighting alongside him as adults, and one of their sons was left in the care of Edwin's second wife. It might be that Edwin's first wife never left Mercia. Whether she died, or was merely repudiated, Edwin was recorded by Bede as entering into negotiations to marry a Kentish princess.

Bede relates that when Edwin first sent to ask for her hand, he was told that it was not lawful for a Christian princess to marry a heathen. Edwin's reply was that he would not prevent the lady from worshipping and he would allow all who came north with her to practise their faith. He did not dismiss the possibility that at some later stage he would himself convert, and so the marriage was agreed.[9] We are told that the princess's name was Æthelburh, and in a comment which invites us to step more intimately into this long-ago world, Bede also tells us that she went by a nickname: Tate.[10]

Tate's father was King Æthelberht of Kent, who was the third *Bretwalda*[11] listed by Bede and was recorded as being the first of the English kings to convert to Christianity. His wife was Bertha, who was the daughter of the king of the Franks, but it is not clear whether she was Tate's mother, because although Bede implies it, an examination of the dates suggests that Bertha would have been in her sixties by the time of

Tate's birth.[12] Links to the Continent are, however, suggested by Tate's actions after the death of her husband. Whether or not Bertha was Tate's mother, it seems certain that Æthelberht was her father, and he was an important and powerful king. By the time of the wedding negotiations, however, it was her brother Eadbald who was king of Kent.

Bishop Paulinus accompanied her on her journey north and Bede credits him with baptising vast numbers of the Northumbrian population. Whether Tate's Christianity was pivotal seems to be open to some debate[13] and although Edwin promised to put no obstacles in her way he did not promise initially to convert himself, and it does seem that Paulinus, rather than Tate, was the driving force behind the mission but, as I have proposed elsewhere, the marriage was important for Edwin in other ways. If, as suggested, Edwin's first wife was abandoned before Edwin left Mercia, it should be noted that she was related to Penda, the pagan king of Mercia and enemy of Edwin's. It is documented that Penda waged war on the king of Wessex because that king had repudiated his wife, Penda's sister.[14] It is perfectly possible that something similar happened with Edwin and that he too set aside his first – pagan – wife when it suited him to do so.

Edwin was a political beast, who whilst in exile had received sanctuary in Mercia and married a Mercian princess, but no military aid seems to have been forthcoming and so Edwin moved to East Anglia where Rædwald had become the fourth *Bretwalda* after the death of Æthelberht of Kent and was powerful enough to help Edwin overthrow Æthelfrith. It is easy to imagine that, once safely back in Northumbria, Edwin repudiated his Mercian wife and, with Rædwald now dead, sought alliance with Kent and through that alliance, access to trading links with Frankia. It might be that Edwin's new wife's status had little to do with her religion and everything to do with the fact that she was the sister of the Kentish king[15] for it seems to have taken a while for Edwin to convert and it is not clear whether King Eadbald of Kent was even a Christian himself at the time of the marriage.

As an ambitious and aggressive king, who expanded Northumbria at the expense of the erstwhile independent British kingdoms, Edwin had his enemies. On the same night upon which Tate gave birth to their first child, a daughter named Eanflæd, an assassin sent from the court of the West Saxons made an attempt on Edwin's life.[16] The assassin, who had dipped his blade in poison, rushed at the king who was saved by a devoted thegn,[17] although the blow was so forceful that the blade went through the thegn and wounded the king. Edwin, having been told that his wife was safely delivered of a daughter, promised that he would renounce his paganism if God would save his life – although he added the caveat 'and victory over the king who had sent the assassin' – and that he would allow the child to be baptised. No wife, newly delivered of her first child, would welcome the news that her husband had just been attacked in his own hall, but we are not told of Tate's reaction to this startling event.

Edwin was indeed victorious over the West Saxons, and Bede then tells us that he made it his mission to learn all he could about the new faith. While Edwin was deliberating, the pope wrote letters to the royal couple.[18] In the letters, the pontiff refers to the conversion of Tate's brother, Eadbald of Kent and talks about her husband's continued worship of idols. From this it seems clear that at the time of Tate's wedding to Edwin, her brother was still a pagan.[19] In which case, Bede's report that it was not lawful for a pagan to marry a Christian princess would seem to echo the sentiments of the Church leaders rather than those of the Kentish king.

Tate's value as a bride, then, was not specifically her Christianity. It has been noted[20] that Eadbald was not as powerful a king as his father, but he might have controlled London; a single gold coin of *c.* 650 exists which might bear his name, and this is unusual because coins at this time did not carry the names of kings. Historian Barbara Yorke has pointed out that none of Æthelberht's successors exercised the same level of authority outside Kent which he had enjoyed, but Kentish power was not necessarily diminished.[21] Eadbald, like his father, married into the Frankish royal family. Bede tells us that in Edwin's reign, the roads were so safe that one could walk from coast to coast, i.e. from the east to the west, without fear of being robbed. Northumbria was powerful under Edwin – he was named by Bede as the fifth *Bretwalda*, taking over this position from Rædwald of East Anglia – and the marriage between him and Æthelburh 'Tate' symbolised a prestigious and important alliance between Northumbria and Kent. Edwin, as the new *Bretwalda*, would have been attractive to Eadbald, and the Kentish king, continuing the links with Frankia, would have been useful to Edwin. Æthelburh 'Tate' was the glue which held the alliance together. Given that at the time of her marriage both her husband and her brother were still pagans, Tate's status was primarily that of a Kentish princess with Frankish blood.[22]

No doubt, however, it was perceived by the Church that her role would also be that of proselytiser. The pope's letter to her makes clear that she should be united with her husband by faith as well as flesh and he asks her to send word of the conversion of her husband and his people, urging her to work and to pray toward that end. 'The unbelieving husband shall be saved by the believing wife.' But still Edwin prevaricated. Bede gives us several chapters relating to the decision, including the well-known story about the life of man being likened to the flight of a sparrow through the great hall, where men cannot know what has gone before or after, and of Edwin's high priest burning his temple and all the pagan idols within. Eventually Edwin was baptised, in York according to Bede, but by the British priest Rhun, according to Welsh monk Nennius in the ninth-century *Historia Brittonum*.

How much influence Tate had in the conversion process remains open to debate. The pope clearly believed that she was capable of influencing her husband about such matters, but Bede gives her little credit, citing learned debate and divine visions as the main reasons for Edwin's choice.[23] The pope also wrote to her in the most respectful manner, recognising her status as Edwin's partner and speaking of 'all the nation that is subject to you.' He sent her gifts; a silver mirror and an ivory comb adorned with gold. Were these gifts symbolic? One argument is that they were an appropriate accompaniment to a request for her to become involved in secular matters of state, but on the other hand they might indicate that her role of queen was viewed more as a domestic spiritual adviser.[24] Gifts aside, it seems that the pope thought her capable of influencing her husband, even if Bede attributed his conversion to other factors.

Successful or not, was Tate merely a 'peace-weaver' bride, a symbol of the power and importance of Christianity? Can we glimpse the woman, rather than the political pawn? We know that she had at least four children, but in a rare personal comment, we learn from Bede that not all of them survived. Apart from Eanflæd, the daughter born on the night of the assassination attempt, we learn that, 'Other children of [Edwin's] by Queen Æthelburh were baptised later on [after Edwin's baptism], namely Æthelhun and a daughter Æthelthryth and a second son Uscfrea; the first two were snatched from this life while they were still wearing the chrisom.'[25] The chrisom was the christening gown; it is unlikely that this entry records the children's death during baptism, but probably means that they died a short matter of days or weeks afterwards and the Christening robes were used as shrouds.

For all that she was a high-status princess and then queen, Tate endured more than perhaps her fair share of misery. When Edwin was killed, in battle against Cadwallon of Gwynedd and Penda of Mercia, she and Bishop Paulinus, accompanied by a brave thegn of Edwin's, fled Northumbria. Bede tells us that 'there seemed no safety except in flight' and Paulinus took the queen and her children and returned to Kent. These were troubled times for Northumbria, with various short-lived claimants coming forward to take the thrones of Deira and Bernicia. Bernicia was claimed by Eanfrith, the eldest son of Æthelfrith, who had been in exile with the Picts. Deira was claimed by the cousin of Edwin and Acha, who had fled when Deira was attacked. Bede wrote disparagingly of both these kings, saying that they reverted to idolatry.[26] Both of them were slain by Cadwallon of Gwynedd, who was then himself killed in battle.

Into the political vacuum stepped a man who became revered as a saint. Oswald, who slew Cadwallon, was the son of Æthelfrith of Bernicia but, significantly, he was also the son of Acha, princess of Deira, sister of Edwin. His lineage made him acceptable to both parts of Northumbria.[27] So, whilst we do not know what happened to Acha, we know that her royal blood continued to be important. Not only had she been prized as a royal Deiran bride, but two of her sons became mighty Northumbrian kings.

Unfortunately, this meant that Tate was no longer safe in Northumbria, hence her flight with Paulinus and her surviving children. These were her daughter, Eanflæd, her son, Uscfrea, and Edwin's grandson from his son by his Mercian wife. The children were not safe because of their connection to Edwin, who had caused Oswald and his brothers to flee. But it seems that they were also not safe in Kent, even though that kingdom was ruled by Tate's brother, because we are told by Bede that she sent the male children to the king of the Franks. They both died there, still in infancy, and were buried 'with honour due to royal children and Christian innocents.'[28] One can sympathise with the terror and heartache endured by Tate, firstly as she saw two of her children buried a short time after baptism, having to flee from the north, and then hearing of the deaths of her son and step-grandson while they were also still children, especially cruel when she thought she was sending them to safety.

We hear virtually nothing more of her – according to some sources, she brought back treasures to the Church of Canterbury and Paulinus, who returned with her, became bishop of Rochester, while others say that she accepted land from her brother Eadbald and founded a monastery at Lyminge in Kent[29] – but her legacy remained every bit as important as Acha's, and for the same reason.

Oswald married a West Saxon princess, although she may not have been his first wife. Her name was Cyneburh and Oswald stood as sponsor for her father's baptism. She might be identified with the first abbess of Gloucester, although we must wonder, if this is the same woman, how she ended up in Mercia, the land of her husband's enemies.[30] It is likely that we would know even less about her had her marriage not also been the occasion of her father's conversion.

Oswald ruled successfully over the whole of Northumbria, one of his first acts being to defeat and kill Cadwallon of Gwynedd. He was then himself killed in battle, by Cadwallon's ally, Penda of Mercia. He was succeeded by his brother, Oswiu. Whereas Oswald was clearly acceptable to both the Deirans and the Bernicians, Oswiu's status is a little less clear. It is usually accepted that he also had Bernician and Deiran blood in his veins, being Oswald's full brother and therefore the son of Æthelfrith and Acha. This might not have been the situation though and there could be a case for suggesting that Acha was not, in fact, his mother, as will be discussed in a moment. Whilst less lauded by Bede than the saintly Oswald, Oswiu seems to have been a wily king, and he strengthened his claims to both kingdoms by marrying a Kentish princess, just as Edwin had done. But this Kentish princess was special, for she was in fact Eanflæd, the daughter of Edwin of Deira and Æthelburh, 'Tate' of Kent.

Eanflæd was a valuable acquisition. When Oswald was killed, his brother Oswiu did not succeed to the whole of Northumbria.[31] Edwin's cousin, who had gone into exile and then briefly emerged to hold Deira for a short while before being killed by Cadwallon, had a son named Oswine. His Deiran credentials were impeccable, and Bede wrote effusively about him: 'A man of great piety and religion [who] ruled the kingdom of Deira for seven years in the greatest prosperity, beloved by all.' He was 'tall and handsome, pleasant of speech, courteous in manner, and bountiful to nobles and commons alike.' It might, of course, have all boiled down to a matter of timing. Perhaps Oswine was more successful because Cadwallon, the king-slayer, was dead by the time he claimed Deira, and perhaps we should not read too much into Oswiu's parentage and rights to Deira. But, without Cadwallon to cause chaos, Oswine managed to hang on to power for seven years, at which point Oswiu decided that he had had enough of this rival. Bede tells us that both kings raised an army but that Oswine, realising that he was outnumbered and outmatched, withdrew and disbanded his army, whereupon Oswiu arranged for him to be killed by a man whom the victim had assumed was a friend.[32]

Significantly, the murdered king was Queen Eanflæd's second cousin. Bede tells us that to atone for the crime, a monastery was built in which daily prayers were to be said for the souls of both the murdered and the murderous kings. The chronicler known as Florence of Worcester says specifically that 'Queen Eanflaed built a monastery which is called In-Getling [Gilling] on the spot where King Oswine, the son of her father's cousin ... was unrighteously slain'.[33] It was surely an interesting scene at court when Eanflæd confronted her husband about the murder and demanded recompense. She must have been a formidable woman.

However, the marriage and the murder did little to aid Oswiu in his determination to take control of Deira, for in fact the Deiran throne then passed to the son of the late King Oswald, although it is by no means clear if he was ruling independently of Bernicia.[34]

So how influential was Eanflæd and why was she so attractive to Oswiu? Acha's Deiran blood had clearly made Oswald more acceptable to Deira and in wooing a Deiran princess Oswiu must have hoped to acquire similar credentials. Eanflæd's blood was important; he could not hope to rule both Deira and Bernicia without her, and the fact that he felt the need for this marriage might suggest that Acha, the captured princess of Deira who began our story, was not, in fact, his mother. To explore this theory, we need to look at what we know about the woman who is usually assumed to be Acha's daughter. She was a lady by the name of Æbbe and her career will be examined later in this section.

Æbbe's parentage is unclear. Bede refers to her as the 'uterine' sister of Oswiu, which would suggest that she was a half-sister who was born of the same mother i.e. Acha gave birth to Æbbe and Oswiu, but they had different fathers so that only one of them was the offspring of Æthelfrith of Bernicia. We know that Eanflæd was the daughter of Edwin, and we presume that Oswiu was the son of Æthelfrith. If Oswiu was also the son of Acha, then he and Eanflæd would have been first cousins, because Acha and Edwin were brother and sister and as cousins the couple would have been too closely related to be married. Yet, as has been pointed out,[35] the marriage was approved by the Church, suggesting that in fact Oswiu might not have been Acha's son. This being the case, Oswiu would only have Bernician, and not Deiran, blood in his veins and it would explain why he had trouble asserting his authority in Deira, and why the marriage to Eanflæd mattered so much.

Oswiu seems to have struggled, even so, to gain control over the southern kingdom of Northumbria. The building of the monastery in Oswine's memory might have had little to do with Eanflæd's status as queen and everything to do with the fact that she was kin to the murdered king; her status, then, might have been less that of Oswiu's consort and more that of Deiran princess.[36] Eanflæd's Deiran pedigree might not have aided Oswiu's claims as much as he had hoped, but it helped her son Ecgfrith become a strong ruler of both the kingdoms. She was influential in other ways, too, and proved that she was far more than a mere 'peace-weaver' with good blood.

The *Life* of St Wilfrid, written by a monk known as Eddius Stephanus, describes how, at the age of 14, Wilfrid left his father's house – his mother was dead and his stepmother was harsh and cruel – in search of the religious life and, having clothed and armed himself and his servants in suitable fashion, presented himself to Queen Eanflæd. The queen commended him to Cudda, a monk at Lindisfarne and, after a year or two when Wilfrid wished to visit Rome, on Cudda's advice Queen Eanflæd equipped him for his journey and sent him to Eorcenberht of Kent, her nephew, asking that he might stay under his protection until trustworthy fellow-travellers could be found for him.[37]

It seems as though Eanflæd operated her own household, distinct from that of the king and that Wilfrid's early career flourished under her patronage rather than her husband's. But, as was mentioned in the introduction, this might be because queens had close associations with the monasteries generally. It might also have had to do with the fact that, despite having been born in Northumbria, Eanflæd was raised in Kent and, like Wilfrid, she practised her Christianity according to the Roman tradition. Her Kentish connections enabled her to ensure Wilfrid's safe passage, but also led to conflict regarding the date of Easter, which she celebrated at a different time from her husband, whose religious instruction had come from the teachings of the British (Irish) tradition. It meant that while she was fasting during Lent, in her separate household, he was celebrating Easter.[38] The issue was eventually resolved at the synod of Whitby in 664, in which another influential lady of this extended family, Hild of Whitby, played a role (see below, p. 20).

But, earlier in Oswiu's reign, he had other, more pressing, matters to occupy his mind. Penda of Mercia was snapping not just at his heels but encroaching on Northumbrian territory as far north at times – according to Bede – as Bamburgh. We are told that Oswiu was 'exposed to the savage and insupportable attacks of Penda.'[39] Bede then goes on to relate how Penda did not accept Oswiu's 'gift of peace' – some might say 'bribe' – and describes the circumstances leading up to the final showdown at the battle of *Winwæd* (probably somewhere near Leeds) at which Oswiu was victorious and gave his and Eanflæd's baby daughter Ælfflæd to the Church in thanks. Only in passing does Bede mention that Oswiu's son by Eanflæd, Ecgfrith, was at the time a hostage in the Mercian kingdom. We are not told how this came about, nor are we told how Eanflæd felt about it. We do know that the child was in the care of Penda's wife, Cynewise (in fact this is the only reason that Bede ever mentions her name), so maybe it softened the blow for Eanflæd knowing that at least her young son was in the care of another woman who also had children. As to how she reacted to the battle, much depends on whether or not Penda was the aggressor. It has been argued that he was not,[40] in which case we can only wonder how Eanflæd felt that her husband jeopardised the life of their son, who must have been only 10 years old or so in 655, the date of the battle.

Oswiu seems to have had a slightly cavalier attitude, and not only to his children's lives. We know that he was not averse to arranging the murder of his rivals and we are told by Bede that at the battle of *Winwæd* his nephew, son of the late King Oswald, was on the side of the enemy. Given that this son was at the time at least nominal ruler of Deira, he might have had cause to be wary of Oswiu.

Oswiu had a chequered marital history. Fighting alongside him at *Winwæd* was his son and subsequent king of Deira, Alhfrith. An adult at the time of the battle, he cannot have been Eanflæd's son, and it is likely that his mother was Rhianfellt, a princess of the British kingdom of Rheged (now part of modern-day Cumbria). Presumably Oswiu met and married her when he was in exile. Alhfrith had a sister, Alhflæd. It might be that Oswiu's association with Rhianfellt encouraged the loyalty of the inhabitants of Rheged to the Northumbrian throne once Oswiu succeeded there. Oswiu, like Edwin before him, appears to have set aside his first wife once he gained the Northumbrian throne, and the likelihood is that Rhianfellt never left her homeland. The English sources do not mention the marriage but there is an entry in the Lindisfarne *Liber Vitae* which appears to confirm her existence at least. Oswiu also had a son by an Irish princess whom he named Aldfrith and who eventually became king of Northumbria.[41]

The children by Rhianfellt played a curious part in proceedings, both marrying into the family of their father's enemy, Penda of Mercia. The circumstances of these marriages remain a mystery. Bede informs us of them only because of their perceived part in the conversion process. Alhfrith married Penda's daughter, Cyneburh, and Alhflæd married Penda's son, whose name was Peada. The emphasis of Bede's narrative is squarely upon the conversion and baptism of Peada[42] and we do not know if these brides were viewed as 'peace-weavers'. If they were, it was a flawed plan, because despite being brothers-in-law, Alhfrith and Peada found themselves on opposing sides of the battlefield in 655. Cyneburh's fate after her father's defeat is not recorded – the monk Hugh Candidus credited her as a co-founder of the monastery at *Medeshamstede* (Peterborough) and she and her sister were said to have been buried at the monastery she founded at Castor in Northamptonshire, so presumably she went home to Mercia[43] – but there is a strange postscript to the story of Peada and his wife, Alhflæd.

After the Northumbrian victory, it seems that Peada was allowed to remain king of a small portion of Mercia, but in the Easter of the following year he was poisoned. One version of the *ASC* says that Peada died, while another, the E version, says specifically that he was 'slain'. Hugh Candidus records that Peada's wife was 'enticed by the devil to kill him.' Bede says that Peada was 'most foully murdered in the following spring by the treachery, or so it is said, of his wife during the very time of the Easter festival.'[44] The *Liber Eliensis* omits the qualifier 'or so it is said'.

We cannot ignore the fact that Alhflæd was the daughter of Oswiu. Was she pressured to kill her husband? Or was she just the victim of a tradition which blames women for the murder of kings? It is difficult to see why, following his resounding victory at *Winwæd*, Oswiu would have not only spared Peada but allowed him to reign, only to order his disposal less than a year later.

Alhflæd, mentioned seemingly only as a means to tell a political or religious story, promptly disappears from the record and we do not know what happened to her. She would not be the last royal woman in Anglo-Saxon England to be accused of murder. Was she 'leaned on' by her father to eliminate a man who might become a focus of Mercian resistance? There do not appear to have been any reprisals, but it is hard to imagine that she would have been allowed, or even that she wished, to remain in Mercia after her husband's demise, so presumably she returned to Northumbria. This was an interesting family dynamic, because whilst Penda and Oswiu were mortal enemies, three of the former's children married offspring of the latter, and yet none of these marriages brought about peace between the two kingdoms. Did Alhflæd simply walk away having murdered her husband the king? It seems unlikely, and this was certainly not the fate of her half-sister, and indeed sister-in-law, Osthryth, who appears to have died for much less of a crime, as we shall discover in a moment, for Alhflæd's was not the last of the marriages between the two families.

Eanflæd and Oswiu had at least two daughters, one of whom, Osthryth, was also married to a member of the Mercian royal family. Her husband, Æthelred, became king of Mercia in time, and was one of the few kings of this period to die in his bed, rather than on the battlefield. He abdicated in favour of his nephew and lived out his retirement in a monastery. His wife, however, fared less well. In circumstances once again hidden from our view, she was killed by the Mercian aristocracy.

Henry of Huntingdon, an Anglo-Norman chronicler, called her death 'a scandalous crime' in which she was 'barbarously murdered'. What could have been the reason? There is a theory that she might have been involved in a plot to destabilise the Mercian regime. An ancient tribe in what was once an independent kingdom, the *Hwicce*, had obscure origins and it was suggested by historian H.P.R. Finberg that they were somehow linked to the Bernician royal family. A prince of the *Hwicce*, named Oshere, was killed and the idea was put forward that Osthryth was complicit with him in an attempt by the *Hwicce* to overthrow their Mercian overlords, but other historians have rejected this link between the *Hwicce* and the Bernicians.[45]

There is evidence, though, to connect Osthryth to the monastery of Fladbury in the territory of the *Hwicce*. Her husband had apparently given the monastery to the bishop of the *Hwicce*, but the chronicle of Evesham Abbey reported that Æthilheard of the *Hwicce* had then forced the bishop to surrender it on the grounds that the king had no right to give it away because it had been Osthryth's property. The same chronicler said that Ceolred – son of King Æthelred and his eventual successor – was not the son of Osthryth and that Æthilheard of the *Hwicce* claimed Fladbury as her kinsman and heir. However, this is not indisputable proof that Osthryth was a member of the *Hwicce* royal family and she probably gave the land or endowed the monastery for her sister, Ælfflæd, after whom Fladbury was named (see below Part VI p. 133).

Discounting a connection between Osthryth and the *Hwicce* also removes a possible motive for her murder. Did the Mercians simply despise her; was she an awful woman? We do know that, along with her husband, Osthryth was revered as a saint at Bardney Abbey and arranged for the bones of her uncle, St Oswald, to be moved there. Bede records that, 'The inmates did not receive [the honoured bones of her uncle] gladly. They knew that Oswald was a saint but, nevertheless, because he belonged to another kingdom and had once conquered them they pursued him even when dead with their former hatred.' Perhaps here, then, is a hint of an alternative motive for her murder, with the nobles supporting the monks of Bardney, although it seems a rather disproportionate response.

Bardney was in the small kingdom of Lindsey, an area over which Mercia and Northumbria had tussled for supremacy. Perhaps Osthryth's placement of Oswald's remains was part of a wider political strategy to gain the sympathies of Lindsey for Northumbria?[46] She must have been a fearless and determined lady, to press on with the translation in the face of such recalcitrance. Perhaps she had a forthright manner which made her less than endearing. It has been noted, though, that her co-founding of Bardney, along with her husband, is one of the few times when Bede mentions the involvement of a queen as an equal partner in such endeavours.[47]

It is likely that her translation of her uncle's remains occurred after the battle of the Trent.[48] Her husband, who was the son of Penda of Mercia, continued, as had his brother before him, to wage war on Northumbria. He was probably very young at the time his father lost his life at the battle of *Winwæd* and he would have known, and might even been a playmate of, the young Northumbrian hostage, Ecgfrith, who succeeded his father Oswiu as king of Northumbria. In 679 Æthelred of Mercia fought and defeated Ecgfrith's forces at the battle of the Trent, and whilst

Ecgfrith was not killed, his brother, Ælfwine, was. Ælfwine was a youth of around 18, and Bede said that he was beloved in both kingdoms, indicating that he had spent time in Mercia, perhaps visiting his sister Osthryth, which suggests that they were close.

It cannot have been easy for Osthryth, married to the enemy of her father. The sources differ regarding the date of her marriage[49] but whether it took place before, or to heal the rift caused by, the death of her brother she was in an unenviable position, her husband being responsible for the death of her beloved brother.

Her husband is recorded as having had only one son, but there is some confusion over whether the boy, Ceolred, mentioned above, was also the son of Osthryth.[50] If she had other children, we are not told. Mystery surrounds her murder, and we have no idea where she was buried, nor who was left behind to mourn her.

Osthryth was the last of Oswiu's offspring to marry into the Mercian family, but his other children also made dynastic marriages. Aldfrith, briefly mentioned above, was his – possibly illegitimate – son by an Irish princess. It might be that Aldfrith was conceived while Oswiu was still married to Eanflæd. According to genealogical tradition, Aldfrith was the illegitimate son of Oswiu by Fin, the daughter of an Irish king who died in *c.* 604, which would mean that Aldfrith would have been born around 630 and consequently in his fifties when he became king in 685. Yet he married and had a number of children, one born in *c.* 696, so it is more likely that his mother was, in fact, the granddaughter of the Irish king and that she and Oswiu met around the time that he was seeking Irish support against the forces of Penda, and therefore while he was married to Eanflæd.[51] If so, one wonders how his queen reacted to this. If the suggestion is correct, and Oswiu conducted an affair round about the time that he was gathering forces for his final showdown with Penda, then in her married life Eanflæd had to endure the murder of her second cousin by the orders of her husband, the giving up of her son as a hostage, her husband's fathering of an illegitimate child, and her baby daughter being promised to a nunnery, of which more in a moment. She would also have known of the death of her son, Ælfwine, at the battle of the Trent. The murder of her daughter Osthryth in 697 mercifully happened after Eanflæd's own death, which probably occurred sometime after 685 but, assuming she still had all her faculties, she would have been aware of the death of her son Ecgfrith, too, who was killed by the

Picts in 685. It hardly seems likely that, however willing or unwilling a bride she might have been, she would have envisaged such personal heartache when she set off to Northumbria from Kent to marry Oswiu.

Aldfrith eventually succeeded his father as king of the Northumbrians and his story is strongly connected with those of his female relatives. His wife, though, was a West Saxon princess by the name of Cuthburh, a sister of King Ine of Wessex. There is no mention of her in the *Historia Ecclesiastica* but Bede was primarily interested in women only insofar as their piety affected Northumbria. Cuthburh was instrumental in founding the first West Saxon monasteries but this would have been of no particular interest to Bede.[52] The twelfth-century Anglo-Norman chronicler William of Malmesbury recorded that she 'was given in marriage to Aldfrith, king of the Northumbrians, but the contract being soon after dissolved, she led a life dedicated to God, first at Barking, under the abbess Hildelith, and afterwards as superior of the convent at Wimborne.' William's notes echo the *ASC* which tells us that Cuthburh founded the monastery at Wimborne, and that she had been married to Aldfrith but that they separated 'during their lifetime'.

Aldhelm, abbot of Malmesbury, who might have been a relative of Cuthburh's, wrote a treatise called *De Virginitate* and dedicated it to Hildelith, the second abbess of the monastery at Barking, which was a double house. Little is known of Hildelith, but it appears that she, like many religious women of the time, was well-educated and had influential contacts, including St Boniface, an English missionary. Boniface wrote to the abbess of Thanet in around 717 saying, 'Thou didst ask me, dear sister, to send you an account, as the venerable Abbess Hildelith gave it to me, of the wonderful vision seen by the man who recently … died and came back to life.' Clearly Hildelith and Boniface knew each other. Bede described Hildelith as a 'devoted servant of God' who 'was most energetic in the observance of the discipline of the Rule [of St Benedict] and in the provision of all such things as were necessary for the common use' and Aldhelm imagined Hildelith and the nuns 'racing curiously through the open fields of books.' In his dedication, Aldhelm mentions a Cuthburh, and it is assumed that this lady is the same Cuthburh who had been married to Aldfrith and later founded Wimborne Abbey. Aldhelm seems to be addressing a number of 'noble ladies-turned-nuns' who had been released from their marriages and it seems that this practice was not uncommon. There is, however, no conclusive evidence that the two women named Cuthburh are one and the same lady,[53] but it is not a huge leap to assume that Cuthburh at some point left her husband and was, for a time, in the monastery at Barking before founding Wimborne.

Queen Eanflæd, too, ended her days in a nunnery. Her husband King Oswiu's various children either succeeded him or ruled as sub-kings under him. Alhfrith, his son by Rhianfellt of Rheged, ruled Deira for a while before disappearing from the records abruptly and it has been suggested that he might have been killed whilst in rebellion against his father;[54] they had certainly clashed over religious matters.

The tensions between those who followed the Roman tradition and those who preferred the Irish form of Christianity – specifically the Ionan tradition associated with St Aidan and the monks of Lindisfarne – were formally addressed at the synod of Whitby. One of those present was Hild, a relative of Queen Eanflæd's and, although she was brought up in the Roman tradition, she seems to have favoured the Ionan argument. Whitby was her monastery, and it was into her care that the infant Ælfflæd, daughter of Oswiu and Eanflæd, was given when she was promised to the Church after the victory at *Winwæd*.

Hild would have known Eanflæd when she was a child. Hild and her sister, Hereswith, were the daughters of Hereric, the young nephew who had fled with Edwin and who was killed while in exile, probably at the hands of the king of Elmet. Bede tells us that Hereric married a lady named Breguswith, and about a dream which she had when her husband was 'living in exile under the British king [of Elmet] … where he was poisoned.'[55] In the dream, Breguswith was searching for her missing husband, but could find no trace of him. In the middle of her search, however, she found a necklace under her garment and, as she looked at it, the necklace spread a blaze of light and the dream, Bede concluded, 'was truly fulfilled in her daughter Hild; for her life was an example of the works of light, blessed not only to herself but to many who desired to live uprightly.'

Hild was baptised at the same time as King Edwin, who was her great uncle, so it may be assumed that perhaps she was brought as a child back to Northumbria after the death of her father. (No more is heard of Breguswith.) Hild went to East Anglia for a while – her sister Hereswith married an East Anglian prince, probably Æthelric, brother of King Anna[56] – but this was not until her sister had gone abroad to live as a nun, so presumably Hild spent her formative years at the Northumbrian court, where she would have known the young Deiran princess, Eanflæd.

According to Bede, Hereswith had retired to live as a nun in the Frankish monastery at Chelles, and he said that Hild's intention was to follow her there – although the dates are subject to debate, since Chelles was not founded until later – but she was persuaded by Bishop Aidan to return to Northumbria and founded the monastery at Hartlepool, breaking with the tradition of English noblewomen going abroad to fulfil their religious vocations, as well as demonstrating the closeness of the relationship between Hild and Aidan, who visited her frequently. It was at Hartlepool that she took custody of the infant Ælfflæd, but two years later Hild founded the monastery of *Streaneshealh* – sometimes *Streanœshalch* – on land which Oswiu had gifted to the Church. It has usually been identified as Whitby.[57]

We learn much about Hild from Bede, including the fact that she was so beloved by all that they called her 'mother', but not whether she was ever married before taking the veil. He says that she was 33 when she became a nun.[58] He does not call her a virgin, but then neither does he tell us of any husband. What we are told, however, is that she was highly educated and influential. Five future bishops are said to have been educated by her and the likelihood is that she assembled a vast library at Whitby. Styli and book-clasps found during excavations show that a great deal of writing was undertaken there. Definitive evidence has recently come to light that women were scribes. Examination of dental calculus of a female skeleton discovered in a medieval monastery revealed traces of blue pigment. Detailed analysis showed these blue flecks to be lapis lazuli, an expensive and rare pigment used in the scriptorium. The conclusion was that the woman had been painting and licking the tip of the brush. Pigment made from lapis lazuli was reserved for the most luxurious illuminated manuscripts, and the likelihood is that this woman was a trusted and skilled illuminator. Whilst this monastery can be dated no earlier than the tenth century, it is clear that we should banish all notion that only men produced the manuscripts of the period.[59] Excavation at Whitby meanwhile also revealed that far from being a small site, consisting of a few cells, it was in fact a major settlement and it was the venue for the synod in 664 which decided once and for all which of the Christian traditions would take precedence and settled the calculation method for the date of Easter.[60]

At the synod, convened and presided over by King Oswiu, those arguing for the Roman tradition included Oswiu's son, Alhfrith. Although

Oswiu eventually pronounced in favour of the Roman argument, it might have been this disagreement between father and son which resulted in the latter's attack on his father and subsequent disappearance.[61] Also in the Roman camp were Wilfrid, the bishop who had been sponsored by Queen Eanflæd and educated by Hild, and Queen Eanflæd, who sent her chaplain, Romanus, as her representative. Oddly, Hild was in the other camp, along with Colman, the bishop of Lindisfarne, despite her having been brought up in the Roman tradition. As mentioned already, there is some doubt as to whether Edwin was baptised by Paulinus in the Roman tradition or by Rhun in the British, and consequently whether Hild was baptised by Rhun, and her hostility towards Wilfrid was described by William of Malmesbury who said that Hild attacked him with 'venomous hatred'.[62] There might, of course, have been some personal animosity which went unrecorded. Wilfrid certainly had the ability to rub people up the wrong way.

Hild survived for many years after the synod but was struck down ten years later by the illness which eventually killed her. With his love of symmetry, Bede tells us that she died at the age of 66 – having been in pain for several years – so she spent exactly half her life as a nun. He records that 'so great was her prudence that not only ordinary people but also kings and princes sought and received her counsel when in difficulties' and that: 'All who knew Hild ... used to call her mother because of her outstanding devotion and grace.' Her death was, according to Bede, revealed in a vision at another monastery at Hackness which Hild had built that same year. A nun there saw the roof of the house roll back, revealing a light shining down from above. In the beam of light, she saw the soul of Hild ascending to heaven.[63]

According to William of Malmesbury, her relics were sent to Glastonbury in the reign of King Edmund in the early tenth century.[64] Florence of Worcester praised her, saying that she 'inculcated justice, devotion, continence and other virtues; but chiefly peace and charity.' He goes on to say that, 'In a monastery governed by this abbess lived Cædmon, that celebrated monk, who received from heaven the free gift of poetical inspiration.'[65] It seems that Cædmon had received no formal training but was able to compose religious songs and poems. One night while he was tending the cattle he dreamed that someone was standing by him, telling him to sing, which he did, in praise of God. The next day he told his master the reeve of the gift he had received, and together they went to Abbess Hild who received him into the holy community. In the earliest days of the conversion process it is perhaps astonishing that it was Hild, a woman, who was responsible for the education of bishops. Her sympathetic encouragement of Cædmon and her reputation as 'mother' to all who knew her reveal a learned yet gentle woman. Her attendance at the synod of Whitby, however, shows a woman also of determination.

After the synod of Whitby and the disappearance of Alhfrith – Oswiu's son by a previous wife – Eanflæd's children began to take centre stage. Her son, Ecgfrith, was married at what must have been a young age to a woman who was older than him and who had been married before. There is little else in the records regarding Eanflæd's life. Perhaps she exerted influence over her young son as later queen mothers were to do, but Ecgfrith was a married man, albeit a young one, for some ten years before his father's death and as we shall see, his wife was a formidable character. We should not assume any hostility between mother-in-law and daughter-in-law, however; we are told that Eanflæd bequeathed five acres of land to her daughter-in-law.[66] After Oswiu's death in 670, Eanflæd entered the monastery at Whitby, where in 680 after the death of Hild, her daughter Ælfflæd became abbess, either solely or jointly with her mother. It must have been here, at the monastery, that Eanflæd and Ælfflæd received the news that their son and brother, Ælfwine, mentioned above (p. 16) had been killed in the battle of the Trent – they might even have received his body for burial at Whitby – and where they learned, six years later, of the death of his brother, Ecgfrith.

This triumvirate of holy women, Hild, Eanflæd and Ælfflæd, all part of the same Deiran royal family, was hugely influential. Eanflæd and her daughter oversaw the translation of Edwin's remains to Whitby. Eanflæd was herself later buried at the abbey and it might be that the intention had been to establish a royal mausoleum there. With the cult of Edwin of Deira and the burial of Oswiu of Bernicia, Whitby could well have symbolised the unification of Northumbria.[67] Whitby played a part in the promotion of saints; Ælfflæd had been instrumental in the translation of Edwin's remains, and somewhere between 704 and 710, a biography of Pope Gregory was produced there.

Like her mother and her cousin and predecessor Hild (they were second cousins), Ælfflæd was not only a powerful abbess but she was politically influential too. Ælfflæd had been entrusted to Hild's care when she was still a tiny infant, moving with her from Hartlepool to

Whitby. By the time she succeeded as abbess, her brother Ecgfrith was king of Northumbria. They were both descended from the Deiran and Bernician lines.

She was also an educated woman. A letter survives in which she wrote to the abbess of the monastery at Pfalzel near Trier in Germany recommending a nun who was on pilgrimage with the words, 'We commend to your highest holiness and customary piety, strenuously with all diligence, N, the devoted handmaid of God and religious abbess',[68] evidence that she was competent in Latin and that she had contacts on the Continent.

Ælfflæd also had close associations with St Cuthbert. Bede, who describes her as a 'holy handmaid of Christ' who looked after her house with 'motherly love, adding to her royal rank the yet more noble adornment of a high degree of holiness', relates how she was seriously ill and at the point of death.[69] 'How I wish I had something belonging to my dear Cuthbert', she said, believing that she would then be healed. Not long afterwards, someone arrived with a linen cincture (girdle) sent by Cuthbert. She wore it and, two days later, she was completely well. In 684 she summoned Cuthbert to discuss the possibility of his becoming a bishop. At the meeting she asked him how long her childless brother, Ecgfrith, would remain on the throne, and who should rule after him. Cuthbert replied that she knew the identity of his successor who lived over the sea on an island. She realised that he was referring to Aldfrith, her illegitimate half-brother.

The following year, in 685, Ecgfrith died and was indeed succeeded by Aldfrith. At first glance it seems hard to argue that Ælfflæd was in any way flexing her political muscles here, because it was she who asked Cuthbert about the succession, and it was Cuthbert who hinted at Aldfrith's name. However, it has been argued that in asking the question, the abbess was testing Cuthbert's loyalty to her family.[70] She certainly had political 'clout'; after the battle at *Nechtanesmere* (unidentified) in which Ecgfrith was defeated by the Picts, the former bishop of the Picts, Trumwine, was expelled and lived under Ælfflæd's command at Whitby. Cuthbert remained a friend and, sensing that his end was near, he made a tour of his diocese and visited 'that most noble and holy virgin Ælfflæd'.[71]

Her influence was felt at the end of Aldfrith's reign, too. Aldfrith's son and eventual successor, Osred, was only about 8 years old when his father died. (It is not clear whether Cuthburh who, as we saw earlier, separated from Aldfrith at some point to become a nun, first with Hildelith at Barking and then at Wimborne, was Osred's mother.) When Aldfrith died, he was initially succeeded by a man name Eadwulf who, according to William of Malmesbury, 'plotted to obtain the kingship.'[72] In 705 at the synod of the River Nidd, Ælfflæd's testimony was of paramount importance. Like Hild before her, she had been hostile to Wilfrid and her influence was such that when Archbishop Theodore of Canterbury, a champion of Wilfrid's, urged peace to be made between Wilfrid and King Aldfrith, he wrote not only to the king, but to the abbess, too. At the synod Ælfflæd, having clearly had a change of heart about Wilfrid, testified in his favour saying that, on his deathbed, Aldfrith had urged that his successor should come to terms with Wilfrid.[73] An agreement was reached, with the archbishop giving his advice while 'Abbess Ælfflæd gave them hers.'[74] Whilst the main focus of the synod was the settling of the affairs of Wilfrid, the author of the *Life* of Wilfrid said that Osred was able to rule because of the support of, *inter alia*, Abbess Ælfflæd.[75] It is clear that she was in a position of huge influence and her presence at Aldfrith's deathbed indicates a strong relationship between the two members of the royal family. She is mentioned in both the *Lives* of Cuthbert and Wilfrid, but obviously had secular as well as religious power.

Wilfrid had connections not just with Ælfflæd's half-brother Aldfrith and her nephew Osred, but with her full brother, Ecgfrith, too. Wilfrid's career in the Church began with his sponsorship by Queen Eanflæd and it was her Kentish connections which smoothed the way for him to spend a year in Kent before embarking on a pilgrimage to Rome. When he returned from Rome, he struck up a friendship with Alhfrith, eldest son of King Oswiu, who was at the time the under-king of Deira and who championed Wilfrid at the synod of Whitby. It seems that Alhfrith was keen for Wilfrid to be installed as bishop of Deira (York) but he was given Ripon instead. Shortly after the synod of Whitby, Wilfrid became archbishop of York but could not be consecrated because the see of Canterbury was vacant at the time. He had to go abroad, to Compiégne.

While he was away, an argument broke out between Alhfrith and his father, Oswiu, possibly connected to the fact that Oswiu had appointed someone else to the archbishopric of York. When Wilfrid returned, he retired to his monastery at Ripon, occasionally conducting duties in the midland kingdom of Mercia. In 669 Archbishop Theodore restored Wilfrid to York and Oswiu died the following year. Wilfrid had lost his champion, Alhfrith, but at least Oswiu was no longer king, to stand in his way.

Unfortunately for Wilfrid, Oswiu's successor, Ecgfrith, became every bit as hostile as had his father. Much of this antipathy was centred around the bishop's perceived influence over Ecgfrith's wife, Æthelthryth, to whom he had been married when still a relatively young man.

Æthelthryth was the daughter of King Anna of East Anglia (who was killed by Penda of Mercia, nemesis of Oswald and Oswiu.) She came from a family whose women were strongly religious, many of them venerated, and who are the focus of Part II of this book. She was married twice, the first time to a man named Tondberht who was of the elusive tribe known as the South *Gyrwe*. Little is known about the South *Gyrwe* and it is not clear whether the land at Ely upon which Æthelthryth eventually built her abbey was originally land belonging to East Anglia or whether it was dower land given to her by Tondberht.[76] Tondberht must have been at the least a high-ranking ealdorman, perhaps even of royal blood, for his bride was of high status and he must have been deemed worthy. Perhaps the marriage symbolised the absorption of the territory of the South *Gyrwe* into the greater kingdom of East Anglia.[77]

The *Liber Eliensis*, a history of the Isle of Ely, was compiled at Ely and in praise of Æthelthryth, and it recorded her life in great detail but is not without its inaccuracies. It says that her mother was Hereswith, sister of Hild, but according to a ninth-century genealogy of the East Anglian kings, Hereswith married not King Anna, but Æthelric, his brother.[78]

Æthelthryth's first marriage lasted only a few years and she was apparently still a virgin when Tondberht died. Given what we know of her later life and the fact that, according to the *Liber Eliensis*, she resisted for some time before agreeing to her first marriage, it is perhaps surprising that she agreed to the second. It is also interesting to note that this indicates a certain amount of choice in the matter of marriage. She had retired to Ely and been a widow for five years before her marriage to Ecgfrith of Northumbria. There were links, of course, to the royal house of Northumbria, for her aunt Hereswith was a Deiran princess and was related to Queen Eanflæd, Ecgfrith's mother. There might have been political considerations, too. Having been dominant over Mercia for three years following the battle of *Winwæd* in 655, Oswiu faced a rebellion three years later and Penda's son, Wulfhere, became king of Mercia. An alliance with East Anglia was timely. So the second marriage might have been for political expediency, but there is little evidence that the same applied to her first marriage and it has been pointed out that not all of her sisters were obliged to marry.[79]

As mentioned previously, Ecgfrith was young, perhaps around 15 years old when he married Æthelthryth in 660. If Æthelthryth was old enough to marry for the first time in *c.* 652, then she would have been older than Ecgfrith by some margin, perhaps as much as a decade. Like other royal women before her, it seems she kept her own household. Bede tells us that a monk named Owine travelled with her from East Anglia and was the 'chief of her officers and the head of her household'.[80]

Æthelthryth's early years in Northumbria coincided with the most successful of Wilfrid's career, but his downfall was partly the result of his association with the royal couple. In the *Life* of St Wilfrid, we are told that 'the pious King Ecgfrith and Queen Æthelthryth were both obedient to Bishop Wilfrid in everything,'[81] but Bede records that she refused to consummate her marriage and it appears that in this, her determination to remain a virgin, she was encouraged by Wilfrid; indeed it seems that Wilfrid himself informed Bede of his role in the matter. In around 672, Æthelthryth became a nun, and Florence of Worcester recorded that she received the veil from Wilfrid. Bede is quite matter-of-fact in his retelling of the story which he says he received first hand from Wilfrid, and he gives only the bare facts: that at length and with difficulty Æthelthryth gained her husband's permission to enter a monastery, staying first with Abbess Æbbe at Coldingham Abbey and then becoming abbess of Ely. He then goes on to relate how she would never wear linen, only woollen garments and ate very little. After seven years, she died of the plague and was buried in a simple wooden coffin, 'in the ranks of the other nuns'. It might even be the case that Ely was the first monastery to be founded in eastern England, so in this, Æthelthryth was something of an innovator.[82]

Bede was clearly impressed by her devotion and humility and he wrote a poem in praise of Æthelthryth, comparing her to earlier saints such as Eulalia and Agatha and writing that:

> She, pledged to God her spouse, twelve years had reigned,
> When in the cloister was she pledged to God.
> To heaven devoted, there she won new fame,
> And breathed her last, to heaven devoted there.
> Veiled in the tomb sixteen Novembers lay,
> Nor rots her virgin flesh in the tomb.

Much was made of the fact that her flesh remained uncorrupted and it was taken as a sign of her virginity. Whether she had always envisioned a life devoted to God we cannot be sure, for she herself admitted to a certain vanity in her youth. In later life she was afflicted with a neck tumour and according to Bede she welcomed the pain, saying that when she was a young girl she was in the habit of wearing an unnecessary weight of necklaces and she thought that the discomfort from the tumour was a method by which she could be absolved of the guilt of her vanity. Miracles were associated with her clothes – devils were expelled from the bodies of those who touched them – and her coffin healed those with eye troubles after they had prayed with their head resting on it.

But what of her initial escape from the clutches of her husband? There are various stories, in contrast to Bede's short summation that she left after 'some length and difficulty'. At one point, we are told, Ecgfrith offered Wilfrid land and riches if he would persuade the queen to consummate the marriage, but it is perhaps more likely that Wilfrid's position at court depended on the queen, rather than his having influence over her.[83] The *Liber Eliensis* tells a dramatic tale in which Ecgfrith, having acquiesced initially to her request for a divorce, began attempts to remove her forcibly from the convent. The abbess of Coldingham advised Æthelthryth that her only option was to escape. The king set off in pursuit, but Æthelthryth and her two lady companions climbed to the top of a steep hill where divine intervention caused the water levels to rise, cutting off the hill and keeping the holy virgins hidden for seven days. The king could not get near, and eventually returned to York. Unfortunately the nuns on the rock began to suffer from extreme thirst. The abbess prayed for them and in answer to her prayers, a spring of water gushed forth and provided the nuns the means with which to slake their thirst.[84] The *Liber Eliensis* makes clear that this story was not based on the writings of Bede but came from those who knew the area of Coldingham and were witness to the events.

That abbess of Coldingham was, in fact, Æbbe, the daughter – perhaps – of Acha princess of Deira who, early in the seventh century, had been married to Æthelfrith of Bernicia and was the mother of Oswald and possibly Oswiu.

A twelfth-century source says that Æbbe received the veil from a bishop of Lindisfarne who died in 661, so she must have become a nun before that date. She was a friend of St Cuthbert and, in Bede's *Life* of the saint, we are told that she sent for him and asked if he would come and exhort the community at Coldingham. He did so, staying for a few days and showing them 'the way of righteousness in deed as well as word'.[85]

Coldingham is perhaps most renowned for having been the centre of a scandal. An Irish abbot of Iona, Adomnan, who became a close friend of Aldfrith, King Ecgfrith's successor, visited Coldingham where, according to Bede, he found the members of the community, men and women alike, sunk in slothful slumbers or else 'they remained awake for the purposes of sin. The cells which were built for praying and for reading were haunts of feasting, drinking, gossip, and other delights; even the virgins who were dedicated to God put aside all respect for their profession and, whenever they had leisure, spent their time weaving elaborate garments with which to adorn themselves as if they were brides.' Adomnan's vision was that the monastery would be destroyed by fire, which indeed it was, but Bede admitted that Abbess Æbbe was herself unaware of the abuses and that it was after her death that the community fell back into their old ways. The abbess was not blamed specifically; Bede said that she was 'disturbed by the prophecy' and was reassured that the terrible punishment would not happen in her lifetime.[86]

Though she was the aunt of King Ecgfrith, her sympathies appear not to have lain with him, but rather with his first wife and her friends. Æbbe was a friend of Wilfrid's and not only did she assist the flight of Æthelthryth, she was instrumental in securing Wilfrid's release from incarceration.

It is hard to know whether the story of Ecgfrith chasing after Æthelthryth should be taken seriously. It is perfectly believable that he would have been glad to be rid of a wife, older than him, who refused to give him children. It has been suggested that the argument might have had more to do with property than conjugal rights. Before she left her marriage, Æthelthryth had given Wilfrid a gift of land, on which he had built a church 'to the glory of God and the honour of St Andrew' at Hexham.[87] Ecgfrith's second wife was Iurminburg, and the royal couple was recorded going on a progress through the kingdom and visiting Æbbe at Coldingham at a time when relations between the king and Wilfrid had deteriorated to such an extent that Wilfrid had been imprisoned at Dunbar.

During the visit to Coldingham, the queen became ill, being possessed by a devil and found at dawn with the muscles of her limbs tightly contracted. Abbess Æbbe, concerned that the queen was dying, confronted her nephew, Ecgfrith, and told him that he had imprisoned Wilfrid unfairly and that he must loosen his bonds, and either reinstate him as bishop or at least allow him to leave the kingdom. The king did as he was told, releasing Wilfrid, who set off for the south, and the queen recovered.[88]

Little is recorded of Iurminburg – Bede's *Historia Ecclesiastica* does not even mention her – and she is sometimes confused with a woman of similar name who hailed from the Kentish royal house featured in Part II and who married into the Mercian royal family. Her name suggests that she might have been related to the Kentish, or even the Frankish, royal families but her origins are unknown. Iurminburg was described as a 'she-wolf [who] corrupted the king's heart with poisonous tales about Wilfrid' and it was noted that she disapprovingly considered Wilfrid's retinue of armed followers to be equal to that of the king.[89]

According to William of Malmesbury, Wilfrid was 'kind and friendly to everybody', that 'abbots and abbesses made him master of their possessions while he was alive, and when dying named him as their heir' and that as a result, 'an unhappy jealousy crept into the hearts of Queen Iurminburg and some of her courtiers, who cast envious eyes upon Wilfrid's great wealth.' We are told that she stole a reliquary of Wilfrid's and that while Wilfrid was imprisoned, 'Queen Iurminburg, tinder and spark of the whole blaze … joined day and night in one round of feasting, and carried the reliquary around with her in triumphal procession, exulting in these spoils which she had taken from [Wilfrid]' and it was in direct consequence of this that she fell ill at Coldingham.[90]

She is mentioned in Bede's *Life* of St Cuthbert, in which Cuthbert finds her at Carlisle, where she has been waiting at her sister's convent during Ecgfrith's last, fatal campaign against the Picts. He tells the queen that she must travel at daybreak two days from the time of their conversation, to the 'royal city' because he has had a vision that the king has been slain. His prediction is proved and the king and all his bodyguards have been slaughtered by the Picts. Shortly afterwards Cuthbert gives the veil to the widowed queen.[91] This is all that we really know about Ecgfrith's second queen, but it is clear from just this small amount that before retiring to – presumably – her sister's monastery she was politically active, able to influence the king, and one other piece of information confirms that she was not the only one in her family with a low opinion of Wilfrid; after his release, we are told, he did not stay long in the south because the wife of the king of the West Saxons was Iurminburg's sister, and she 'detested' Wilfrid.

It is hard to know why some members of the royal family were hostile to Wilfrid. Perhaps Ecgfrith and Iurmenburg's dislike stemmed from the fact that Wilfrid's loyalties lay elsewhere, with Oswald's family, and that he might have transferred his allegiance to an unknown member of that line when he lost his patron Alhfrith and that there is significance in the fact that it was Æbbe, a kinswoman of the Bernicians, but one who also had strong Deiran connections, who secured his release from prison.[92] However, the same could be said of Ælfflæd, whose father was Bernician and whose mother was Deiran, and yet as we have seen, she seems to have followed her kinswoman Hild in her hostility towards Wilfrid. There seems no obvious reason for Hild's antipathy but it is certain that Wilfrid was a man who elicited strong reactions from those with whom he had dealings. It has been put forward that Wilfrid's power was much diminished by Æthelthryth's departure and that it was she who was instrumental in keeping his status so elevated.[93] When she left, so did he, and it is clear that Ecgfrith's new wife's opinion mattered a great deal to the king. Royal women certainly seem to have had the ear of their male kin.

We have more information about Æbbe which does not pertain to Wilfrid. She is the subject of a story recorded by the thirteenth-century chronicler Roger of Wendover which, though full of delicious detail, is anachronistic and must be viewed with suspicion, but is nevertheless too entertaining to ignore. Roger describes how Æbbe, hearing that invaders were 'ravishing holy women and consuming everything in their way,' with 'an heroic spirit' and in an effort to preserve the virgin chastity of the nuns, took a razor and cut off her nose, together with her upper lip, whereupon all the others of the community did the same. Seeing the nuns thus horribly mutilated, the invaders quickly went away, but before they left, they set fire to the monastery and the abbess and all within 'attained the glory of martyrdom.'[94] The problem with this lurid tale lies with Roger's assertion that the incident occurred in 870, at the height of the Viking raids, nearly 200 years after Æbbe's death.

Although she is known as Æbbe of Coldingham, there is some uncertainty about the location of her monastery, originally said to have been at *Coludi urbs* (St Abbs Head, Berwickshire). Here, high up on a place now known as Kirk Hill, it is thought that the original monastery, a collection of 'beehive' huts, was built in the mid-seventh century. St Abbs is about two miles from Coldingham, where a later, Benedictine, monastery was built for a community of monks in the eleventh century. A visit to St Abbs Head reveals that dragging construction materials up to Kirk Hill would have been a difficult undertaking, and life on the headland would have been bleak indeed. The proximity to Coldingham would explain the naming of Æbbe's monastery, of which all traces have been lost.

In March 2019, results were published of radiocarbon dating which shows that material sent for analysis from a dig at Coldingham Priory can be dated to between 660 and 880. There is a high probability, therefore, that there was an original Anglo-Saxon monastery on the same site, directly underneath the remains of the later medieval priory.[95] Investigation is ongoing, but it could yet prove that Æbbe of Coldingham's abbey was indeed further inland than St Abbs and situated in Coldingham itself.

Miracles were associated with Æbbe, with a man named Henry reported to have had a vision in the twelfth century in which he was instructed to build an oratory to St Æbbe on St Abb's Head. A surviving document records forty-three ensuing miracles, of which nearly all were healing miracles. The cult associated with St Æbbe was not unique. It has been noted that the ubiquity and the persistence of the royal cult was characteristically Anglo-Saxon.[96] The miracles attributed to Æbbe, and to Æthelthryth to whom she gave her courageous assistance, are detailed more fully in the appendix of this book.

We have already seen Bede's devotion to Æthelthryth, and his description of the miracles associated with her plain wooden coffin, and how the first book of the *Liber Eliensis* gives rich detail about her life, albeit sometimes inaccurately. Her cult was cultivated a little sooner than that of her erstwhile protector, Æbbe, for it was Æthelthryth's sister, and successor as abbess of Ely, who translated Æthelthryth's remains from the common graveyard to a position within the church more befitting her status. (In the later Middle Ages a fair held at Ely on her feast day proved so popular – ribbons which had touched the shrine were sold in quantity – that the quality of items became poor and this is where the word 'tawdry' originated; a corruption of the saint's name used to describe items of inferior workmanship.)

This sister who arranged Æthelthryth's translation was named Seaxburh, and she was abbess of Ely until her death at a 'good, late age'.[97] She was described as a virago and was clearly fondly remembered at Ely. But her early story is connected with the royal house of Kent.

Part II

The Saintly Royal Family of Kent

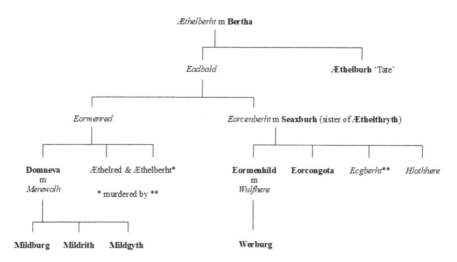

The Royal Family of Kent.

> It was at Ely that the most blessed lady Æthelthryth first established a religious house for the handmaids of God. After her death, her sister Seaxburh … mother of the most holy virgin Eorcongota, grew old as a nun and as the abbess in the same place. She was succeeded as abbess by her other daughter, Eormenhild … These three ladies were abbesses in unbroken succession, and they were followed by many emulators of their leadership and piety right down to the time of the Danes.[1]

Æthelthryth and Seaxburh were the daughters of King Anna of East Anglia and they had two more sisters, named Æthelburh and Wihtburh. All four were venerated as royal saints. Æthelburh became a nun in Frankia, at the monastery of Faremoutiers-en-Brie, the house where her

31

stepsister was abbess. Bede described her as having lived 'a life of great self-denial, also preserving the glory of perpetual virginity which is well pleasing to God.' She wished to build a church in the monastery but died before the works could be completed. When the brothers raised her bones they found her body untouched by decay.[2]

A little more is known about Wihtburh, although even the author of one of her *Lives* confessed to an amount of ignorance concerning this particular saint. It was said that she was buried at the monastery at East Dereham in Norfolk until her bones were 'shamelessly purloined' by the monks of Ely in the latter part of the tenth century.[3] According to one tradition, she was the youngest of King Anna's daughters but Bede makes no mention of her, despite giving details about her sisters in his *Historia Ecclesiastica*. An eleventh-century register states that she was Anna's daughter, and an entry in the *ASC* for 798 says that her body was found 'all sound and undecayed in Dereham, fifty-five years after she departed from this life',[4] but if she died in 743 it makes it less likely that she was a daughter of Anna's, who died in around 654. According to the *Liber Eliensis*, a later abbot, Richard, saw a vision of Wihtburh on his deathbed, and the *LE* also states that Wihtburh, Æthelthryth and Seaxburh were sisters. In Book One, Anna's six children are listed, the daughters being Seaxburh, the first-born, an 'incomparable woman', Æthelburh, Æthelthryth and Wihtburh. But it then goes on to state that their mother was Hereswith, when this is not the case for, as we saw in Part I, it is likely that Hereswith was in fact married to Anna's brother. The *LE* is not always reliable and it appears that the monks were not above changing the facts to suit their own purposes, perhaps claiming Wihtburh despite her not having been a daughter of Anna's.[5]

The identity of the eldest sister, Seaxburh, is not in any doubt. She was remembered as the successor of Æthelthryth at Ely and, as was mentioned briefly at the end of Part I, she arranged for the translation of her sister Æthelthryth's undecayed body, from the simple wooden coffin in which she was buried to one made of white marble. When she retired to Ely, the *Liber Eliensis* tells us that she was greeted by her sister Æthelthryth, and 'queen greeted queen; sister conducted sister within, amid festive dancing. They wept profusely for joy, and, as there was true love between them a double happiness resulted.' They clearly had a close bond. Despite this, Bede says very little about Seaxburh, and he seems to mention her almost in passing in his hurry to talk about her daughter,

Eorcongota, who, he says, 'deserves special mention.'[6] She was a nun at Faremoutiers-en-Brie like her aunt, Æthelburh, and it was said that on the night of her death, 'many of the brethren of that monastery, who were in other houses, declared that they at that time distinctly heard concerts of angels singing, and the sound as it were of a great multitude entering the monastery.'[7] It might be pertinent that unlike her sister Æthelthryth, whom Bede applauded for retaining her virginity through two marriages, Seaxburh came to the religious life only after having become a wife, queen, mother and regent and it is fair to say that Bede took much less interest in women who did not preserve their chastity. This might be the reason why he chose to focus on Seaxburh's daughter, rather than on her.

At Ely Seaxburh, who oversaw the translation of her sister's uncorrupt body, apparently foresaw the day of her own death and was buried behind her sister[8] and, as we saw at the start of this section, was succeeded by another of her daughters, Eormenhild. Seaxburh's offspring played important roles and were extremely influential; it is Seaxburh's life as a married woman where we are given more information, and it is through her marriage that the family of Anna of East Anglia became linked to the esteemed royal family of Kent.

In a fragmentary text it is recorded that Seaxburh and her daughter Eormenhild were nuns at Milton Regis in Kent. At Sheppey, a house attached to Milton Regis, Seaxburh built a monastery which was thirty years in construction. For the same length of time, we are told, she had been acting as regent for her son, King Hlothhere of Kent.[9] In other versions of her *Life*, it is said that the son for whom she acted as regent was in fact called Ecgberht. In the group of texts known as the *Legend of St Mildrith*, considerable detail is given concerning the Kentish royal house, and Seaxburh's time at Ely is not even mentioned.[10] For a woman to be regent at a time when there was much unrest and hostility between the kingdoms is remarkable, and if we are to believe that the regency lasted thirty years, it is even more striking. So how did this 'daughter of East Anglia' come to be so involved in Kentish politics?

Bede makes much of the close links between the royal houses of East Anglia and Kent. Kentish princesses made valuable wives, as we have seen with the example of Æthelburh 'Tate', daughter of Æthelberht, wife of Edwin of Northumbria and of her daughter, Eanflæd. Bede also includes a story about a thegn named Imma, and the aftermath of the battle of the Trent in 679 in which the young son of Oswiu and Eanflæd was killed. Imma had been captured by men loyal to the king of Mercia but was able to call upon the help of Hlothhere of Kent, because he, Imma, had once been a thegn of Queen Æthelthryth who, being the sister of Seaxburh, was thus Hlothhere's aunt. The *Liber Eliensis* specifically states that Imma was her butler, so it is likely that here is another case of a member of the queen's household having travelled with her to a new kingdom. That he could call upon the aid of his mistress's nephew the king of Kent, speaks perhaps of her influence.[11]

We have already been introduced to the famous daughter of Æthelberht of Kent, Æthelburh 'Tate' and briefly to her brother, Eadbald, who succeeded their father as king of Kent. Here, in the *Legend of St Mildrith* texts, we are told the name of Eadbald's queen, Ymme – the only place where this is mentioned – and we are given details of his children.

It seems that Eadbald's eldest son was Eorcenberht and it was this eldest son, who succeeded his father as king of Kent, whom Seaxburh married. Eorcenberht ruled Kent from 640–664, but the date of the marriage is not known. Hlothhere was the youngest son of Eorcenberht but it is not certain whether Seaxburh was his mother. The other son for whom she might have been acting as regent, Ecgberht, was alleged to have committed murder with far-reaching consequences for another branch of the family, as will be examined below. Of Seaxburh's daughter and granddaughter, the information is less controversial.

Seaxburh's daughter Eormenhild was said by William of Malmesbury to have succeeded her mother as abbess of Ely. It seems she made less of an impact on the hagiographers and chroniclers than had her mother and, indeed, her cousin; nevertheless the few facts known of her life are worth recounting.[12] Presumably she considered herself to be Kentish and lived there until the time of her marriage. This was to King Wulfhere of Mercia, son of Penda the warlord who had been such a thorn in the sides of the kings of Northumbria.

After Penda's defeat at the battle of *Winwæd* in 655, Wulfhere went into exile – at presumably quite a young age – and for three years, Oswiu of Northumbria was in control of Mercia but, in 658, a number of Mercian ealdormen rose up in rebellion and Mercia regained its independence, with Wulfhere as king.

Unlike his father, Wulfhere was a Christian, and like so many kings before him it seems he looked to the influential royal house of Kent for a bride. Wulfhere was of such a different religious persuasion from his father that it is probably less than coincidence that he sought a wife who could help him forge links with the Kentish court and through there, links with the Franks.[13] There is some doubt though, over whether his marriage to Eormenhild was his first. There is a charter concerning the foundation of Gloucester Abbey, which seems to suggest that a lady named Cyneburh, sister of the king of the *Hwicce*, was the first abbess of Gloucester and that she was succeeded by a kinswoman of hers, a woman named Eadburh, who, before retiring to the abbey, had been the wife of King Wulfhere. Presumably, then, Wulfhere repudiated one of these wives in order to marry the other and it is usually assumed that it was Eadburh whom he married first and that the charter's assertion that Eadburh was Wulfhere's widow must be wrong, because Eormenhild outlived Wulfhere to become abbess of Ely.[14]

Bede does not mention Eormenhild or her daughter, who also became a saint. The point has been made that had he had such information, he would certainly have used it, and that perhaps we must suspect that she and her daughter never existed,[15] but plenty of other sources do talk about her. One of the texts incorporated into the Mildrith Legend, *þa halgan*, says that Eormenhild was buried at Ely along with her mother Seaxburh and her aunt, Æthelthryth,[16] and as the quoted lines which opened this section show, William of Malmesbury believed it too. Eormenhild may well have had a Christianising influence on Mercia. The eleventh-century hagiographer, Goscelin of St Bertin, said that she had planned to live the religious life but was dragged reluctantly into marriage, the sweet-natured girl being unable to escape the snares of the world, but by her mediation 'Kent and Mercia were made as one kingdom.'[17] Goscelin relates that although Wulfhere was a Christian, the new religion was still in its infancy in Mercia. Eormenhild, 'the handmaid of God ... by her sweetness, her soothing encouragements, and her obliging ways softened untamed hearts, and bestirred them to the taking up of Christ's sweet yoke.'[18] He also said that her husband obeyed her desires and petitions and yielded to her advice.

When Wulfhere died in 675 Eormenhild went back to the southeast where she was credited with enabling the abbey at Ely to flourish 'thanks to the good works and miracles brought about by the saintly women, namely Æthelthryth, Wihtburh, Seaxburh and Eormenhild.' She is mentioned in a charter of 699, issued by King Wihtred of Kent, and confirming privileges of the Kentish monasteries so we know that she died sometime after that, but the only other fact about her life on which the sources seem to agree is that she was the mother of Saint Werburg. We are told that she 'preferred that her only daughter be betrothed to God, rather than to an earthly realm.'[19]

There is, incidentally, a curious entry in a record concerning Stone, in Staffordshire, where two sons of Wulfhere were said to have been killed by their father, who, having apostatised, found them at prayer and killed them 'with his own hands'. When the sad news was relayed to Queen Eormenhild, she arranged for their bodies to be entombed in a stone monument. Wulfhere, it is said, was tormented by guilt and grief until he was absolved by St Cedd. This baffling tale comes from the seventeenth-century antiquarian William Dugdale and is extremely unlikely to be true. There is no indication that these boys were sons of Eormenhild, but had she suffered the loss of her sons by the hand of their father, or even been aware of the murder of her stepsons, we might imagine that she would have left Wulfhere for the religious life during his lifetime, and that such a bereavement might have been mentioned by her hagiographer and/or the *Liber Eliensis*.[20]

It is possible that Wulfhere had another son, named Berhtwald, who is otherwise unknown except for an entry in the *Life* of Wilfrid, where he is named as a nephew of King Æthelred (Wulfhere's brother and successor), and William of Malmesbury's *Gesta Pontificum Anglorum* which says of King Æthelred of Mercia: 'The same king has by his brother Wulfhere a nephew called Berhtwald' but it cannot be said – even supposing he truly existed – that this Berhtwald was the son of Eormenhild.[21] We should perhaps eliminate these three sons, and say that so far as we know, Eormenhild had only two children, her son Coenred – who eventually succeeded his father as king – and her daughter Werburg.

William Dugdale, as well as reporting the murder of the two boys, also said that Werburg, daughter of Wulfhere and Eormenhild, 'lived and died' at Chester while the *Liber Eliensis* is clear that 'King Wulfhere's queen, Eormenhild, the daughter of Eorcenberht and Queen Seaxburh, bore him a daughter, St Werburg who … entered the monastery of her great aunt, the blessed Æthelthryth [where] she performed many miracles.'[22] So, did she live in Chester, or did she retire to Ely?

A clue may be found later in the *Liber Eliensis* where it is recorded that her uncle, Wulfhere's brother and successor, Æthelred, upon hearing of her holiness, took her from Ely and put her in charge of

Hanbury (in modern-day Staffordshire) and Threekingham (in modern-day Lincolnshire). So it seems that having been trained by her aunt Æthelthryth at Ely, her reputation was such that she was 'headhunted' by her uncle, but this is still a long way from Chester.[23] According to the *Life* of Mildburg, written in praise of the life of her cousin, Werburg was buried in Hanbury. The *Life* of Werburg, on the other hand, says that she died at Threekingham, although she was initially buried according to her wishes at Hanbury, and her relics were at Chester by the time the *Life* was written. However, although *þa halgan* also records the moving of her remains to Chester, no explanation is given. Her importance was not just as a Kentish princess, for the Mercian royal family began to claim and promote their own saintly kin, and it was her cousin, King Ceolred, son of her uncle Æthelred, who commanded that her remains be elevated nine years after her death.[24] The *Life* of Werburg points out that in fact she 'blossomed' from four kingdoms: from Frankia through her great-great-grandfather's marriage to Bertha, from East Anglia through her grandmother Seaxburh, from Kent through her grandfather and from Mercia through her father. According to the *Life*, she was generous to the poor, tender and compassionate to the afflicted, and she was abstinent, faithful and patient.

Among the many miracles attributed to her, perhaps the most well-known is that told by William of Malmesbury. He said that she owned a strip of land where the crops were being eaten by wild geese.[25] Werburg told the bailiff to shut the geese up in his house and, whilst the bailiff thought it an odd request, he obeyed. He then stole one of the birds for his supper, fearing no reprisal. The next day Werburg commanded the geese to fly off but they did not, instead crowding round her feet and complaining loudly. She realised something was amiss, questioned the bailiff and obtained his confession. She then made a sign of healing and the bird sprouted new feathers and sprang back to life. William of Malmesbury went on to say that Werburg's powers were such that the prayers of all were granted, especially those of women and children.

Werburg was unusual among most of the Kentish members of her family in returning to Mercia rather than living out her days in Kent or Ely. She was, presumably, born in Mercia and her heritage shows the prestigious connections the royal house of Kent was able to make through various marriages; her mother Eormenhild was not the only daughter of Kent to migrate to Mercia after her marriage.

Eormenhild was the daughter of Seaxburh of East Anglia and Eorcenberht of Kent. According to some sources, Eorcenberht had an elder brother, Eormenred, who was disinherited when their father Eadbald left the whole Kentish kingdom to Eorcenberht. Other sources suggest that there might have been some power-sharing, but there was one reported incident which was to have far-reaching consequences for Eormenred's daughter, a lady known as Domne Eafe, or Domneva.

Domneva was also known by two other names, and this has led to a certain amount of confusion. Historian Patrick Sims-Williams showed that all the texts agree that her name was Domneva, or some variant thereof, but Florence of Worcester and William of Malmesbury called her Eormenburg.[26] She has been identified with an abbess, Æbbe (Domneva, or Domne Eafe, seems to have been the Latin form of Æbbe) in a number of charters relating to the minster at Thanet. D.W. Rollason drew attention to the fact that three of the Mildrith Legend texts said that Domneva had an alias, Eormenburg, but that a charter dated to the late seventh century is witnessed by Æbbe and Eormenburg, both assumed to be daughters of Eormenred of Kent and clearly separate women.[27]

Like her cousin Eormenhild, who married Wulfhere of Mercia, Domneva also strengthened ties of kinship between Kent and Mercia when she married a man named Merewalh. Merewalh's identity and paternity have been the subject of long debate. He has been assumed to have been another son of Penda of Mercia, but much has been made of the fact that his name suggests a possible Welsh/British connection and does not alliterate with his father's – unlike, for example, Penda's son Peada.[28] Certainly Merewalh's own family was alliterative, with all the children, male and female, having names beginning with M. The only source which states that he was Penda's son is the document known as the *Testament of St Mildburg* (his daughter) where King Æthelred of Mercia, son of Penda and brother of Wulfhere, is referred to as her uncle. Merewalh was prince of an area of Mercia which might originally have been a separate tribal homeland of the people known as the *Magonsæte*. According to one source Merewalh already had two young sons, Merchelm and Mildfrith, when he converted to Christianity and began looking for a new bride.[29] Together he and Domneva of Kent had daughters, Mildburg and Mildrith – and might have also had another daughter named Mildgyth – and a son, Merefin, who died whilst still only a child.

The marriage appears to have lasted for a little over a decade before Domneva left Mercia and returned to Kent.[30] The circumstances under which she left are recorded in detail in the Mildrith Legend and in one version of the *ASC*.[31] The story concerns Seaxburh's son Ecgberht, who allegedly murdered Domneva's brothers, whose names were Æthelred and Æthelberht. It is possible that the murders had something to do with the dynastic disputes arising from the disinheritance of Domneva's father, Eormenred. Of the murders, William of Malmesbury – who could have been using an independent source – reported that Ecgberht's servant, Thunor, deceived the princes with daily kisses, then while hugging them stabbed them, and buried them deep in a pit right under the king's throne, where no one would think to look.[32] But the king was scorched by divine fire, which caused him to dig away the stones, and the earth opened up and swallowed Thunor alive. Whether he directly ordered the killings, or was merely guilty of failing to stop his servant from committing murder, King Ecgberht was deemed liable. A *wergild* (man price) was owed in compensation, and Ecgberht paid this *wergild* to Domneva in the form of land on Thanet for her to found a monastery. According to one version of the Mildrith Legend, Domneva requested that she have as much land on Thanet as her tame hind could run around. As the hind ran, it was followed by the king and the court, but Thunor – still alive in this version – attempted to stop the animal and was swallowed by the earth. When the hind had finished running, Domneva was able to claim forty-eight hides of land, compensation had been duly paid, and Thunor got his comeuppance.[33]

Seventh-century traditions allowed for royal couples to separate in pursuit of the religious life and, just as Eormenhild would have been unlikely to stay with Wulfhere had he really murdered her sons, so Domneva would have been free to leave Merewalh even without her brothers being murdered. Were their deaths really the catalyst, and is the story true? If it is, it shows a shrewd woman who was wily enough to ensure the maximum grant of land for her religious foundation.

According to Bede, in 676 King Æthelred of Mercia devastated Kent. The *Testament of St Mildburg* refers to him as Mildburg's uncle and, in the eighth century, connections between the families were emphasised again when a later king of Mercia mentioned in a grant to Minster-in-Thanet his love for his 'blood-relationship to the venerable abbess Mildrith'. It is possible that by attacking Kent, King Æthelred was seeking vengeance for the killings of Domneva's brothers and an intriguing footnote to this story is that in the eleventh century some relics of a saint named Æthelred lay in the church at Leominster founded by Merewalh. Perhaps this was one of Domneva's murdered brothers.[34] One other consideration is that if the story is true, and that Seaxburh was Ecgberht's mother, then given that her date of death is usually considered to be *c.*700 and the killings took place before 676, she must surely have been aware that her son, or stepson, was guilty of murdering his cousins. Yet, as with so much of this period of history, we are not told her reaction to this cataclysmic event.

It seems that Domneva took her daughters with her to Kent, initially at least, and as H.P.R. Finberg pointed out they were probably quite young when, as he put it, their mother 'quitted Mercia for the more bracing air of Thanet.'[35] Of the shadowy daughter named Mildgyth, there seems to be no further information than that she was buried somewhere in Northumbria, where she spent her life and worked many miracles. Sir Frank Stenton said that she was a nun at Eastry but other historians have questioned whether she even existed.[36]

Mildrith was sent abroad, to receive her education at Chelles.[37] Goscelin related a story that while she was there, the abbess attempted to force her into marriage with one of her kinsmen. When Mildrith refused to acquiesce, she was put in a hot oven, but miraculously managed to escape. The abbess then beat her so viciously that her hair was torn out. Mildrith sent some of this hair to her mother as an SOS signal. Domneva sent a rescue party, although Mildrith refused to leave until she had collected some holy relics from her room. The delay meant that they were pursued and were only successful in escaping because the tide turned. When she at last returned to Kent and set foot on land, Mildrith left the imprint of her shoe on the rock at Ebbsfleet and transferred to it healing powers. No doubt her mother was pleased to see her again; Mildrith entered Domneva's house at Minster-in-Thanet and eventually succeeded her as abbess.[38] She appears on the witness list of a charter issued by King Wihtred of Kent in 716 and in 724 she was granted land by his son.

The rulers of Kent continued to grant land to her as late as 733, so the abbey was clearly favoured by successive kings. Between 675 and 780 Minster also received toll-remissions on ships, demonstrating that the abbey was actively involved in trade between London and the Frankish ports. One of the texts of the Mildrith Legend calls the monastery 'very famous' and records that the relics of the murdered princes, her uncles Æthelred and Æthelberht, were translated there.[39]

Like her cousin Werburg, Mildrith's sister Mildburg stayed in Mercia rather than returning to her mother's homeland in Kent and became abbess of Wenlock sometime between 674 and 690 and according to the *Testament of St Mildburg* was still alive in 727 and possibly as late as 736. Before she became abbess at Wenlock it had been under the auspices of the abbot of St Botulf's at *Icanho* (in East Anglia) and an abbess whose name was Frankish: Liobsynda, or Liobsind. It seems that Liobsind was the first abbess and was brought over from Chelles. We know that Mildrith was educated at Chelles, and it is possible that Mildburg also spent some time there.[40] It is likely that Merewalh was paving the way for his daughter to take over the abbey which was, like the Frankish monasteries, a double house. A curious mix, then, produced a house in Mercia, on the Welsh border, founded initially by East Anglians and styled on Frankish models.

The monastery at *Icanho* had been founded by Botulf and the *Testament of St Mildburg* recorded that the abbot of *Icanho* gave Mildburg Wenlock and other estates. Patrick Sims-Williams suggested that the likely scenario was that the community at St Botulf's had acquired the land from Merewalh and made it over to Mildburg. The siting of Wenlock is interesting, given that it was on the border between the territory of the *Magonsæte* and that of the *Wreoconsæte* and it has been propounded that it was built from, or upon, the remains of an earlier Roman building there.[41]

It seems that Mildburg also had connections with Llanfillo, near Brecon.[42] On the face of it, this is not easy to explain, but during the seventh century relations between the Mercians and the Welsh had been good – Penda and Cadwallon of Gwynedd had fought as allies against the Northumbrians – and there is a possibility that perhaps Mildburg's father Merewalh was indeed a Welshman after all, given land for service by Penda, or that perhaps he was Penda's Welsh son-in-law, by dint of his first marriage, rather than his son.[43]

The *Testament of St Mildburg*, as we saw briefly above, offers insights into her other family relationships. The document is styled as a testament, although there are no bequests contained within it. The most likely author is Goscelin but it is written as if dictated by the lady herself. It describes grants of land made to her by Merchelm and Mildfrith, sons of

Merewalh by his first wife, and they address her as their sister, '*germana ac soro*', and although she refers to them as her brothers, '*germana*' often means half-sister.[44] In a charter dated somewhere between 709 and 716 (S 1800) Mildburg was granted land by King Ceolred – son of King Æthelred of Mercia and possibly of his wife Osthryth, mentioned in Part I – but neither of her half-brothers witnessed the grant so perhaps by then they were both dead.

Ceolred might have granted land to the monastery but we should not assume from this that relations between the abbess and the king, who was her cousin, were anything approaching cordial. King Æthelred abdicated the throne and went to Rome in pursuit of the religious life, and probably had an inkling that his son was not throne-worthy, for he nominated his nephew, a son of his brother Wulfhere, to rule after him. This son of Wulfhere's ruled only a few years before he, too, retired to Rome.

King Ceolred was not popular. Reports of his depravity reached the ears of St Boniface. Boniface wrote that Ceolred showed by 'wicked example an open display of these two greatest sins in the provinces of the English … that is, debauchery and adultery with nuns and violation of monasteries.' In the same letter, Boniface describes the death of Ceolred who, 'feasting in splendour amid his companions' was suddenly sent mad 'by a malign spirit … so that without repentance and confession, he departed from this light without a doubt to the torments of hell.'[45] Boniface had received the details from a visionary monk at Wenlock who had seen the awful punishments awaiting the king upon his death. An interesting aside here is that the presence of a monk at Wenlock shows that this was indeed a double house.

The writing style of the *Testament of St Mildburg* is similar to Aldhelm's *De Virginitate* which, as we saw in Part I, was dedicated to Hildelith. Hildelith was in contact with Mildburg's monastery because it was she who told Boniface about the vision of Ceolred's death.[46] Boniface explains in a letter to the abbess of Thanet (Eadburh, successor to Mildrith) how it was told to him that the visionary had died and come back to life, but not before witnessing the terrible fate of others, including King Ceolred who was fated to suffer the torment of demons.[47] It has been suggested that it was Mildburg herself, Ceolred's cousin, who was responsible for circulating the story. Perhaps there was loyalty to the *Magonsæte* which was felt keenly; the royal family descended from Merewalh seems to have petered out and in a couple of generations it had lost power, being absorbed into and subject to the kingdom of Mercia. Thus there is every reason to suspect that there was no love lost between Mildburg and Ceolred. It is not clear exactly when Mildburg died, but William of Malmesbury related how, when her tomb was broken into, an odour of fragrant balsam wafted through the church and miracles ensued.[48]

The contrast between what we know of those who became saints and those who did not is marked. As D.W. Rollason observed, the saints descended from King Æthelberht of Kent or linked to him by marriage number no fewer than nineteen, but of the history of Merewalh's family beyond his saintly Kentish daughters there is no trace.[49] Merchelm succeeded his father – he is styled *rex* in the *Testament of St Mildburg* – and his brother Mildfrith was commemorated on a monumental inscription commissioned by a later bishop of Hereford. The inscription named Mildfrith's consort as Cwenburh, and she was described as his fair wife, but nothing more is known of her; she is merely a name on a stone.

The family of the princes of the *Magonsæte* died out, and the links with Kent evaporated, but this was not the end of the story of powerful women living in Mercia.

Part III

Murder in Mercia and Powerful Royal Daughters

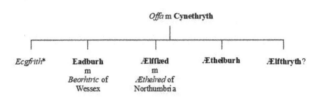

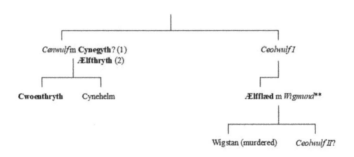

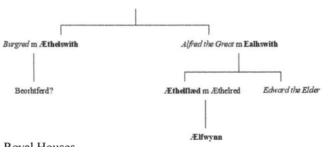

The Mercian Royal Houses.

The direct descendants of Penda ruled in Mercia until 716 but with the death of Ceolred the crown passed between various branches of the royal family, often with bloody coups and rival claimants being exiled. One of the strongest kings during this period was Offa, and much of what we know of his reign comes from the dealings he had with the emperor Charlemagne, with whom he seems to have felt equal in status. Offa came to power in 757 having driven out a king who ruled after his predecessor, King Æthelbald, had been murdered. Clearly aware that kingship could be lost as quickly as it could be won, he set about strengthening the kingdom, absorbing smaller, hitherto independent units, such as the erstwhile kingdom of the *Hwicce*, and the kingdom of the South Saxons, into Mercia. He had more complicated dealings with the larger, more powerful, kingdoms – Kent and the kingdom of the West Saxons – but he was no mere barbarous warlord and his family were important figures during his reign.

Offa married a woman named Cynethryth, although it is not recorded when the marriage occurred. She only appears in the charter witness lists after *c.* 770 and it has been argued that the marriage might not have taken place very much before this date, considering that the children known to have been born to the couple married in the late 780s and 790s.[1] It is not known where she came from or whether she was even Mercian, but it is possible that her name might provide a clue.

With the death of Ceolred the line of succession through Penda's descendants had been broken and neither Offa nor his two predecessors had any direct links with the previous king. Given that Penda had a wife named Cynewise, and daughters named Cyneburh and Cyneswith, it is just possible that the Cynethryth who married Offa might have been of Penda's line, and as such her bloodline would have been important in strengthening Offa's claim to the throne. Making assumptions based on name alliteration is always problematic, however, and this can never be more than conjecture; many West Saxons had names which also alliterate with hers. Some have gone so far as to suggest that she was the queen and Offa was her consort, citing the fact that in some cultures, for example the Pictish, rule descended through the matrilineal line, but this might be stretching a point.[2] Whatever her heritage, she was an important woman and far from being a 'token' queen; she was pivotal in Offa's determination to strengthen his kingdom and ensure that their son, Ecgfrith, succeeded him as king of Mercia at a time when sons rarely succeeded their fathers.

Cynethryth was the first Mercian queen since the ill-fated Osthryth (mentioned in Part I) to attest charters and she did so on a regular basis until Offa's death. She exercised joint lordship with Offa over the Mercian monasteries and she retained possession of the lucrative Cookham monastery after his death, which led her into dispute with the archdiocese of Canterbury.[3] She attested as the mother of Ecgfrith, even appearing in charters without him, before he reached his majority, after which he seems to have replaced her on the lists.[4] As will be discussed elsewhere, a queen's status was significantly enhanced by being the mother of an atheling.[5] She was also the only known queen, not just of Mercia, but any queen in England, to have coins struck in her name.[6] Although she was only shown wearing a diadem on one of the coins issued in her name, her title is clear: '*regina M*'. Surviving examples of the coins are versions of Offa's own, adjusted to show her name in place of his and they were possibly modelled on those of a Byzantine empress. She clearly enjoyed high status, and the monk and scholar, Alcuin, wrote to Ecgfrith reminding him that he should learn authority from his father and compassion from his mother, and 'from him how to rule the people with justice, from her to feel pity for those who suffer.'[7]

Cynethryth continued to play a prominent role during her son's kingship, witnessing two of his charters despite having been absent from the witness lists for some years. Perhaps this indicated a takeover, or merely the strong presence of a mother whose young son was now king. Her authority was clear though, for Alcuin also asked that the king send greeting to her; he would have written to her himself but knew that the king's business kept her too busy to read letters. Cynethryth was referred to as 'queen', 'queen of the Mercians' and 'queen of the Mercians by the grace of God'.[8]

It seems likely that Cynethryth was vital to Offa's determined efforts to secure his dynasty. Whether or not her background strengthened his claims, her titles and the issuing of coins in her name most certainly bolstered his position. But while her bloodline might have been important, it was clearly not enough for Offa. He went further still, arranging for their son not only to succeed, but to be anointed while he, Offa, was still alive. His efforts were all for naught, however, because Ecgfrith lived for only a matter of five months after his father's death, at which point Cynethryth embraced the religious life. There are two ways of viewing this: either Ecgfrith died of natural causes and his mother, bereft and without any reason to stay at court, went sadly to start a new life as a religious. Alternatively, given the murky circumstances which surrounded many of the changes of regime in this period, she perhaps suffered the knowledge that her son, on whom so much hope had been pinned by his parents, was murdered. Either way, it is likely that Cynethryth carried deep sorrow with her when she left the court for the cloistered life.

Times had changed for the abbeys and there was not the same proliferation of female royal saints. The double monasteries began to decline, perhaps in part because as royal endowments they were becoming too rich and too powerful. Mercian kings claiming monastic land as hereditary property ruffled the feathers of the churchmen. Offa built up quite the property portfolio, naming Cynethryth as his heir. She became abbess of Cookham, but the archbishop of Canterbury claimed the rights to it, and Cynethryth had to enter into an agreement whereby in order to keep Cookham she had to give away another monastery and a number of large estates attached to it at a place named *Bedeford* in Kent. She was given a different monastery as compensation at *Pectanege*.[9] Cynethryth was seemingly in control of a wide number of religious foundations and a lady named Cynethryth was recorded as abbess of Winchcombe, too, although it is not certain that she and Offa's widow were one and the same.[10] It has been thought by some that one of her daughters, Æthelburh, was the abbess of Fladbury, although this seems not to have been the case and the assumption is based on the witness list of a spurious charter.[11] This confusion over her tenure as abbess of Fladbury, though, is the least contentious of the tales regarding Cynethryth and her children.

Whether or not her disagreement with the Church had any bearing on the opinions of the later chroniclers, Cynethryth was not kindly remembered. Offa's reign is notable for the building of the famous dyke, his dealings with Charlemagne and for the murder of Æthelberht, king of East Anglia. One argument with Charlemagne resulted in a trade embargo and might have come about because of an arrangement for one of Offa's daughters to marry Charlemagne's son. Offa, considering himself equal to the emperor, also wished for his son Ecgfrith to marry one of Charlemagne's daughters. A similar situation might have sparked the murder of the East Anglian king, for in some versions of the tale, the East Anglian king was visiting Mercia seeking the hand of one of Offa's daughters.[12]

The *ASC* records merely that 'Offa had Æthelberht beheaded' but, typically, the later chroniclers embellished the story. The twelfth-century chronicle of John of Worcester says that he was slain 'by the wicked urging' of Cynethryth. Roger of Wendover goes into yet more detail, claiming that when Offa asked his wife for advice on the marriage proposal, she replied: 'God has this day delivered into your hands your enemy, whose kingdom you have so long desired; if, therefore, you secretly put him to death, his kingdom will pass to you and your successors for ever.' He goes on to relate how the queen arranged for a pit to be dug underneath a seat where their guest would sit. The victim was plunged into the pit and stifled by the queen's executioners. According to the earliest version of Æthelberht's *passio* (account of a martyr), the grieving fiancée, Cynethryth and Offa's daughter, Ælfthryth, took herself off to the monastery at Crowland.[13]

Given that Offa was at pains to bring southern England under his control, and the fact that there is some evidence that the East Anglians were minting their own coins and asserting independence, it is more than likely that this was a political murder. Why, then, did the later chroniclers blame Cynethryth? It might have something to do with the origin of the cult of St Æthelberht and the fact that the story, as told by the earlier chronicles, was harmful to Offa's reputation and therefore it was expedient to shift the blame onto the queen.[14] We know that she wielded power – her name on coins is evidence of this – and Alcuin referred to her piety, which seems an unlikely word to use if she had been accused or suspected of anything so heinous as murder, but it is a trope frequently used by later chroniclers to show women of power abusing that privilege to incite or commit murder; as we shall see, Cynethryth was not the last royal lady to be accused of murder, and the next accused was one of her daughters.

As well as their son, Ecgfrith, Offa and Cynethryth had a number of daughters. One, mentioned above, was Æthelburh. It seems that she was not the woman of the same name who was abbess of Fladbury, but it is likely that she was an abbess, perhaps in charge of another of Offa's family houses.[15] She is known to have corresponded with Alcuin, who wrote to her upon the death of her brother-in-law, Æthelred, king of Northumbria: 'Some of this ruin has brought you hot tears, I know, for your beloved sister. Now she is widowed she must be urged to soldier for Christ in a convent, that her temporal grief may lead to eternal joy.'

In another part of the same letter, he says that Charlemagne's wife has sent a small gift of a dress, a touching piece of information which helps to bring these characters to life.[16] That Alcuin could speak of 'hot tears' shed for a sister who had been widowed means these sisters must have been very close and the gifts sent by the emperor's wife show that the arguments between Offa and Charlemagne did not stop the women of the two families acting towards each other with kindness and sympathy.

The sister who was widowed upon the death of the Northumbrian king was Ælfflæd. The political situation in Northumbria at this point was a troubled one. Æthelred had already taken the throne and been expelled once, before regaining the throne and driving out his rival in 790. In 792 he married Ælfflæd, daughter of Offa, and we know that the ceremony was held at Catterick in modern-day North Yorkshire. The eleventh-century chronicler Simeon of Durham even furnishes us with the date: 29 September. Such was the power of Offa that marriage to his daughters was a prestigious and strategic move, designed to guarantee Mercian protection in times of strife. It did not help Æthelred much though and he was murdered just four years later. Alcuin wrote to Ælfflæd's mother-in-law expressing his condolences and, as we have seen, to her sister.

We know that prior to her marriage, Ælfflæd witnessed charters and in one, S 127, she was described as unmarried. However, this is the same spurious charter mentioned above, which named her sister Æthelburh as abbess of Fladbury. Possibly, then, given that she was not married to Æthelred until 792, she might have been the daughter who was originally destined to marry the son of Charlemagne. It is hard to imagine that she had much choice about either of these marriages. When Simeon of Durham recorded the wedding, he called her a queen but whether he meant that she had previously been a queen, as some have suggested, is doubtful. There is no suggestion that the marriage arrangements with Charlemagne's son went ahead. What is not in doubt is that she was widowed in 796 after the death of Æthelred, but there is no record of her life after that. It is probably safe to assume that she ended her days in a monastery or living quietly on her estates. However it was that she lived out her days, it is likely that it was in a less dramatic fashion than that of her sister, Eadburh.

Offa had managed, or nearly managed, prestigious marriages for two, possibly three, of his daughters: the proposed union between Mercia and the emperor Charlemagne, Ælfflæd's wedding to the king of Northumbria and most infamously, Eadburh's marriage to Beorhtric, king of the West Saxons. Offa and Beorhtric were allies against Ecgberht, a rival to the West Saxon throne who had been exiled by Offa and given refuge in Frankia. Eadburh married Beorhtric in 789 and according to the *ASC* Beorhtric had supported Offa because of this union.[17] Clearly, then, this was a political marriage. No children are recorded, but this might be because Beorhtric was not succeeded by his own kin, but by Ecgberht, who returned from exile and succeeded to the kingdom upon Beorhtric's death. There is no suggestion in the *ASC* that there was a battle, but it remains a possibility. It does record the death of another man which might seem insignificant but may be important because, according to Asser, the tale was much more complicated, and sinister. The *ASC* entry says that 'In this year King Beorhtric and Ealdorman Worr died.'

Asser was not a post-Conquest chronicler, like the ones who accused Cynethryth of murder. He was a Welsh monk living in the court of King Alfred the Great, commissioned to write a life of the king. Ecgberht was Alfred's grandfather, so Asser was writing only two generations after the events, and contemporary to the *ASC* at this point. He was adamant that Beorhtric had not died on the battlefield, or even in the comfort of his own bed, but at the hand of his wife, Eadburh of Mercia. Asser's story about Eadburh is excoriating and runs over several chapters. It was Eadburh's fault, he said, that the wives of West Saxon kings were no longer called 'queen' because she brought a 'foul stigma' on all the queens who came after her, and Asser says he heard the tale of her 'very great wickedness' from Alfred himself. Apparently, as soon as Eadburh had earned the king's (her husband's) friendship, she began to behave tyrannically in the manner of her father and loathed all of her husband's advisers. She denounced them at every opportunity and attempted to deprive them of power. If this failed, she killed them by poisoning them. This happened to a young man who was dear to the king and, on this occasion, King Beorhtric accidentally also took the poison, with the consequence that both he and the young man died.

The story continues: Eadburh, unable to remain in England, went with 'countless treasures' to the court of Charlemagne, who then told her to choose between him and his son and she chose the son, he being the younger of the two. The emperor informed her that had she chosen the father, she could have had the son, but because she had not, she would have neither. He did, however, give her a large convent where she could be abbess. This was not the end of her story though, because she continued to live recklessly and was eventually caught 'in debauchery' with a man of her own race and, having been ejected from the abbey, ended her days in poverty, dying a 'miserable death' in Pavia, Italy.[18]

This tale contrasts wildly with the simple entry in the *ASC* yet there are clues that might suggest there is an element of truth in it, because of the comment that 'Ealdorman Worr died' along with Beorhtric. Could this man, Worr, have been the adviser who was poisoned alongside the king? There is some evidence for Eadburh's having ended her days on the Continent. As we shall see, she would not be the last royal lady of Mercia to die at Pavia – Italy being a popular pilgrims' destination – and there is an entry in the Reichenau *Liber Vitae* dated between 825 and 850 recording that there was a convent in Lombardy whose abbess was called Eadburh.[19]

Truth or no, Asser's remarks have been described as 'malicious'.[20] What reasons could he have had for besmirching her reputation? Whatever the manner of his death, Beorhtric of Wessex was succeeded by his rival, Ecgberht, founder of the Alfredian dynasty. There would be every reason for Alfred's biographer to point to the chaos and instability of the reign before Ecgberht's. Eadburh may well have been 'an active representative of Mercian interests at the West Saxon court' and one might also consider the time at which Asser was writing;[21] by Alfred's reign, Mercia was no longer a kingdom but was still strong. There was an alliance with Wessex, but perhaps it was politic to downplay the status of royal women at this point, something which will be considered in more detail later when we look at the life of Alfred's daughter Æthelflæd, Lady of the Mercians.

There is one other possible explanation, though it is very tenuous. Dynastic struggles in Mercia in the eighth and ninth centuries saw to it that sons rarely succeeded fathers to the throne. The make-up of the Mercian kingdom, developed from a confederation of individual tribes and kingdoms, meant that there was often more than one contender for the throne who had no kinship tie with the previous incumbent. Historians have noted links between some of these families because of the alliteration of their first names. Given that at one time or another, Mercia was ruled by several kings whose name began with B, it is just possible that Beorhtric – king of Wessex but married to the daughter of the powerful Offa, king of Mercia – might have been a member of another branch of the Mercian royal family, and was ruling Wessex as a puppet of Offa's. This is nothing more than conjecture, but it might explain why the official biographer of Alfred was keen to record that the reign ended badly. There might have been reluctance to mention Beorhtric's origins, and so the blame had to fall squarely upon his wife.

Little else is known about Eadburh. Perhaps we can deduce how old she was when she died; if she was still alive in Lombardy as late as 850, sixty-one years after her marriage, she either lived to a ripe old age or was married very young. Alternatively, perhaps the earliest date of the Reichenau *Liber Vitae*, 825, is the more accurate one. She witnessed charters as a queen and one which might be authentic, where she is styled *regina*, is also witnessed by the ealdorman Worr. Clearly, these two knew each other, but whether we can assuredly say that he died at her hand, must be open to doubt.[22]

What can be stated with certainty is that the governance of Mercia remained unstable. Offa's ambition for his son Ecgfrith to succeed him was realised, but Ecgfrith reigned for only five months before dying. There is no suggestion in the records of foul play, but it remains a possibility. The kingship then passed to another branch of the royal house. Offa was descended from Penda's brother, while the new king might have been descended from Penda's sister, although he made strong claims on land in the territory of the *Hwicce*, too. Whatever his origins, King Cenwulf was an effective, long-reigning monarch. He, like Offa before him, claimed Church lands as his family property, a policy which strained relations with Canterbury and which would have ramifications for Cenwulf's daughter who, like Eadburh, would be accused of murder. In this case though the charge was not mariticide, but fratricide.

There seems no doubt that our next royal lady, Cwoenthryth, was the daughter of King Cenwulf, but the identity of her mother is not known. Cenwulf might well have been married twice; a charter of 799 appears to show a wife, Cynegyth, but it is unreliable at best. Her name is alliterative with the known children of Cenwulf, but alliteration as a device for proving familial links can only ever be speculative. Another woman, Ælfthryth, witnessed charters perhaps as early as 804, and as *regina* in 814.[23]

King Cenwulf had as tight a grip on southern England as had his predecessor, Offa, but it was his argument with the archbishop of Canterbury which was to have repercussions for his daughter. Cwoenthryth was named as his heir, not to the throne, but to his property. Her date of birth is unknown but she witnessed a charter as 'the king's daughter' in 811 and it was probably at some point after this that she entered the religious life and became abbess of the family house at Winchcombe.[24] Winchcombe, in the region of the *Hwicce*, was especially associated with this branch of the royal family; it was the burial place of Cwoenthryth's father and brother. The annals of Winchcombe claimed that the convent of nuns was founded by Offa in 787, while Cenwulf founded the monastery of monks there in 798. Thus it could be contended that it was Cenwulf who established the double monastery of which his daughter became abbess.[25]

The argument that Cwoenthryth inherited centred around the king's claim to the lands, which Wulfred, archbishop of Canterbury, insisted belonged to the Church. Cwoenthryth inherited not only Winchcombe in Mercia from her father, but houses in Kent, too: Minster-in-Thanet and Reculver. She cannot have overseen all three sites in person – Reculver is some 175 miles from Winchcombe – but she was clearly in charge of a wide network, and presumably reliant on deputies to act for her in her absence. With the double houses providing the nuclei for growing settlements, she would have been a powerful woman in charge of huge revenues and responsible for organising hospitality to the king's entourage whenever he travelled. Along with industry, literacy would have thrived and it appears that Winchcombe was used as a repository for the royal family archives. The tussle for these lucrative lands and properties was at times unedifying. At one point, it seems that Wulfred might have forged documents in the Church's favour.[26]

After Cenwulf's death, in 821, the argument continued. The Mercian throne passed to Cenwulf's brother, Ceolwulf, but he reigned for only two years before he was ousted by a new king, not of the same line. Archbishop Wulfred, at one point suspended and threatened with exile, had been restored. He was back at Canterbury, and Cwoenthryth no longer had a relative on the throne of Mercia. Councils were held in 824 and 825 at *Clofesho*,[27] where Cwoenthryth's right, not to be an abbess – this was never in dispute – but to hold the lands, was debated. Judgement was made, perhaps unsurprisingly, in Wulfred's favour.[28] Cwoenthryth remained in possession and in charge of Winchcombe and came to an agreement whereby she remained abbess of the Kentish abbeys but had to surrender the Kentish houses and recognise Wulfred's authority over them and the associated lands.[29]

Cwoenthryth's power had emanated not from marriage alliance, but from her control of the monasteries in Kent, in direct opposition to Canterbury. It is clear that she was viewed as a powerful and dangerous rival, keeping Mercian royal interest alive in Kent and collecting taxes which were destined for Mercian, not Kentish or Church coffers.

It is not known when Cwoenthryth died, but presumably she lived out her days as abbess. Why was she not remembered in the same glowing terms as other powerful abbesses who also oversaw centres of learning, such as Hild? Her spat with Wulfred would not have helped, but it was mainly because of later stories told about her and her alleged involvement in the murder of her own brother.

We can look to William of Malmesbury for one of the more lurid accounts of the murder. Apparently, when King Cenwulf died, he left his son, Cynehelm – better known as Kenelm – to his sister to bring up, because the boy was only 7 years old. She, however, had designs on the kingdom herself and ordered a servant, named in one source as Æscberht, to dispose of the boy.[30] The servant took the boy hunting, killed him, and hid his body in some bushes. The crime was revealed when a dove flew over the altar of St Peter's in Rome and dropped a parchment which detailed the whereabouts of the boy's body. A message relaying the martyrdom was sent by the pope to Mercia and Kenelm's body was recovered and brought back to Winchcombe for burial. Cwoenthryth, hearing the chanting of the priests and the shouts of the people, looked out of the window in horror. She then recited the psalm they were singing, but backwards in the form of a spell, in order to avoid discovery. But she was struck by divine retribution, and her eyes were torn from their sockets so violently that William of Malmesbury declared that, in his day, there were still blood spatters on the psalter from which she had been reading. In one version of the story, Cwoenthryth was not only deprived of her sight, but was punished by death.[31]

Is it really possible that Cwoenthryth ordered the murder of her brother and was then allowed simply to continue living as an abbess? If the murder occurred shortly after the death of her father, surely it would have been mentioned in her dispute with the archbishop of Canterbury? The stories about the murder come from a later period and there is no evidence that Kenelm was ever king of Mercia, although there is some which suggests that a brother of Cwoenthryth existed, and pre-deceased his father.

There are charters dated 799 and 821 which are witnessed by a Cynehelm, described as *Cenelm filii regis* (S 156) and *Kenelmus filius regis* (S 184) but they are not considered to be authentic. There was a senior ealdorman called Cynehelm at the Mercian court, attesting charters until 812, although he is never described as the king's son, for example in S 165 of 811: '*Ego Cynehelm dux consensi et subscripsi*'. It is possible that Cenwulf had a son, and the likelihood is that this son died before he was able to succeed to the throne, but the story of his murder, contained in the eleventh-century *Life* of Kenelm must be taken with a large pinch of salt. The person named in the charters would not have been a small child in 821, and the *ASC* does not record such a man even briefly succeeding his father. Since Cenwulf was buried at Winchcombe, it would be logical that any son of his would also have been interred there and, with the story of his martyrdom, the family gained a saint and the church was able to claim holy relics. At a time when churches had a need for possession of such, Kenelm's story seems to have met these requirements, taking the facts of a young prince's death and turning them into a legend of murder and sanctity and, at the same time, tainting the reputation of his sister the abbess. In later times, monks were living in single-sex houses and required to be celibate. Nuns too, were cloistered separately, the houses ruled by male priors, and a reminder of the days when abbesses were in charge of both the male and female religious was perhaps not a welcome one.

King Cenwulf was succeeded not by his son but by his brother, Ceolwulf, and Cwoenthryth was succeeded as abbess of Winchcombe by Ceolwulf's daughter, her cousin Ælfflæd. Ælfflæd can be seen in action in her capacity as abbess in charters relating to a grant given to a man named Wullaf. In around 825, Cwoenthryth had granted land at Upton – part of Cenwulf's inheritance belonging to Winchcombe – to Wullaf's father, to be held for three generations. Ælfflæd then confirmed this in *c.* 860, extending the grant to Wullaf and for three more generations. Both of these charters are now lost but were referred to in a charter of 897 (S 1442) when a dispute between the churches of Worcester and Winchcombe was settled, in the presence of Alfred the Great, his brother-in-law Æthelwulf, and his son-in-law, Æthelred. Wullaf was forced to give up all hereditary rights and was leased the land but for his lifetime only, whereupon the land would be given to Worcester.

This seems to mark the only appearance of Ælfflæd in the charter records, but later saints' *Lives* name her as not only the daughter of King Ceolwulf, but the wife of a subsequent king, Wigmund. Her importance in the history of Mercia was not as abbess of a rich foundation, but as a member of more than one branch of the royal family.

For most of the eighth and ninth centuries, as we have seen, Mercia was beset by dynastic struggles. Rarely did son succeed father and, if he did, the reign was short-lived. Between the death of Offa in 796 and the death of the last Mercian king in *c.* 878 there were more than a dozen reigns. Cenwulf ruled for twenty-five years, but others ruled for short periods, some had their reigns interrupted, and few succeeded or preceded members of their own branch of the family. Cenwulf's brother, Ælfflæd's father Ceolwulf, ruled for two years before being replaced by a man named Beornwulf, who was killed in battle a few years later and succeeded by a man called Ludeca. He was killed in battle and succeeded by Wiglaf, who reigned twice, having his kingship interrupted by Ecgberht of Wessex, the man whom Offa had forced into exile. Wiglaf's son was Wigmund. According to Thomas of Marlborough, a thirteenth-century prior and chronicler of Evesham, Wigmund married Ælfflæd.

What we know of Ælfflæd comes from the stories concerning yet another murdered child of royalty, and the tale of the martyrdom of Wigstan shows how important her bloodline was in these times of dynastic power-play.

The long and complicated succession can be broken down for simplicity into the families of those kings whose name began with C and those whose names began with B. The kings whose names began with W were affiliated to the C kings through Ælfflæd. She was the daughter of a C king – Ceolwulf – and the wife of a W king – Wigmund – and her son had the alliterative name Wigstan. Wigstan was the grandson, therefore, of two kings.

The story goes that when Wigmund, who might have co-ruled with his father for a short while, died, his son Wigstan did not wish to become king, preferring the religious life. The chronicle of John of Worcester gives the date of his murder as 1 June 849, and says that a kinsman of Wigstan's, a man named Beorhtferth, son of the next king of Mercia,

Beorhtwulf, was the assassin. Wigstan's body was taken to Repton, Derbyshire, where his grandfather, Wiglaf, had been interred.

Why would a man who had renounced the throne be killed? Thomas of Marlborough said that Beorhtferth wanted to marry the widowed Queen Ælfflæd, and that Wigstan had refused to give his permission. We are not told the precise relationship between the two men, although some versions of the story say that Beorhtferth was Wigstan's godfather, but if we rely on the alliteration of the names, it is safe to assume that they came from rival branches of the royal family. Perhaps the story about Wigstan's decision to give up the throne is untrue? There is no clear evidence that his father, Wigmund, was ever actually king. Perhaps his widow was acting as regent for the young Wigstan, who took exception to the proposed marriage on the grounds that it would weaken his own claim to the throne.[32] It appears that Beorhtwulf wished to strengthen his claim to the kingship by marrying his son Beorhtferth to Ælfflæd; clearly her bloodline was pivotal to his case. Indeed, her first marriage might have come about from similar considerations. King Wiglaf had become king after the death of the obscure Ludeca, but in marrying Ælfflæd, the daughter of Ceolwulf, his son Wigmund linked the family to the previous ruling house, suggesting that her heritage was equally important to the family of her first husband as it was to her prospective second spouse.

With the martyred Wigstan out of the way, it may be assumed that Beorhtferth continued with his plan to marry Ælfflæd but, if he did, we are not told.[33] In fact, nothing more is known of him, and precious little of her, beyond her subsequent post as abbess of Winchcombe. There is, however, an interesting post script to her story. Beorhtwulf was succeeded, officially, by another B king, Burgred, who married the sister of Alfred the Great, and we will look at her story in a moment. But Burgred had a rival, who issued charters in Mercia and was perhaps considered more of a legitimate king than Burgred. This man was Ceolwulf II. He is most famous for having allied with the Vikings who occupied Repton in the 870s and forced Burgred to flee, but there may be a clue to his heritage in his name; it is possible that he was the son of Ælfflæd.[34] If so, then it shows clearly how a woman barely mentioned in the sources was nevertheless a daughter, wife and mother of kings and a crucial player in the power politics of the age.

It is not clear what happened to Beorhtwulf, or even how he died, but he disappears from the records in 852, to be replaced not by his son,

Beorhtferth, but by Burgred. This was the era of the Viking invasions, and Beorhtwulf had been allied with Wessex against the invaders. One of Burgred's first acts as king was to attack Wales, with West Saxon assistance. He also married into the illustrious West Saxon family, and his marriage to Æthelswith, sister of Alfred the Great (who was at that time not yet king) was no doubt a political rather than a love match. According to Asser, they were married after Easter at the royal estate of Chippenham, and the marriage was conducted in 'royal style'.[35] This was not the only such union of the period and, while the other matches compared favourably to the last such marriage, that between the 'murderous' Eadburh of Mercia and her supposedly poisoned husband Beorhtric, they could not escape the consequences of that alleged incident. For, while Burgred married a West Saxon princess, her brother Alfred married a Mercian princess when he became king, and the status of these two brides was far from equal.

Little is recorded of Alfred's sister Æthelswith, but where her name does appear, she is described as *regina* and in one charter she is styled 'queen of the Mercians' and acts alone as grantor of fifteen hides of land in Berkshire.[36] It is rare for a queen to be found gifting land in her own name. An item survives which speaks a little of her largesse and is a tangible link to a woman who lived so long ago. An exhibit in the British Museum, it is a gold ring inlaid with niello – a black metallic alloy mixed as a paste and worked into the engraving lines – and measuring around 2.6cm in diameter. It bears an inscription, *Æthelswith Regina*, but it is too big to be worn on a woman's finger and the inscription probably marks the name of the giver, not the owner. Even so, to stand and look at this piece of jewellery is to feel a connection with the woman who, even if she never wore it, must surely have seen it and personally handed it to the recipient.

In 868 her brother Alfred of Wessex married Ealhswith of Mercia, and there were other possible connections between the two courts. Also in 868, a certain Beorhtferd *filius regis* (son of the king) attested a charter of King Æthelred of Wessex, the brother whom Alfred would succeed (S 338a). Given the alliteration, and the fact that Æthelred had sons too young to inherit when he died, it is possible that this Beorhtferd, rather than being Beorhtferth son of Beorhtwulf, was a son of King Burgred's, and perhaps of Æthelswith's. If so, he could not have been more than about 14 when this charter was issued, and it is clear that he did not succeed his father. In 873–4, Vikings over-wintered at Repton and Burgred was deposed and forced to flee overseas. Back in Mercia, Burgred had been replaced as king by Ceolwulf II, possibly the son of Ælfflæd, and he issued two charters in 875. He seems not to have lasted very long as king, and the next leader of Mercia to emerge was not a king, but an ealdorman.

Presumably Queen Æthelswith and any children went with Burgred into exile but it is impossible to piece together what happened to the family between the expulsion and the recorded deaths of Burgred and his wife. According to Asser, Burgred went in 874 to Rome and died there not long afterwards, in the Saxon Quarter. Æthelswith, however, died in 888 in Pavia, seemingly whilst on pilgrimage. We can only surmise, therefore, that she lived on in Rome for over a decade after having been widowed.[37]

Her counterpart in Wessex fared better, although she was never accorded such high status as Æthelswith. She was never called 'queen', seemingly because of the alleged murderous tendencies of Eadburh the poisoner. However, her predecessor, Wulfthryth, wife of Alfred's brother, King Æthelred, might have been a consecrated queen as she is given the title *regina* in the only charter in which she appears and another sister-in-law, Judith, whose story we shall look at in Part VI, was an anointed queen.[38]

Ealhswith, wife of Alfred the Great, appears to have come from an illustrious Mercian family, but not only was she never a queen, Asser did not even mention her by name. He said that her mother was Eadburh – not to be confused with Eadburh, daughter of Offa and legendary poisoner – and that the elder lady was from the 'royal stock of the king of the Mercians'. He had often seen her with his own eyes and said that she was a 'notable woman who remained for many years after the death of her husband a chaste widow until her death.'[39] That husband, Ealhswith's father, was said to be a man named Æthelred *Mucil* (or *Mucel*) of the *Gaini*. Presumably the *Gaini* were one of the many ancient tribes of Mercia. Asser stated that the family was royal, and it is possible to identify Ealhswith's family through charter evidence.

Æthelred *Mucil* may be identified with the man who attested two charters in 868, the year the wedding took place.[40] Given that one of these charters was Mercian, and one was West Saxon, it is an indication of the close connections between the West Saxon and Mercian courts at this time, an alliance which was to prove invaluable during the crisis of the Viking invasions. Another charter, concerning Ealhswith's brother,

Æthelwulf, gives further insights into the family's roots. S 1442 outlines his responsibilities towards the monastery at Winchcombe. As we have seen, Winchcombe was regarded as a family possession by King Cenwulf and ownership was also claimed by his daughter, Cwoenthryth, so perhaps there was some link between the family of Ealhswith and that branch of the Mercian royal family. Æthelwulf is mentioned in the *ASC* which recorded the death in 901 of 'Ealdorman Æthelwulf, the brother of Ealhswith, King Edward's mother'. Ealhswith was not to be recorded or remembered as a queen – she did not attest any charters – but as a daughter, sister, and a mother. Quite why she did not attest any of her husband's charters must remain a mystery. Perhaps Alfred simply did not wish her to. This might be an explanation, but he was happy to allow his daughter to attest a charter of his in 889.[41] Royal wives and daughters regularly attested charters; perhaps Asser's statement about the status of Wessex queens was not designed to invalidate rival claims, but to explain away the specific treatment of Ealhswith whom, it must be remembered, he did not even name. It is a great irony that the wife of one of the best-known Anglo-Saxon kings was kept out of the records, not by the later chroniclers, but by those amongst whom she lived.

Asser did, however, record and name her children. They were Æthelflæd, the first-born (of whom more in a moment), Edward, two other daughters, Æthelgifu and Ælfthryth,[42] and another son, Æthelweard. Asser then makes a poignant remark, saying that in his list he leaves aside 'those who were carried off in infancy by an untimely death and who numbered ...'. How many? We do not know. As historian Simon Keynes points out in the notes to his translation, the numeral, if it was there, is unreadable.[43] Though rare, Asser's is not the only remark on this subject. We saw in Part I Bede's mention of seventh-century Queen Æthelburh 'Tate', two of whose children died in infancy and were buried in York. Even if still-births or infant deaths were common, there is no reason to think that they were not distressing.[44]

Ealhswith might also have had to contend with the presence at court of an illegitimate son of Alfred's, who could have been conceived after Alfred's marriage. Alfred's will contained a bequest for a man named Osferth who is described as the king's kinsman. He also appears in a charter of Alfred's son Edward (S 1286), where he is styled *frater regis* (brother of the king). Could he really have been an acknowledged illegitimate son of Alfred's? If so, Ealhswith must have had to suffer with fortitude his continued presence at court, for he attested a great number of charters. But the nature of his relationship to Alfred is by no means clear. His name suggests that he might have been related to the family of Osburh, Alfred's mother. Alternatively, he might have been a son of Oswald *filius regis* who attested at least three charters and might have been a son of Alfred's brother Æthelred. Asser is hardly likely to have mentioned a natural son of his beloved patron, but Osferth's identity must remain an enigma.[45]

Asser said that two of the royal children, Edward and Ælfthryth, were 'at all times fostered at the royal court' and were left under the care of tutors and nurses. We cannot assume though that the other children were not treated similarly. Education was important to Alfred and it seems unlikely that only some, rather than all, of his children would have 'attentively learned the psalms' and read books 'in English, and especially English poems'.[46] The sad reporting of the losses in infancy of a number of other children and the careful nurturing of the surviving offspring suggest a close family relationship, adding to the mystery of why Ealhswith should have been so overlooked by her husband and his biographer.

Ealhswith's two eldest surviving children, Æthelflæd and Edward, would grow up to form a working partnership which saw them pushing back the frontiers of the Danelaw (the areas settled by the invaders) and retaking towns overrun by the Vikings, but Ealhswith did not live to see the full extent of their success, dying three years after her husband in 902. The other children did well: Ælfthryth married a count of Flanders, while her sister, Æthelgifu, became abbess of her father's foundation at Shaftesbury. Æthelweard, the youngest, attested many of his brother Edward's charters and was generously provided for in Alfred's will.[47]

Ealhswith, despite being ignored by Asser, was, nevertheless, also treated generously in her husband's will, becoming the beneficiary of three important estates, including one at the place of his major victory over the Danes, at Edington, and another which was Alfred's own birthplace at Wantage. It might have been after Alfred's death that Ealhswith founded the abbey of St Mary at Winchester, more commonly referred to as Nunnaminster. The New Minster (Winchester) *Liber Vitae* named her as the builder of the abbey and she was buried with her husband – after his bones had been moved there by his son, Edward – in the New Minster. A tenth-century metrical calendar describes her as 'the dear and true Lady of the English'. To be styled Lady of the English, rather than simply of Wessex, was to be recognised as a queen in a way in which she was never acknowledged in life and puts her on a more equal standing with her husband, in memory if not in life.[48]

Her famous first-born, Æthelflæd, was never a queen, though she ruled a kingdom in all but name. It is often bewailed that little in modern times has been written of her, but the truth is that for all her fame, there is scarcely any information about her life. Whilst the post-Conquest chroniclers fell rather in love with her, the only information contained in the *ASC* is the annal known as the Mercian Register, which focuses on her life and covers the years 902–918.

After the flight of Burgred, Mercia had been ruled, briefly, by Ceolwulf II whose cause of death is unknown, but might have come about as a result of a campaign against the Welsh. The next leader to emerge was Æthelred, an ealdorman who seems to have made no claim to the throne, but ruled Mercia nevertheless.

Continuing the long-standing link between the two kingdoms – especially important now that only Wessex and 'Free' Mercia could put up any resistance to the Vikings – Æthelflæd, daughter of Alfred of Wessex, was married to Æthelred of Mercia in around 886 or 887. The first recorded interaction between Alfred and Æthelred is in 886 when Alfred occupied London and, according to Asser, restored it 'splendidly – after so many towns had been burned and so many people slaughtered.'[49] He then entrusted it to the care of Æthelred (London was traditionally a Mercian town) and perhaps the marriage was the seal on this new working arrangement.

There does not seem to be any suggestion that Alfred installed Æthelred as leader of Mercia, despite Henry of Huntingdon's assertion that London was *given* (my italics) to the ealdorman. It is likely that he was much older than his bride and was already a tried and tested warrior, acceptable to the Mercians as a leader, for it is doubtful that at this point, even with the Viking threat so near, the Mercians would have tolerated a leader imposed on them from without.[50]

It is clear that in the early days of their marriage, Æthelred was an active leader and there is little mention of his wife. He is recorded as being a joint sponsor with Alfred when Hasteinn the Dane was baptised as part of a truce arrangement in 893, and a near contemporary chronicler[51] said that after the battle at Farnham in Surrey when the

Danes were besieged on Thorney Isle, 'Earl Æthelred lent his aid to the prince [Edward].' With Alfred occupied in Exeter, Danish armies were engaged at Buttington by the forces of Æthelred of Mercia and the ealdormen of Wiltshire and Somerset. The fight against the Vikings was clearly being fought on three fronts, with Alfred, his son Edward, and his son-in-law Æthelred being mentioned in the chronicles as active in the struggle to push back the invaders.

Something changed, however. In 902, after Alfred's death, Edward faced a rebellion by his cousin, who allied with a rival member – possibly a relative of the B kings – of the Mercian royal house. There is no mention of Æthelred's having taken any part in the ensuing battle, even though his leadership might have been threatened by this revolt. In 907, according to the *ASC*, 'Chester was restored' and the Vikings driven out, but we are not told by whom. Given its location, one would expect this campaign to have been conducted by Mercian troops. In 909, Edward gathered Mercian and West Saxon troops and went harrying in Northumbria, but again there is no mention of his brother-in-law. When, in 910, those Northumbrian Vikings, presumably in retaliation, came south, at the ensuing battle at Tettenhall, deep in Mercia, there is again no mention of Æthelred. Since we know that he died in 911, we must assume that he was ill for some time beforehand. An Irish annal, known as the *Three Fragments*, and not considered hugely reliable, recorded that he was incapacitated in some way but still able to give strategic commands to his wife, stating that when Chester was overrun, messengers were sent to the 'King of the Saxons, who was in a disease and on the point of death.' It suggests that it was his wife, Æthelflæd, who held sway at this point.

Yet there is no indication in the English annals that she took his place in any military capacity before his death. The Mercian Register records no campaigns of any kind in the years 902–911 which could be attributed to her and it does not paint her as any kind of 'warrior woman'. In fact it does not even mention her by name until it records that in 910 she built a *burh* (fortified town) at an unidentified place named *Bremesbyrig*. It does appear, though, that the year 902 marks a turning point, being both the first entry in the Mercian Register and the first point at which it becomes clear that her husband was no longer militarily active.[52]

The idea has been put forward that the A version of the *ASC* at this point was a Wessex court chronicle, detailing the actions of Edward, whilst the

Mercian Register, sometimes termed the Æthelflæd annals, concentrated on her 'rule'.[53] Certainly the main chronicle virtually ignores her, identifying her only as Edward's sister. Even so, the Mercian Register focuses not so much on any war-like proclivities, but on her building and refortification programme, a programme which was nevertheless to prove crucial in the joint campaign of brother and sister in their attempts to push the Vikings out of northeast Mercia. It is an impressive list – 912 *Sceargeat* and Bridgnorth, 913 Tamworth and Stafford, 914 Eddisbury and Warwick, 915 Chirbury, *Weardbyrig* and Runcorn – and it is not random. Charted alongside Edward's activities, it shows a strategic and concerted campaign, by which she was fortifying specific towns which then enabled him to push back the Vikings in other areas.[54] The *burh*-building mainly occurred in the years after Æthelred's death. Perhaps this was a more acceptable way for a woman to lead, instead of taking part in pitched battles. The building programme also increased apace after Æthelflæd became sole ruler. Had nursing her husband during his illness kept her closer to home during those years? Edward did not attempt to take direct control over Mercia when Æthelred fell ill and one reason might be that he was simply too stretched, so close to the beginning of his reign, fighting the enemy from without (the Vikings) and within (his cousin). But if this is the case, then the Mercians, too, must have been hard-pressed and yet Æthelflæd only fully emerges after the date of her husband's death. It is plausible that she stayed near to him during his long incapacitation. We know that she was a compassionate woman, because of the record of what happened at Derby.

After 915 the nature of her activity changes somewhat, no longer restricted to defence, and we are told that in 916 she sent an army into Wales, the implication being that it was to avenge the death of an abbot who had been slain. In 917 her forces took Derby – where four thegns who were 'dear to her' were killed within the gates, showing how much she valued those around her – and in 918 she peacefully took control of Leicester. That same year the people of York pledged allegiance to her. Whilst there is no direct suggestion that she wielded a sword, she was clearly recognised as a leader. Leicester was particularly important, being one of the 'Five Boroughs' which were of crucial strategic significance.[55] The tide was turning.

If we want stories of her active participation in the military engagements then we need to look beyond the English sources to the

Three Fragments. In 918 the second battle of Corbridge saw the Dublin Norseman Ragnall once more pitched against the Scots and the English Northumbrians. The *Three Fragments* says that Æthelflæd directed the battle, ordering her troops to cut down the trees where the 'pagans' were hiding. 'In this manner did the queen kill all the pagans, so that her fame spread abroad in every direction.' It appears that as well as partnering her brother in an extensive and well-coordinated attack on the Danes, she was conducting her own campaign against the Norse. It should perhaps be noted that Corbridge is some 200 miles from Leicester, and that Æthelflæd is known to have been in Tamworth in June. Could she really have taken Leicester, fought at Corbridge, and been in Staffordshire all before midsummer? By 918, she would have been around the age of 50.

If she was fighting, where did she learn to do it? She certainly does not appear to have had a role model in her mother, who was kept out of the limelight and the records. Asser spoke of the royal children being educated, but not of the daughters being taught to wield swords. A glance at some other sources might provide clues.

The post-Conquest Anglo-Norman chroniclers spoke highly of her. Henry of Huntingdon was inspired by her actions to write:

> Heroic Elflede! great in martial fame,
> A man in valour, woman though in name:
> Thee warlike hosts, thee, nature too obey'd,
> Conqu'ror o'er both, though born by sex a maid.
> Chang'd be thy name, such honour triumphs bring.
> A queen by title, but in deeds a king.
> Heroes before the Mercian heroine quail'd:
> Caesar himself to win such glory fail'd.

Another poem, *Judith*, written in Old English, was thought by some to have represented Æthelflæd, but although the poem talks about 'Judith' in glowing terms – she is white and shining, noble and holy, courageous, and has *wundenlocc* (curly hair, a sign of beauty) – the idea that this stylised woman is in fact the Lady of the Mercians has been discredited. It seems unlikely that the poem has Mercian origins, and it was in fact written in the West Saxon dialect. Other contemporary sources merely call Æthelflæd the 'Lady of the Mercians' and it is only the later, post-Conquest, chroniclers such as Henry of Huntingdon who regard her as a heroine.[56]

Henry was clearly enamoured of her, but he got somewhat muddled when talking about her family. He thought that Æthelred was Æthelflæd's father and that Ælfwynn was her sister, when in fact they were her husband and her daughter respectively. This confusion, and a line in the Mercian Register, might assist us further. The Mercian Register, when talking about what happened after the death of Æthelflæd, says that her daughter Ælfwynn succeeded her briefly, but was then deprived of authority by Edward of Wessex. Tellingly, it calls Ælfwynn 'the daughter of Æthelred, Lord of the Mercians'.

It might be that there was a lost annal, one which placed greater emphasis on Æthelred and his status. If Henry of Huntingdon was relying on this lost annal, it might explain his confusion about the succession.[57] So in answer to the question: where had she learned to fight, if indeed she ever did, it is possible that she watched and learned from her husband. He must have been a great warrior to have been accepted as leader of men used to being ruled by kings. In this light, the fragmentary annals begin to ring true, when they speak of her taking advice from him regarding the siege of Chester, and of her leading the fight against Ragnall.

The Irish and Welsh annals called her a queen, whilst the English ones did not. Was her activity deliberately suppressed by the English chroniclers? This seems unlikely; if they were so against the idea of a woman leader then this would reflect the thinking of the time and she would never have been allowed to rule in the first place. The title of queen and the question of whether she should have been called one, should not vex us unduly. She was not a queen simply because her husband was not a king. She and her husband issued charters, but the coinage of the early tenth century was struck in Edward's name. Nevertheless, it is a very peculiar moment in history, showing a woman leading an erstwhile kingdom whilst having no regal title. The scant information we have about her keeps her on a par with the other royal women whose stories are told in this book. But it is not in keeping with the anomalous and unique situation which saw a woman ruling a country. The paradox presented by her story did not seem to trouble the earlier chroniclers; the Mercian Register presents the bare facts of her achievements with a laconic economy and expresses no surprise that a woman should have led a kingdom in such a fashion and for so long.

When Æthelred died, Edward took control of London and Oxford, but left the rest of Mercia alone. Perhaps, as suggested above, he was being stretched too thinly to take control of the whole of 'Free' Mercia. He had already seen one attack on his kingship, led by his own cousin alongside an atheling of Mercia. Why not simply appoint another ealdorman to rule Mercia? It seems that his sister might have been the only person whom he could trust. This speaks greatly of his opinion of her and leads to the conclusion that she must have had remarkable personal qualities.

Her 'warrior' reputation comes from the *Three Fragments* and from the later chroniclers, but she was an effective administrator, too. She issued charters in her own name which show her granting land to the nobility and she witnessed charters issued by Werferth, bishop of Worcester.[58] She and her husband were benevolent, moreover, releasing a religious community from its obligations to the royal court and restoring land to the community at Wenlock. They also intervened in a case over a monastic estate which the bishops at Worcester had been trying to recover for some years.[59] In 909 the bones of St Oswald were translated from Bardney to Gloucester and if this was done at Æthelflæd's behest, as seems likely, then it was a shrewd move on her part.[60] An English saint was now safe in a strong Mercia, away from overrun Viking territory. There is no doubt that her husband was ill at this point; Edward was harrying Northumbria so it might be that he brought the relics back and into her hands for safe-keeping. The minster in Gloucester dedicated to St Peter was renamed St Oswald's, and it was here that Æthelred was buried. Although Æthelflæd died in Tamworth, her body was taken back to Gloucester and she was buried at St Oswald's, alongside her husband. She perhaps, ultimately, felt more affinity to her mother's homeland than her father's and despite the arranged nature and age gap of the marriage, was clearly a devoted wife, too.

Æthelflæd had only one child. William of Malmesbury said this was because her labour had been so difficult that she 'ever after refused the embraces of her husband.'[61] The notion of her adopting a celibate life might have appealed to William, but equally there is every likelihood that Æthelflæd had other children who were perhaps still-born or did not survive infancy.

We do not know when Ælfwynn was born. Her name appears in three charters, the earliest of which is dated 903.[62] Thus, all we can deduce about her age when her mother died is that she was somewhere between the age of around 15 and 30. According to the Mercian Register, she succeeded her mother but was then 'deprived of all authority' by Edward, three weeks before Christmas, in 919. It might be that the entry is wrong, and that this occurred in 918. Even so, it would mean that between 12 June when her mother died, and December, Ælfwynn ruled Mercia. Why did Edward wait? More pertinently, why did the Mercians not resist his overthrowing of their new leader?

This time there was to be no ealdorman appointed to rule Mercia. Edward took direct control. Perhaps, after all, it had been the limitations imposed upon him by the Viking onslaught which had prevented him from doing so earlier, but it might also speak of the strength of character of Æthelflæd and the fact that the daughter was not of the same calibre as the mother. The question must remain: why did the Mercians accept the rule of a woman? It must, in part, be testament to her personal qualities.

Ælfwynn's situation was no less anomalous than her mother's. Here, for the first and last time in pre-Conquest England, a woman succeeded a woman. Yet she was not given leave to continue her rule. What was her status? She was not called 'Lady of the Mercians' as her mother had been, but the daughter of Æthelred. When Edward died, Mercia went to his eldest son Athelstan whilst Wessex went to Athelstan's eldest half-brother Ælfweard who, conveniently, died just sixteen days later. The statue of Æthelflæd outside Tamworth Castle famously shows her with her arm round a small boy, her nephew Athelstan, who was, apparently, brought up by her in the Mercian court. There is no contemporary evidence for this; the assertion comes to us from William of Malmesbury. Athelstan was said to have been with his father when he died on campaign in Mercia however and if he was brought up in Mercia, then it would have made him more acceptable to the Mercians. It has been suggested that the idea was for Athelstan to marry Ælfwynn. [63] As first cousins they were too closely related for the marriage to be sanctioned by the Church however, but it does prompt the question: why was Ælfwynn unmarried? Was her mother aware of plans to marry her daughter to Athelstan and was she against the match; was she going further, and preparing Ælfwynn to take over from her in an active role against the enemy? We only have one source suggesting that Æthelflæd raised Athelstan and it does not seem from her own charter evidence that she considered him her heir. It has been pointed out that by choosing her daughter to succeed her she would continue the dual identity of Mercia and Wessex and the link between the two families. [64]

We know virtually nothing of Ælfwynn's life but we do know that she witnessed a charter of her mother's, issued at *Weardbyrig* (unidentified but possibly in Shropshire) in 915, when Æthelflæd was in the midst of her intense *burh*-building programme. Even if Ælfwynn had been born late in the marriage – and it seems implausible that she would have been conceived after her father fell ill in around 902 – she would not have been there as a small child accompanying her mother. Most likely she was a young adult at the very least. Given that it would have been far safer for her to remain in the Mercian heartland, there could well have been a specific reason for her presence at *Weardbyrig*, that of watching and learning from her mother.

Whatever the intentions, they did not come to pass and Ælfwynn disappears from the records after her removal from Mercia. A later charter (S 535) records a grant by King Eadred made in 948 to a religious woman named Ælfwynn. It would be nice to be able to say that this is Ælfwynn of Mercia, but there is no convincing evidence to link these two women. Nor is it likely that another prominent Ælfwynn, who was named foster mother of the future King Edgar, Eadred's nephew, was in any way connected to Æthelflæd's daughter.[65]

If the mother's life was a paradox, in that she was a remarkable woman barely remarked upon by the chroniclers, then the daughter's life was even more of an irony: the only female ruler of the period to succeed a female ruler, who barely merits a mention and disappears from the records months after having begun her rule.

Part IV

Serial Monogamy: Wessex Wives and Whores?

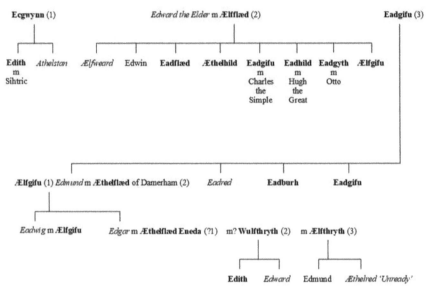

Wessex in the Tenth Century.

Athelstan, who ruled Mercia briefly and then the rest of England, was the eldest and possibly illegitimate son of Edward the Elder, although it might be that his parents were briefly married. In which case, Edward had three wives in total, who between them bore him fourteen children. Edward set the precedent for the serial monogamy practised by kings of the tenth and indeed part of the eleventh centuries. It was an era where the status of their wives as mothers began to matter a great deal.

Athelstan's mother, Ecgwynn, barely emerges from the shadows. Some said she was a concubine, while others said she was a wife. Sometimes she was described as high-born and sometimes as being of lowly birth. If we can believe the chroniclers, her status was important; Athelstan's accession was not universally approved.

The sources for Ecgwynn all come from post-Conquest chronicles.[1] The chronicle originally ascribed to Florence of Worcester called Ecgwynn a noblewoman, but William of Malmesbury said that she was of humble origin. He tells a story of a shepherd's daughter who, having had a vision, was taken in by a former nurse of the English kings. Here, Edward the Elder paid a visit to his erstwhile nurse and became 'deeply enamoured' of the young shepherd's daughter, spending one night with her during which Athelstan was conceived.[2] William tells the tale in the context of explaining the succession dispute in Wessex after Edward's death. A nobleman named Alfred led the opposition, claiming that Athelstan was an illegitimate son of a woman of low birth. William hints that Athelstan's half-brother, Edwin, was also part of this opposition and was exiled by Athelstan, put to sea in a boat from which he then plunged to a watery death.

Taken in isolation, the tale seems clearly to show that Athelstan was not considered a worthy claimant to his father's throne in Wessex. Indeed, add it to the fact that when Edward died, it was his eldest 'legitimate' son, Ælfweard, who was designated his heir in Wessex, while Athelstan was given Mercia, and it is hard to conclude anything other than that Ecgwynn was, regardless of her class, no more than a concubine and not a wife. It is also interesting to note that if Ælfweard had been considered the legitimate heir, it should have followed that after his death, his full brother Edwin would have been chosen king. That Athelstan was rumoured to have disposed of Edwin might speak volumes about the strength of his claim.

However, elsewhere in his *Chronicle of the Kings of England*, William of Malmesbury stated that Ecgwynn was an 'illustrious lady' when listing Edward's 'wives'. More telling is William's assertion that Athelstan had been adored by his grandfather, Alfred the Great, and that when he was a young boy he had been given by Alfred a 'scarlet cloak, a belt studded with diamonds, and a Saxon sword with a golden scabbard'. William also said that Alfred 'made him a knight' which is anachronistic, since technically no such rank existed in pre-Conquest times, but if it signifies some sort of investiture, it would suggest that his royal status was somehow acknowledged by Alfred.[3] It seems that the slurs cast on Ecgwynn's social standing and marital status had more to do with the disputes after Edward's death and perhaps served to explain why Athelstan, as firstborn, was not designated heir to both kingdoms. Whether or not Ecgwynn was Edward's wife, the stories prove that the status of a king's mother was just as, if not more, important than the might and strength of the king when it came to establishing throne-worthiness, but we must bear in mind that the only information we have comes to us from later sources, from chroniclers writing with the benefit of hindsight and who were not all in agreement.

Ecgwynn also bore Edward a daughter, although her identity is far from clear. Roger of Wendover names her as Edith, the sister whom Athelstan married to Sihtric, the Norse king of the Northumbrians. William of Malmesbury, whilst giving the same story, does not name her, and neither does the *ASC* although it mentions the occasion of her marriage. Roger of Wendover went on to relate that after Sihtric's death, and having preserved her virginity, Edith retired to the monastery at Polesworth, which was in Mercia. She was venerated as a saint and if she was, indeed, Athelstan's full sister then her return to Mercia, rather than Wessex, might make sense on two counts: that she, like her brother, was brought up at the Mercian court and that their mother, Ecgwynn, might have been Mercian herself.[4]

Whatever Ecgwynn's nationality and status, she was replaced when Edward married Ælfflæd, whose identity has also been debated. It is not known when Ecgwynn died, nor precisely when Edward married Ælfflæd, but it might have been before the death of his father, Alfred. A grant made in 901 at Southampton has an impressive witness list, including many dignitaries of the period, and seems to show Ælfweard, the younger half-brother, taking precedence over Athelstan.[5] If so, then two things may be inferred: that Ælfflæd's status as wife outranked that of Athelstan's mother Ecgwynn, and that if Ælfflæd's son Ælfweard was on a witness list in 901, her marriage to Edward took place at least as early as 900. Perhaps it was at this point that Athelstan was sent to Mercia to be brought up away from the West Saxon court.

It is possible that what is known as the Second (Coronation) *Ordo* was first used for Edward's consecration as king in 900. It included a queen's *ordo* which may have been designed for Ælfflæd, indicating that the pair were already married by this point. However, historians have also argued that it was drawn up for Athelstan's coronation.[6]

Ælfflæd was clearly important, whether or not she was married to Edward before he became king, for it seems that her children took precedence over their half-siblings. But who was she? Her father was an ealdorman of Wiltshire named Æthelhelm, which was also the name of a nephew of Alfred the Great's. If these were one and the same man, as has sometimes been assumed,[7] then the marriage can be viewed as a political move designed to strengthen Edward's candidacy for the throne following Alfred's death. However, this identification of Ælfflæd's father would also mean that she and Edward were first cousins once removed, and thus the marriage would be unacceptable on the grounds of consanguinity, being within the prohibited degrees of kinship.

Another argument against this identification is that Æthelhelm, Alfred's nephew, had a brother, Æthelwold, who – as seen in Part III – rebelled against Edward, claiming a right to the Wessex throne (he and his brother were sons of Alfred's elder brother who had been king before Alfred, but they were infants when their father died). Given what we know about the importance of royal marriage and the throne-worthiness conferred on the children by the status of the wife, it seems unlikely that Edward would have acknowledged the strength of that branch of the family by marrying into it, for in an attempt to boost his own credentials he would have been admitting their importance and thereby in fact undermining his own claim.

It is interesting to note, however, that Æthelwold's mother, Wulfthryth, briefly mentioned in Part III, was named *regina* in a charter whereas Edward's mother was not.[8] Edward was declared king after Alfred's death, not Æthelwold, so perhaps we should not read too much into the title of *regina*. We have seen that, according to Asser, the ninth-century West Saxons did not permit a king's wife to be called queen. An alternative title might have been *hlǽfdige*, (lady) which was used for Alfred the Great's wife, Ealhswith. Edward had good reason to stress the status of his mother, and Ealhswith became the 'true', or 'dear' Lady of the English.[9] Edward would hardly have wished to confer similar status to the rival branch of the royal family by marrying into it, although it would not be until later in the tenth century that queens as mothers gained truly elevated status.

Æthelhelm, ealdorman of Wiltshire and father of Ælfflæd, seems then to have been a different man and not related to the royal family. As has been noted it was not usual for athelings to serve as ealdormen and in a charter of 892 which recorded a grant made by Alfred to Æthelhelm, no mention is made of a kinship.[10]

Edward was said by William of Malmesbury to have favoured Athelstan as his heir.[11] Why, then, did Edward marry again, unless he was already at this point a widower? Perhaps his relationship with Ecgwynn, whether formalised by marriage or not, was a love match and she was not of noble enough stock. More importantly, she might have been Mercian. Neither of these things would help Edward when faced with claims from the rival branch of the Wessex royal family. It is easy to imagine – and similar scenarios occurred with earlier and indeed later kings – that Edward put aside his first 'wife' and made a political marriage at the time of his coronation. If Ælfflæd was the daughter of a leading West Saxon nobleman, then Edward would have the support of his father-in-law's men against rebellion from his cousin.

Alas, although Ælfflæd seems to have been important politically, we know little about her life. It is not even known precisely when she died. There is one extant text which suggests that she outlived Edward, but it is not corroborated by any other sources.[12] What we do know is that she had perhaps eight children by Edward and could well have suffered the knowledge that at least two of them died in her lifetime. Ælfweard, as we have seen, survived his father by a mere sixteen days and Edwin drowned at sea, a victim, it appears, of the disputes surrounding Athelstan's kingship. It might have seemed especially cruel that whilst mothers often lost adult sons, neither of these was a battlefield death. Ælfflæd also had six daughters. Two – Eadflæd and Æthelhild – took the religious life, while the other four made prestigious marriages. Their standing was clearly high: Eadgifu married Charles the Simple, king of the Franks, while Eadhild married a Frankish duke, Hugh the Great.[13] Eadgyth and Ælfgifu were, apparently, both sent to Germany so that the future emperor, Otto, could choose one of them as his bride. He married Eadgyth – it was, apparently, 'love at first sight' – and Ælfgifu married another prince. What Eadgyth's sister felt about being rejected by Otto, we can only surmise. Her fate – and indeed her identity – is the subject of some confusion. According to one, near-contemporary, source, having been rejected by Otto, Eadgyth's sister married a 'certain king near the Alps'. The author of the *Life* of Otto named her as Eadgifu. Edward the Elder's daughter of that name though was a half-sister of Eadgyth and would have been a child at the time. William of Malmesbury insisted that Eadgyth had been accompanied by her full sister, Ælfgifu and that she had married Louis, prince of Aquitaine. The 'king' near the Alps might have been Louis, brother of the duke of Burgundy.[14]

In 2010 it was confirmed that bones excavated from Magdeburg Cathedral in Germany were those of Eadgyth. A sarcophagus inscribed with wording suggesting that it contained her remains had been thought to be empty, but partial skeletal remains were found inside it, along with material and other organic residues. Measuring strontium isotopes on a portion of the upper jaw, the scientists were able to establish that this person had not lived her formative years in Germany, but in Wessex. The skeleton appeared to have undergone trauma, as a result of changed circumstances, at around the time her mother is believed to have been repudiated and opens up the possibility that Eadgyth, living with her away from court and possibly in a nunnery, had a marked change in diet at that point.[15] In 936 his father died and Otto was crowned emperor, with Eadgyth by his side as queen. The pair survived a civil war and when she died in 946 it was said that the whole of the German nation mourned her with an intense grief.

These high-ranking diplomatic marriages are redolent of a later medieval or even early modern period and show how valuable these royal daughters were, although it should be pointed out that by the time of their marriages, they were royal sisters, the marriages of all but Eadgifu's taking place during Athelstan's reign. The British Library holds a gospel book which, according to the inscription, might have been a gift from Otto to his brother-in-law, Athelstan.[16]

Whether Ælfflæd knew the fate of her daughters cannot be ascertained. By 920 Edward had married yet again. It is possible that he was a widower by this stage, or that he made yet another political marriage. Ælfflæd might perhaps, if that were the case, have retired to an abbey. The consensus is that she was buried with her daughters Eadflæd and Æthelhild at Wilton but the possibility has been raised that she might have been buried in Winchester. If, as has been suggested, her resting place was the New Minster, refounded by Edward, it might be that she predeceased her husband and was buried at a place dear to his heart, by a grieving husband.[17] If, as I have argued above, Ælfflæd was the daughter of the ealdorman of Wiltshire, rather than Æthelhelm nephew of Alfred, then an association with Wilton would make much more sense. However, there seems to be a strong connection between Edward the Elder's second family and Winchester, specifically his foundation of the New Minster. His father's body was moved there and his mother was buried there, as were his brother Æthelweard and Edward's son Ælfweard. Ælfweard's brother Edwin's rebellion against their half-brother Athelstan was directed from Winchester and embroideries commissioned by their mother Ælfflæd were designed for the bishop of Winchester. On the other hand the primary sources state that Ælfflæd was buried with her daughters at Wilton and a charter of Athelstan's dated 937 (S 438) shows Athelstan granting land to St Mary's Wilton and mentions Ælfflæd's daughter, Eadflæd.

Ælfflæd was evidently an important royal wife and did her duty in providing 'an heir and a spare', even though her sons did not survive long. Yet we know little about her, not the date of her marriage or even of her death. The only extant charter where she appears on the witness list dates from 901 where she is styled not *regina* but 'wife of the king' and attests after her mother-in-law, Ealhswith, (who is styled 'mother of the king', receiving more recognition than she had as wife of King Alfred).[18] She did, however, leave something more tangible which has survived: the embroideries briefly mentioned above. A stole and a maniple, recovered from the tomb of St Cuthbert, were reportedly gifted by Athelstan in around 934 to the religious community at Chester-le-Street. Both have embroidered inscriptions which translate as 'Ælfflæd had this made,' implying that she commissioned the pieces. It is possible that they were not completed during her time as Edward's consort, otherwise they might have gone as intended, to Winchester.[19] Stitched with gold thread and red silk, they are exquisite and in 2017 were on display as part of the St Cuthbert Treasures exhibition at Durham Cathedral.

It is impossible to ascertain why Edward would have repudiated the mother of eight of his children. If he grew tired of her, one wonders why it took him so long to do so. They must have spent a fair amount of time together, but of their relationship, frustratingly, we are told nothing. If the marriage was dissolved so that he could make a new political alliance, it must have been a bitter blow to a woman who had done her duty, lived a blameless life and raised a family with the king. The situation makes more sense if we assume that at this point Edward was a widower.

Whether she died or was put aside, Ælfflæd was eclipsed by her successor. By 920 Edward had married Eadgifu – their first son was born in 920 or 921 – who was to become not only the influential mother of kings but also the grandmother of kings. She would not be the last queenly grandmother to continue to exert influence, as we shall see later.

Eadgifu's father had also been a nobleman; Sigehelm, ealdorman of Kent, fought alongside Edward at the battle of the Holme,[20] where Edward's rebellious cousin was killed. Sigehelm, too, was killed in the battle and this may have informed some of the events which happened later in the century when Eadgifu was the queen-grandmother.

It is hard to know why Edward would have married again if Ælfflæd was still alive. Was one or both of these marriages a love match? Alas, probably not, although his previous relationship with Ecgwynn, given that it offered little politically, was perhaps based on affection. There are no surviving records of wives having been put aside because they were barren; primogeniture, while often *de facto*, was not the recognised system of inheritance.[21] Even so, this would not apply in Ælfflæd's case. Edward had three sons, so this was not a question of needing to marry again in order to beget heirs. Perhaps, like her predecessor, Eadgifu brought to the marriage an alliance which guaranteed support for Edward, this time in the southeast; the struggle against the Viking invaders was still ongoing and Edward spent much of his latter years away in Mercia. Edward had been granted land by his father in Kent so perhaps he had close ties with the area. Eadgifu might also have brought dower lands in Kent to the marriage.[22] Presumably, though, she was considerably younger than Edward – she survived him by over four decades and could have been as much as thirty years younger than him – and she bore him four children. This is remarkable given that she might have been married for as little as five years, and that during much of that time he was away on campaign (unless she went with him and stayed in Mercian strongholds presumably at this point belonging to her stepson, Athelstan.) The possibility cannot be ignored that one of the pregnancies might have produced twins.

Her daughters were called Eadburh and Eadgifu. Eadburh became a nun at Winchester and William of Malmesbury, who described her as 'Eadburh the Happy', relates how she was the architect of her own fate. When she was just 3 years old she had given proof of her future holiness when her father, wishing to ascertain whether she would choose the religious life, laid out a chalice and the Gospels, and some bangles and necklaces. When little Eadburh was brought in by her nurse, she was told that she could choose what she wanted, whereupon she immediately crawled towards the Gospels and chalice. She joined the community of Nunnaminster at Winchester which, having been founded by her grandmother Ealhswith, wife of Alfred the Great, had close ties with the West Saxon royal family.

Osbert de Clare, a twelfth-century monk who wrote the *Life* of Eadburh, focused on a few incidents in particular. One episode shows the prioress beating a nun who was, contrary to rules, reading alone, before discovering, aghast, that the nun in question was Eadburh. The prioress was contrite, not because she had struck one of saintly virtue, but one who was a princess. Clearly Eadburh stood apart and was to be treated differently. It was also considered that she should not undertake such a humble service as shoe-cleaning, as such duties were beneath her, and by doing so, it seems she caused quite a stir. Her father, King Edward, visited the abbey to enquire of her progress and the community was reluctant to divulge details of her behaviour but, when they were pressed to reveal what she had been doing, the king reacted favourably.

Edward appears to have been indulgent towards his daughter and Eadburh also persuaded him to gift an estate at a place called *Canaga* to the nunnery. Until this point, the community had only the estate within Winchester, the original endowment, and this was not enough to meet their needs. Eadburh's presence proved rather useful, and they begged her to appeal to her father, so her worth was less in her virtue than in her family connections.[23]

Elsewhere in his *Gesta Pontificum Anglorum* William of Malmesbury states that some of her bones were held at Pershore.[24] It is far from clear, however, how the community at Pershore came by her relics and there seems to have been some rivalry between Nunnaminster and Pershore. There is some evidence of a Mercian saint of the same name – Adderbury (Oxfordshire) is a place-name derived from Eadburh – and it may be that the relics claimed by Pershore were those of this namesake saint.[25]

In his *Chronicle of the Kings of England*, William said that Edward the Elder brought up his daughters so that, 'in childhood they gave their whole attention to literature, and afterwards employed themselves in the labours of the distaff and the needle.'[26] Thus the royal daughters were literate, but also well-skilled in sewing and embroidery; excellent preparation for their adult lives as royal wives or indeed as religious women.

Each of Eadgifu's sons went on to become kings and it was during their reigns that she was most influential. Widowed in 924, she outlived both of them. When Edward died, as we have seen, Ælfweard, his son by Ælfflæd, briefly succeeded, to be followed by Athelstan. Athelstan did not marry and when he died in 939 he was succeeded by Eadgifu's son, Edmund, who was around the age of 18 when he became king. Edmund married twice; his first wife, a woman named Ælfgifu, bore him two sons, both future kings. Her identity is debateable and her background unknown. A grant by her son, Edgar, in 966, names his maternal grandmother, Wynflæd, so this must have been Ælfgifu's mother. There is an extant will of a tenth-century noblewoman of that name, but it seems unlikely that this is the same lady.[27]

Ælfgifu appears not to have been married for long. Her son Eadwig was probably born around 940, and his younger brother Edgar around 943. King Edmund himself died in 946 – the victim of a brawl, or perhaps a political assassination – having married again, so his first marriage must have ended not long after Edgar's birth. The younger of the royal orphans, Edgar, was fostered by a noblewoman, the wife of the ealdorman of East Anglia, whom we shall meet in Part VI.

Ælfgifu is known as Ælfgifu of Shaftesbury, and William of Malmesbury in particular had a lot to say about her. He said that it was she who built the nunnery there and that her bodily remains were placed there. She was 'so pious and loving that she would even secretly release criminals who had been openly condemned by the gloomy verdict of a jury.' She would also give away her expensive clothes to the needy and she was a beautiful woman who was remembered for the miracles associated with her; the blind, the deaf and the lame were cured after visiting Shaftesbury.[28]

It would be easy to assume that she retired to Shaftesbury in the manner of a number of previous queens, but the short-lived nature of her marriage and the young age of her children suggest another scenario. It is plausible that she died in childbirth, either in labour with Edgar or with a subsequent pregnancy in which both mother and child died.[29] If she did indeed die in childbirth then she cannot have been a nun at Shaftesbury, but merely its benefactress.

Edmund's brief second marriage was to a lady who was known as Æthelflæd of Damerham, that being the name of the place where Edmund gave her land. According to the *Liber Eliensis* she was the daughter of Ælfgar, ealdorman of Essex and was the widow of a Mercian ealdorman, Athelstan, who was known as Athelstan Rota, or 'the Red'. It is usually assumed that he was her second husband. The *Liber Eliensis* makes it clear that she remained 'perpetually in widowhood' although it has been postulated that in fact Athelstan may have been her first, rather than her second, husband.[30] The daughter of an ealdorman, the wife of a king and of an ealdorman, she was rich and well-connected; her sister married the ealdorman Byrhtnoth who was commemorated in the poem *The Battle of Maldon* and both women left detailed wills, which will be discussed in Part VI.

In the grant of land by the king to her at Damerham, Æthelflæd is described as Edmund's 'queen', but she did not witness any of her husband's charters. Her predecessor, Ælfgifu of Shaftesbury, attested a charter of Edmund's but her name is well down the witness list, several places below that of Eadgifu, 'mother of the king'.[31] When Edmund was murdered he was succeeded by his brother, Eadred, younger son of Eadgifu, Edmund's sons being too young to rule.

Eadgifu had remained in the background during her stepson Athelstan's reign, but the succession of her own sons, first Edmund and then more especially the bachelor Eadred, brought her once more to prominence. Eclipsing her daughters-in-law, she attested charters of Edmund's alongside Eadred, for example S 505 in 945, which shows her and Eadred above the bishops on the witness list, and during Eadred's reign as 'mother of the king'. For example, in charter S 551 dated 949, she is styled *regis mater* and again appears above the bishops on the witness list. Whether she had remained at court during the years of Athelstan's kingship, or whether she had retired to her estates, she was clearly at the centre of government during the reigns of her sons and retained her standing as mother of the king despite the presence of two daughters-in-law. Her influence was felt elsewhere, too.

In a charter of 953 (S 562) she is described as *famule Dei* (handmaid of God) and William of Malmesbury relates that St Æthelwold longed for a stricter religious life than could be lived in England and was 'thirsting for exile in France.' It was, according to William, Eadgifu the king's mother, who persuaded Æthelwold to stay. Æthelwold, along with bishops Dunstan and Oswald, was one of the leading lights of the Benedictine monastic reform of the tenth century, a reform movement which became inextricably linked with the politics of the period and had consequences for the royal women.

Eadgifu was remembered as a benefactress at Christ Church, Canterbury – S 1211 is a grant of 959 recording her gift of estates in

Kent – and she held a large amount of land, either bequeathed by her father or gifted to her by her sons.[32] Her Kentish connections no doubt strengthened the West Saxon kingdom; despite her grief at the death of Edmund, Eadgifu's position as 'dowager queen' and mother of kings must have felt unassailable.

In 955 Eadred – who seems to have been ill with a condition similar to that which afflicted his grandfather Alfred – died, probably still only in his very early thirties. The largest personal bequest in his will was to his mother.[33] He was succeeded by his late brother Edmund's elder son, Eadwig, who was then a teenager of around 15. The bitter blow of losing yet another son was no doubt softened by the expectation on Eadgifu's part that she would continue to exert influence, this time as the grandmother, rather than the mother, of a king. Her fortunes took an unexpected tumble, however, when Eadwig found a wife and caused a scandal which, if the chroniclers are to be believed, rocked the monarchy and indirectly led to the temporary division of the kingdom.

When examining the events, it is hard to know whom to feel most sorry for: the doughty grandmother who had held power for so long, seemingly with dignity, or the young girl who was vilified and found herself caught up in a political storm which she probably did not understand. Her name was Ælfgifu, and her greatest misfortune was that her time at court coincided with that of Dunstan, a favourite of the former King Eadred's, an abbot, reformer, bishop and subsequently archbishop. The *Life* of St Dunstan, dating from the late tenth century, pulled no punches in its denunciation of her behaviour. It said that a certain foolish woman of noble birth enticed Eadwig to intimacy, aiming to tempt him into marrying her or else her daughter. On the day of his consecration, Eadwig left the banqueting table and Dunstan was sent to find him and bring him back. The scene that greeted Dunstan was of the king's crown thrown carelessly to the floor, and the king 'wallowing between the two of [the women] in evil fashion, as if in a vile sty.'[34] Other versions of the story add that the king and Dunstan quarrelled, and Dunstan was exiled. Roger of Wendover reported that as he put to sea, the mother was alleged to have threatened that if he ever returned to England, she would have his eyes put out. William of Malmesbury described the incident too, declaring that the king had been caught 'rioting in the harlot's embrace.'

Whether or not these elaborate descriptions have any basis in fact, it is clear that Dunstan was indeed banished by Eadwig and that Eadwig and his young wife were – presumably against their will – divorced a few years later on the grounds of consanguinity. They were too closely related, it seems, although it is hard to believe that no one spotted this at the time of their marriage. However, the possible identity of the young bride holds some clues as to why the marriage was so frowned upon. As I have demonstrated elsewhere the couple, if Ælfgifu's family connections have been correctly identified, were not in fact related within the prohibited degrees, but her bloodline was of significance.[35]

A woman named Ælfgifu left a will, in which it is implied that she had a brother named Æthelweard. This Æthelweard has been identified as the tenth-century nobleman, Æthelweard the Chronicler, who not only provided a near-contemporary account of these times, but also gave one of the few positive accounts of Eadwig.[36] It does not seem implausible that this was because Eadwig was his brother-in-law. More pertinently, Æthelweard's chronicle is dedicated to a woman with whom he says he shares a common ancestor, that ancestor being Æthelwulf, father of Alfred the Great.

If Æthelweard and therefore his sister, Ælfgifu, were descendants of Alfred's brother, Æthelred, this means that they were directly related to the branch of the family which opposed Edward the Elder's succession. Furthermore, this blood-tie directly links them to the rebellious cousin, Æthelwold, who was killed at the battle of the Holme. Not only would such a marriage, in theory, have strengthened the claims of that branch of the royal house over Edward's and his offspring, it must always have been in the back of Eadgifu's mind that the battle of the Holme was also where her father was killed. Could she have resented the appearance of this young woman at court, knowing that she was related to the man who, directly or indirectly, was responsible for her father's death? It is an interesting hypothesis but is weakened by the fact that at this stage, the direct bloodline from Alfred was well-established, and by the lack of direct evidence that either of his brother Æthelred's sons ever married or produced children. This is not to say, however, that Ælfgifu's family connections were not important.

Another proposed family tree – and one which is not mutually exclusive of the first – suggests that she was a relative of Alfred's wife, Ealhswith, descended from the daughter of Ealhswith's brother. Far from being subjugated after the death of Æthelflæd in 918, the Mercians continued to demonstrate a sense of national identity and were to prove pivotal in the election of more than one king in the tenth century. It could be that this bloodline was the important one, the marriage being designed to garner support for Eadwig from the Mercians. Given his young age, however, it is difficult to envisage that Eadwig himself arranged the match. It is equally hard, though, to see who might have been the puppeteer pulling his strings. If his wife was indeed related to the Mercians then it means that she was related to the ealdorman of East Anglia,[37] whose wife was charged with the upbringing of Eadwig's brother, Edgar, and who was so powerful that his epithet was 'Half-king'. But it seems not to have been the Half-king who was controlling Eadwig, if indeed anyone was leading or advising him. His short reign is notable for the amount of land he gave away in an attempt to buy support. It was to do him no good, for the nobility deserted him, including the leading Mercians. Two years after his coronation he lost half his kingdom; two years after that, he was dead.

The depiction of Ælfgifu as, at best, a woman of loose morals had more to do with the lionising of the leaders of the monastic reform movement than any true reflection of her character. She was a victim of circumstance as much as anything else. Whilst it is tempting to view her as the young, new, ambitious queen at court determined to oust Eadgifu the matriarch, it is hard to see how she could have been personally so influential. The rift between her husband and his family, though, was very real. Eadwig not only quarrelled with Dunstan but was accused of depriving his grandmother Eadgifu of her lands and property. The real crime here appears to have been that of a new court faction upsetting the old establishment. Eadgifu, doubtless in no mood to be upstaged by a granddaughter-in-law, and feeling sorely treated by her grandson, was in danger of losing her exalted position as the dominant royal woman at court.[38] It is just possible that she put pressure on the archbishop of Canterbury to annul the marriage before any children were born. In 957 Edgar, younger brother of Eadwig, made a move for the kingdom, which for a while was split – Edgar was declared king in Mercia and controlled Northumbria while Eadwig just about hung on to Wessex – and restored both Dunstan in his position as abbot and some, but not all, of Eadgifu's lands.

Eadgifu was respected by her youngest grandson though and appeared in an important charter of 966, where she witnessed the refoundation of the New Minster, Winchester. This charter will be discussed again, for it contains significant information regarding Edgar's children, but it was to mark his grandmother's last appearance on the public stage.[39] It is not known when she died, but by 966 she had outlived her husband by forty-two years and witnessed the deaths of both of her sons. Edgar did not remain single or celibate and she perhaps retired from court life once he married, although possibly not until his final marriage, which took place around 964 and seems to have been regarded as more legitimate than his previous liaisons. It is not known exactly where she was buried. It has been suggested that she retired to Wilton, but perhaps she was buried in Winchester where her husband was laid to rest.[40] Her dedication to her children by him is undeniable.

It is not clear what happened to the 'harlot' Ælfgifu after her marriage was annulled in 958. She probably lived quietly somewhere on her family's estates. She did not, however, disappear completely from the records. During the 960s she was the recipient of land grants made by Edgar who was now sole king.[41] It is possible that the grants were a gesture towards reconciliation, or perhaps part of his ongoing recognition of the debt owed to the Mercians who gave their whole-hearted support for his kingship bid. As we shall see, Edgar was extremely happy in the company of women and the nature of his reign suggests that he was not one for vendettas or grudges.[42] She was mentioned in a list of those for whom prayers should be said in the New Minster *Liber Vitæ* among 'illustrious women, choosing this holy place by the gift of God, who have commended themselves to the prayers of the community by the gift of Alms' which does not quite square with the image left to us by the writer of the *Life* of Dunstan; nor does her presence on the witness list of an agreement between two churchmen in 956 or 957 where she is styled 'the king's wife'. Also present on the list, and clearly acceptable company for the churchmen, was her allegedly scandalous mother.[43]

Land which Ælfgifu bequeathed to Edgar and his queen was later gifted by them to the abbey at Ely, so she clearly predeceased Edgar, who died in 975.[44] In her will, dated between 966 and 975, she requested that she be buried at the Old Minster, where her husband had been interred.[45] Given that he died only a year after their annulment it seems pertinent to wonder whether she was allowed to attend his funeral but such information was not recorded. Her husband's rule was unsuccessful and short-lived,[46] and the chroniclers concentrated on the golden age of reform and Edgar's strong reign which enabled it. Ælfgifu's will, though, shows her bequeathing jewellery and rich estates, including one to Bishop Æthelwold, which suggests that not all the reformers were opposed to her.

Not all historians agree that the testatrix Ælfgifu was the same woman who had been married to Eadwig, but the will mentions Æthelweard in a way which suggests he is her brother and who has been identified as Æthelweard the Chronicler.[47] This testatrix was also in possession of an estate which had belonged to Æthelfrith, an ealdorman who had married into the Mercian royal family, suggesting that the testatrix is Ælfgifu the 'harlot' and apart from a small number of individuals who appear to be her family members, the rest of her bequests all went to members of the royal family. Of particular interest is the gifting of a necklace of 120 *mancuses* of gold (a *mancus* being around 4.25g), plus an armlet of thirty *mancuses*, and a drinking cup, all to go to 'the queen'. It is possible that this was more than a formal bequest and that she was befriended at court by one of Edgar's wives, who was the recipient of that fine necklace and who knew what it was like to fall foul of the powerful Dunstan.

Ælfthryth, the inheritor of the necklace, was the last and most famous of Edgar's wives. His love life was complicated and is hard to reconstruct with any certainty. The usual narrative is that Edgar had three wives, with some doubt being cast over the middle of the three and whether she was ever officially his wife. However, his first wife is an even more shadowy character and impossible to identify.

Edgar's first wife was said to have been named Æthelflæd, nicknamed *Candida* (White) or *Eneda* (Duck). The chronicle of John of Worcester stated that Edgar had a son, Edward, by her and that she was the daughter of an ealdorman named Ordmær. It was suggested that Ordmær might have been a Hertfordshire thegn.[48] Whoever he was, if he existed at all, he does not appear on any witness lists. That we have no other record of Æthelflæd is not unusual, but the fact that her father cannot be identified presents more of a problem. There is one person of that name who is mentioned in the *Liber Eliensis*, but he is not described as an ealdorman.[49] An Æthelflæd the White is mentioned as a beneficiary in the will of Wynflæd, a tenth-century noblewoman, of whom more in Part VI, but while we learn that she was to receive a 'gown and cap and headband, and afterwards Æthelflæd [was] to supply from her nun's vestments the best she can for Wulfflæd and Æthelgifu and supplement it with gold so that each of them shall have at least sixty pennyworth', there is nothing to indicate that this is the wife of Edgar.[50]

If Æthelflæd *Eneda* existed, and if she was the mother of Edward, then it might be that she died during childbirth or shortly afterwards, in around 962. Her successor is almost as hard to identify, but there is much more information about her. Wulfthryth, the mother of Edgar's daughter Edith, certainly, and his son Edward, possibly, became abbess of Wilton and was later venerated as a saint. She was the subject of much gossip and conjecture. We know that her marriage – if that is what it was – to Edgar must have ended in or before 964, the date when Edgar married his last wife, Ælfthryth. We also know that Wulfthryth was an abbess, but it is not known precisely when she entered the religious life. Many sources state that she was, in fact, a nun when Edgar met and seduced her, and this is where the waters become rather murky.

According to a *Life* of Dunstan, written in the latter part of the eleventh century by Osbern of Canterbury, Edgar seduced a nun of Wilton who gave birth to a son, Edward. This seduction caused Dunstan to impose a seven-year penance on Edgar which delayed his coronation. However, Edgar's supposedly delayed (it was possibly a second) coronation occurred in 973. Seven years before that he was already married to his last wife Ælfthryth, so the timings do not tally.

Another hagiographer of Dunstan, a young contemporary of Osbern's named Eadmer, based his account on that of Nicholas of Worcester, who said that Edward was the son of Æthelflæd *Eneda*. Taking this as fact, Eadmer decided that Edward was not the son of a nun, and that Edgar, a married man, nevertheless sinfully seduced a laywoman who wore a veil in an attempt to avoid the king's attentions:

> For on a certain occasion this same king came to a monastery of virgins, which is located at Wilton, and there, captivated by the beauty of a certain young girl … he ordered her to be brought to him … . While she was being led to him out of fear for her chastity she placed a veil snatched from one of the nuns on her own head … . When Edgar saw her [he said] "How suddenly you have become a nun." He grabbed and dragged the veil from her head.[51]

Goscelin of St Bertin wrote a *Life* of St Wulfhild, abbess of Barking and said that it was she, rather than Wulfthryth, who was the object of Edgar's attentions. She evaded him by escaping naked down a sewer, and so the king took her kinswoman, Wulfthryth, a laywoman being educated by the nuns, instead. Goscelin was however adamant that Wulfthryth became Edgar's lawful wife and that they were bound by 'indissoluble vows'.[52] There is no mention in this version of the wearing of a veil to protect her from the king.

William of Malmesbury adds to the confusion. In his *Chronicle of the Kings of England* he gives the story of the seven-year penance but does not provide any names, reporting that, 'Edgar carried off a virgin who was dedicated to God, from a monastery by force, ravishing her and repeatedly making her the partner of his bed, for which he received a seven-year penance.' In his *Gesta Pontificum Anglorum*, he says it was Wulfthryth who put on the veil and that 'she was not actually a nun, as popular opinion crazily supposes.'[53] So it seems we might have two women, one of whom was a nun and one who was not, or we have Wulfthryth alone who either was, or was not, a nun, who was either married to Edgar or was his concubine.[54]

Perhaps the more pertinent point is whether or not she was Edward's mother? The A version of the *ASC*, a contemporary source, says that Edward was still a child when his father died in 975.[55] Edith was in her twenty-third year when she died, somewhere between 984 and 987, so she must have been born between 961 and 964 (the date when her father married his last wife.) This leaves a very few years for Edgar to have fathered these children so perhaps there is something in Eadmer's idea that he conducted an affair with Wulfthryth whilst married to his first wife. However, given that the *passio* of Edward reported that he and Edith were full, not half, siblings, along with the lack of evidence for Æthelflæd *Eneda*, and Edward's age at the time of his father's death, it is more likely that Edward was the son of Wulfthryth.

It might be that it did not matter whose son Edward was and that what was important was whose he was not; that is to say, he was not considered legitimate by those who supported the son by Ælfthryth after King Edgar died, that son being Æthelred II, the 'Unready'. It is possible that Æthelflæd *Eneda* was a stock character for the narrative of those who supported Æthelred the Unready, casting doubt on Edward's legitimacy much as those opposed to Athelstan had done by disparaging his mother, Ecgwynn.

Wulfthryth might have been Edgar's wife, but she did not witness any charters of Edgar's and her status was eclipsed by that of her successor.

Whatever the nature of her relationship with Edgar, and whether she was the mother of two children or one, it is clear that by 964 the relationship had ended. She retired to Wilton and by 974 she was abbess, although it seems it will never be known whether she decided to leave the court or was set aside by her husband, losing her status as concubine or wife when Edgar married Ælfthryth.[56]

Wulfthryth seems to have been a canny administrator of Wilton. She purchased a collection of relics, and lands which had been granted to her by Edgar were conferred to the nunnery, presumably so that the abbey would retain the lands after her death. She was influential too: Goscelin's *Life* of her daughter, Edith, relates how she brought pressure to bear on King Æthelred when his officers tried to remove a thief who had claimed sanctuary in the church and the royal servants were blinded as punishment, and how she interceded on behalf of two priests imprisoned by the reeve of Wilton.[57]

Her daughter, Edith of Wilton, was also venerated as a saint. She was said to have chosen the religious life for herself formally at the age of 2, an occasion marked by a visit from her father who came with royalty, clergymen and courtiers 'as if to the court of Christ and a heavenly betrothal feast'.[58] Sadly for Wulfthryth, she outlived her daughter who, as mentioned above, died whilst still only 22 or 23. Dunstan was said by William of Malmesbury to have predicted Edith's death when he was consecrating a chapel which Edith had ordered built, bursting into tears and prophesying that she would die within six weeks and saying that he saw a vision of her standing by her own tomb.[59]

Edith is indeed perhaps best known for the cult which grew up around her (see appendix) but most of the information we have about her life comes from Goscelin, who might well have spent time serving as a chaplain at Wilton[60] and one story which he alone relates is that after the murder of her brother, Edward, the noblemen of England offered the throne to Edith. Given that Goscelin names their leader as Ælfhere of Mercia, known to be a staunch supporter of Æthelred the Unready, it seems an improbable tale, especially given that Edward was killed in 978 when Edith would have been no older than 17 and possibly as young as 14 and that queens, of any age, had not been allowed to rule in their own right.[61] Edith, of course, demurred anyway. Perhaps the story was a device merely to show her rejecting, once again, the secular life she had spurned when a child. There is something else to consider here too: that whether or not it is true that the throne was offered to Edith, we know that her mother was still alive at this point and, if she was also the mother of Edward, would therefore have received news that her son had been murdered. Such things are not mentioned by the chroniclers but they cannot have occurred without causing pain.

Edith's seal-matrix survives, and describes her as *regalis adelpha* (royal sister) and it is clear that Wilton benefited from her family connections. Edgar appointed two foreign chaplains for her education and the chapel she ordered built and dedicated to St Denis and which Dunstan consecrated, was richly decorated with gold and semi-precious stones. Edith reportedly favoured dressing in a more ostentatious style than most nuns or abbesses and Bishop Æthelwold castigated her, telling her that Christ had taken no interest or delight in external appearances, rather it was the heart which He asked for. She replied that she had, indeed, given her heart to the Lord, who paid attention to the heart and not the clothing. William of Malmesbury included in his version a comment of Edith's about the bishop's 'ragged furs' which had silenced the bishop.[62] Edith's seal-matrix depicts an image of a woman and whilst this might not be an attempt of a portrait of her it is a reminder perhaps of her legendary penchant for elaborate clothing. Goscelin reported that after a fire in the monastery, whilst many of the nuns' possessions perished, Edith's leather and purple garments survived unscathed, thus vindicating her. This story might have been designed to symbolise the inviolable status of Edith as a holy virgin, but there is no reason to suppose that there is not at least an element of truth and it raises a wry smile to think of Edith steadfastly refusing to take any notice of the bishop's advice on sartorial matters, and it gives just an inkling of her forceful personality.[63]

The reigns of Edward the Elder and those of his sons – Athelstan, Edmund and Eadred – were punctuated by violence: fighting back the Vikings (Edward), establishing control of the wider kingdom (Athelstan), violent death (Edmund) and wresting back control of Viking York (Eadred). Edward's grandson, Eadwig, a teenager when he became king, lost more than half his kingdom when Mercia and Northumbria declared for his brother Edgar.[64] His death – untimely or timely, depending on one's point of view – at the age of just 19 or so, allowed his younger brother Edgar to succeed to the whole of England.

Edgar's reign, in contrast to that of his forebears, was marked not by war – his epithet was The Peaceable – but is remembered chiefly for the Benedictine monastic reform spear-headed by Bishops Æthelwold, Dunstan, and Bishop Oswald, the latter two becoming archbishops during Edgar's reign. We have already seen that Edgar had a somewhat chequered love life and it is not clear whether he was a serial monogamist like his grandfather Edward, or whether he had an affair with Wulfthryth whilst married to another lady, whose name might have been Æthelflæd. We are on more sure ground when examining the details of his last marriage, but this too was mired in gossip and scandal.

Ælfthryth was the daughter of a Devonshire nobleman named Ordgar and, according to the twelfth-century Anglo-Norman chronicler Geoffrey Gaimar, her mother was of royal descent.[65] Her noble connections did not stop there however, for she was also the wife of Ealdorman Æthelwold of East Anglia, whose pedigree was impeccable. He was the eldest son of the man who had become known as Athelstan Half-king, and he was the foster brother of Edgar, who had been given into the care of the Half-king's wife when his mother died during, or shortly after, his birth. Circumstances surrounding Ælfthryth's first marriage are not recorded; we do not know the date, nor whether it was a love match or a political union. She bore her first husband two children – Leofric, the founder of St Neots, who married a lady named Leofflæd, and Æthelnoth – but it is possible that she had little to do with them after the end of her first marriage. This ended with Æthelwold's death in 962, so she must have married him at least eighteen months before that. On the face of it, there is nothing untoward about a widow remarrying two years after the death of her husband, but to some chroniclers the demise of her first husband and the occasion of her second marriage had a macabre connection.

William of Malmesbury says that she met both of her husbands at the same time when King Edgar sent Æthelwold to scrutinise the lady and convey the king's offer of marriage if 'her beauty were really equal to report.'[66] Æthelwold found that the lady was, indeed, as beautiful as had been reported, but he told the king that 'she was a girl nothing out of the common track of beauty' and, having duped the king, married the lady himself. When Edgar caught word of what had happened, Æthelwold fearfully begged his wife to dress plainly but 'she called up every charm by art' and Edgar fell in love with her. He summoned Æthelwold to a wood at Harewood, ostensibly to hunt, and there 'ran him through with a javelin.'

Gaimar put a slightly different spin on the story and in his version Ælfthryth, though impregnated by Æthelwold, did not have the children with him by choice for, 'She did not love him, and she had been told how he had tricked the king.' Here, then, is a slightly more romantic take on proceedings. Gaimar says that Edgar at first refused to believe that he had been tricked, because he had 'no reason to be wary of someone he loved, having himself brought him up at court.' This last point is a reminder that these men did, indeed, have a shared upbringing, not at court but at the home of the Half-king in East Anglia. According to Gaimar, Edgar sent his foster brother to the north and it was there that he was killed.

It seems unlikely that Edgar was responsible for the death of his foster brother. He retained close links with the family, elevating two more of his foster brothers to the ealdormanship of East Anglia. Whilst these later chroniclers might have been basing their stories on rumours circulating at the time it is probable that the tales were fuelled by the gossip and scandal connected to events later in Ælfthryth's career and that her first husband died of natural causes.[67]

Gaimar also suggested that Edgar was godfather to one of Ælfthryth's sons, a fact which was pivotal to the next part of his version of her story. Like Ælfgifu the 'harlot' before her, Ælfthryth managed to incur the wrath of Dunstan, back from exile and dominant in Edgar's government. Gaimar paints the picture: Ælfthryth had come to Edgar wearing a 'hooded robe of fine black worsted [and] a short cloak … lined with grey miniver. Her tunic was of matching silk brocade.' No more than a month later Edgar and the queen were lying in bed and 'around them there was a curtain of fine brocaded silk from Persia. Dunstan came into the king's chamber and stood leaning pontifically against one of the red-painted, panelled bedposts.' Apparently he demanded to know who was lying in bed with the king and was told that she was the queen, to whom the kingdom bent its knee. Dunstan retorted that it was wrongful and that, 'It would have been better for you to be dead than to be wallowing in adultery in this way.' The couple had earned Dunstan's condemnation because Edgar was godfather to her son by her first marriage. Gaimar said that the queen was so angry that she swore lifelong enmity to Dunstan.

Whatever the circumstances of Ælfthryth's marriage to Edgar, it seems it was a legitimate one, and one which gave her much higher status than that of his previous wives. The New Minster charter of 966, mentioned above as being the last public appearance of the redoubtable Eadgifu, also gives insights into the status of Ælfthryth, her children, and of her stepson, Edward.

The family was all there, to witness the refoundation and grant of privileges to the minster, but while Ælfthryth attests as the king's lawful wife, and her first son by Edgar is described as the king's legitimate son, Edward, the son by a previous marriage or liaison, is merely 'begotten by the same king.' The difference is further highlighted by the fact that each member of the royal family has a gold cross against their name, whilst Edward has only the outline of a cross.

Sadly, Ælfthryth's eldest son by Edgar died when he was still an infant. By that time she had another small son, Æthelred, who was to become known to history as the 'Unready'. She spent time away from court at an estate called *Æthelingadene* (the valley of the princes) and as well as her sons being recognised as legitimate heirs, she herself witnessed charters and was styled *regina*.[68]

The monastic reform was gathering momentum and when Bishop Æthelwold produced his *Regularis Concordia* laying out the rules for monastic life he mentioned Ælfthryth by name saying that she should 'defend communities of nuns like a fearless sentinel.' The idea behind the reform was to return the monasteries to adherence to the rule of St Benedict. 'So it came to pass that with the king's consent, partly by the counsels and the acts of Dunstan, partly by the zealous support of Æthelwold, monasteries were everywhere founded .... Some for monks, some for nuns, established under abbots and abbesses living under rule, and the blessed Æthelwold often visited them.'[69] Many lay clerics were evicted, and the nobility began to resent the encroachment on their lands and privileges, as the bishops became more powerful.[70] Although Ælfthryth was later linked to the anti-monastic faction, it is clear from the wording in the *Regularis Concordia* that she and Bishop Æthelwold had a harmonious relationship.

In 973 Edgar had what amounted almost to an imperial coronation. It is unlikely that it was his first coronation, but it was a spectacular occasion.[71] More to the point, Ælfthryth was anointed alongside him, and in this she was the first tenth-century queen certainly to be both crowned and anointed. In his *Life* of St Oswald, the monk Byrhtferth of Ramsey described the coronation feast, saying:

> The queen, together with the abbots and abbesses, had a separate feast. Being dressed in linen garments and robed splendidly, adorned with a variety of precious stones and

pearls, she loftily surpassed the other ladies present; a regal bearing was befitting to her [since after the death of her husband] she had been found worthy to marry the king … . When all these royal nuptials were completed, all went home, blessing the king and queen.[72]

Attesting charters, providing legitimate heirs, and being charged with the welfare of monastic ladies, Ælfthryth was also remembered as a *forespreaca* (advocate), speaking on behalf of women in legal disputes.[73] A letter explains how a woman named Wulfgyth 'rode to me at Combe, looking for me.' The 'me' in question is Ælfthryth, and she goes on to describe how she interceded as female advocate – the word used here is *þingestre* – and helped bring a land dispute between Wulfgyth, her husband and Bishop Æthelwold to a conclusion.[74] The queen was a respectable, dignified woman, conducting herself with Christian decency.

Well, perhaps not quite. The *Liber Eliensis* contains a peculiar tale about an abbot who chanced across Queen Ælfthryth. She was cavorting with horses, and indecently exposed herself to them 'in contempt of the fear of God and the honour of her royal dignity.' She had concocted 'noxious potions' and when the abbot refused to join her in her evil-doings she ordered her serving women to murder him by thrusting heated daggers into his armpits so as not to leave any tell-tale marks. There is no context for this story and elsewhere the *Liber Eliensis* reports that she and King Edgar gave land to Bishop Æthelwold and requested that his *Regularis Concordia* be translated into English.[75] A curious combination indeed of a benefactress who also, allegedly, indulged in the dark arts.

As previously mentioned, Edgar's reign was a peaceful one. His coronation in 973 was marked by the leaders of several other kingdoms around the British Isles paying homage to him. The Viking threat had dissipated, and Edgar and his queen were riding high. But just two years later he was dead, his sons were still young boys, and resentment which had been simmering during his reign came to the boil. The monastic reform, and more specifically the founding and endowment of monasteries in large numbers, had left many laymen feeling displaced. In one instance, Edgar had restored land but commanded that all the thegns who had any land on the estate should conform to the bishop's wishes or give it up; Queen Ælfthryth interceded on behalf of one of the men but managed only to secure for him a life interest in the land, after which it would revert to the Church.[76]

With Edgar's death the land disputes proliferated and it is often said that the two factions were either for the reform or were anti-monastic. Ælfhere, ealdorman of Mercia, had lost a great deal of his land to the Church and his brother had been godfather to one of Ælfthryth's children. He seems to have been an ally of the queen's, despite his having been named by Goscelin as offering the crown to Edward's sister, Edith. Ælfthryth had been a legitimate wife of the king and her sons were legitimate athelings, yet it was her stepson, Edward, who was declared king despite his apparent illegitimacy. Byrhtferth of Ramsey said that he was a youth with an evil temper who 'struck not only fear but even terror into everyone' and beat members of his household and that some preferred his gentler brother.[77] Eadmer recorded that the opponents of Edward challenged the status of his mother, who whilst lawfully married, had not been crowned queen.[78] The habit was clearly then to denigrate candidates for the throne by denying the worthiness of their mothers; the status of royal ladies as mothers of kings was more important than that of wife, as we have seen with the career of Eadgifu and the slurs cast upon Athelstan's parentage. Indeed, Ælfthryth's first appearance in the witness lists was as a mother, not a wife.[79]

Whether there was a rebellion is not clear, for Edward reigned for three – albeit troubled – years. Supporting him, it seems, were the archbishops Dunstan and Oswald and opposing him were Ælfthryth and Ælfhere of Mercia. Yet it should not be assumed that either of these latter two was anti-monastic per se; Ælfhere was a benefactor of Glastonbury Abbey and Ælfthryth, despite having interceded for the layman who lost land rights, was an ally of Bishop Æthelwold, former tutor of Edgar and author of the *Regularis Concordia*. Hugh Candidus, the Peterborough monk, wrote that 'the queen listens to the prayers of the bishop.' Piety and politics seem to have been intertwined, with the bishop being 'virtually a court chaplain'. The New Minster charter, drafted by Bishop Æthelwold, and clearly setting out the queen's status, might have reflected the closeness of their working relationship. We have seen how this charter clearly marked Edward as illegitimate, and yet he secured the throne after his father's death.[80]

With the country in turmoil – the earl of Northumbria was banished, and a comet was regarded as an evil portent – it was an uneasy time and in 978 Edward was killed whilst visiting his stepmother at her house in Corfe. Byrhtferth of Ramsey made no specific accusation, but later chroniclers were in no doubt about where the blame lay. Henry of Huntingdon accused her and, according to Roger of Wendover, when her stepson arrived Ælfthryth 'allured him with her caresses' whilst William of Malmesbury, who maintained that Edward had retained only the name of king but given power to his stepmother and infant half-brother, said that this did not satisfy the queen who made sure that as Edward leaned forward to greet her, her attendant stabbed him. His horse then dragged him through a wood until he was found dead and he was buried 'ingloriously' at Wareham.[81]

Was Ælfthryth a killer; is there ever smoke without fire? Certainly it was said that she founded monastic institutions to expiate her guilt and the murder was seemingly never properly avenged. When her son Æthelred became king he was instrumental in the development of Edward's saintly cult, but was this an admission of guilt or an insurance policy, designed to neutralise suspicion which might cast a pall on the new reign?[82]

Together with Edgar, Ælfthryth had endowed Ely with the land at Marsworth left to them by Ælfgifu the 'harlot' and she feasted with the abbots and bishops on her coronation day, who must presumably have considered her decent, Christian and worthy of anointing. On the other hand, according to Goscelin, she was responsible for the expulsion from Barking of the abbess Wulfhild, kinswoman of Wulfthryth, Edgar's 'nun' and possible rival for Edgar's affections. Murderess or not, it is clear that she was a political beast and, whilst it was said that she founded Wherwell Abbey in compensation for her crimes and eventually died in residence there, the position of the mother of the king was, as already discussed, an exalted one, and Ælfthryth was not ready to retire.

Part V

Dowager Queens and Mothers-in-Law: Wessex in the Eleventh Century

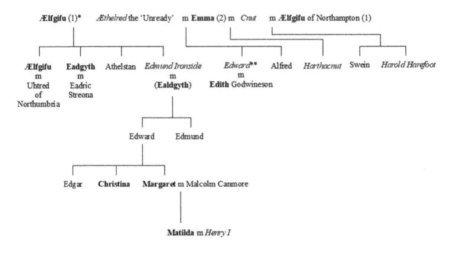

Ælfgifu (1)*   Æthelred the 'Unready'   m **Emma** (2) m Cnut   m Ælfgifu of Northampton (1)

Ælfgifu   **Eadgyth**   Athelstan   Edmund Ironside   Edward**   Alfred   Harthacnut   Swein   Harold Harefoot
m   m   m   m
Uhtred   Eadric   (Ealdgyth)   **Edith** Godwineson
of   Streona
Northumbria

Edward   Edmund

Edgar   **Christina**   **Margaret** m Malcolm Canmore

Matilda m Henry I

*not all children included here   **known as the 'Confessor'

Wessex in the Eleventh Century.

Edward was reburied with all due ceremony, and Æthelred was crowned king. He was, however, still a young child, perhaps around 12 but possibly as young as 9 or 10, and his half-brother's murder – committed in Æthelred's cause, whoever ultimately ordered it or wielded the knife – must have cast a long shadow. Bishop Æthelwold, shrewd politician as well as religious reformer, remained at court as his adviser, and so did Ælfthryth. From Æthelred's accession until 984, there were no athelings and Ælfthryth retained her high status. In four charters she was styled *regina* and her name appears after the bishops in the witness lists, whilst in others she was *mater regis*. With one exception, whenever she was mentioned as the king's mother, her name came after the king's and before the bishops, another example of how the status as royal mother was more exalted than that of royal wife.[1]

Ælfthryth's star appears to have waned a little after 984 (although she was to launch one more comeback a few years later). It may be no coincidence that 984 was the year in which Bishop Æthelwold, her champion, died. It was probably around this same date that Æthelred married for the first time. His marital history, whilst being rather less salacious, mirrors that of his father, Edgar, in that it is difficult to ascertain whether he had two or three marriages, and that his last wife was to prove, like Ælfthryth, to be a formidable queen and queen mother.

John of Worcester said that Æthelred's first wife was called Ælfgifu, and that she was the daughter of an ealdorman called Æthelberht. But just as with Edgar's supposed first wife, there is no evidence of this woman's father; no ealdorman named Æthelberht is recorded elsewhere. Roger of Wendover said that she was a 'woman of low birth'.[2] Ailred of Rievaulx, writing in the mid-twelfth century, said that she was the daughter of a man named Thored, but he did not name her. This is probably Thored son of Earl Oslac who had served Edgar and was banished in 975. Until his banishment, Oslac had been earl of Northumbria, but he and his son both had interests in Cambridgeshire.[3] Thored attested charters in the 980s and his links with the north would have been valuable for a reign which had begun in rather murky circumstances. It is possible that Æthelred was married first to a woman named Ælfgifu and then to the daughter of Thored, but it is generally accepted that this was one woman and, combining the two versions, that she was Ælfgifu, daughter of Thored.[4]

However we can look no further than this for, whoever she was, she did not attest any charters and is otherwise unnamed in the sources. Unlike the previous wives of Edgar, though, she seems to have had an unquestionably legal marriage, for her sons were considered to be legitimate athelings. The eldest son, Athelstan, pre-deceased his father but during his lifetime seems to have been considered the most throne-worthy of the royal children. In a tenth-century noblewoman's will a plea was made to the queen for the testatrix's kinsman to serve 'the atheling' i.e. Athelstan.[5]

If we are to assume that there was only one wife before 1002, then we must also assume that all of Æthelred's children born before that date were also the children of Ælfgifu. She might well have been a northerner, but the children were all given names which carried reminders of their West Saxon royal heritage: sons Athelstan, Ecgberht, Edmund, Eadred, Eadwig and Edgar; and daughters Eadgyth, Ælfgifu and Wulfhild, the first two of whom went on to make almost unprecedented political marriages. Some historians have estimated that Ælfgifu may have had as many as eleven children which is an impressive number, especially given that at least nine of them survived. Athelstan's will is extant and carries important information about his upbringing, of which more in a moment, and Edmund became king, briefly, and is known to history as Edmund Ironside. No slur was made regarding their legitimacy, for though Roger of Wendover said that they were born of a woman of low birth, 'Howbeit [Edmund] redeemed this defect of his mother by the nobleness of his mind and the vigour of his body.' More significant, perhaps, was that this son of Æthelred was an adult when his father died, unlike the sons of Edgar. The brothers' affinity with the inhabitants of the Danelaw would also play a part in events and might strengthen the notion that their mother hailed from this area. But this is to jump ahead.

The atheling Athelstan was buried in 1014 in the old minster, Winchester and was the first non-king to be interred there since the burial of his namesake King Athelstan's half-brother Ælfweard. This interment can be seen as a clear statement of his legitimacy and his precedence as the eldest atheling. In his will he made many bequests, but he asks that all be done in God's name and for the soul of his dear father and 'my grandmother Ælfthryth, who brought me up.'[6] Ælfgifu must have lived until the eleventh century, for her youngest son, Edgar, did not appear on charter witness lists until 1001. We do not know exactly how old the royal children would typically have been when they first appeared on the witness lists,[7] but they might have been very young infants, as is the case with Ælfthryth's young son Edmund who was born after her marriage in 964 and whose name appeared on the previously mentioned New Minster charter of 966. Yet in the 990s the king's wife, mother to all those children, made no appearance in the lists herself, whilst her mother-in-law returned to court and made her presence felt.

Ælfthryth was back, along with her brother, Ordulf, who became an adviser to the king. She witnessed charters alongside her grandsons, although now her name appeared after that of the bishops. Clearly she had a role in rearing the eldest, Athelstan, and her activities were not restricted to domestic matters, either. A lawsuit dated between 990 and 992 (S 1454) involved a noblewoman named Wynflæd who brought witnesses to swear to her ownership of certain estates: 'Then she brought forth the proofs of ownership with the support of Ælfthryth, the king's mother.' The tenth-century will referred to above which mentioned Athelstan 'the atheling' contained an appeal to 'the royal lady', i.e. Ælfthryth. It is possible that she was also responsible for the appointment of Athelstan's foster mother, a lady named in his will as Ælfswith.[8] Her return to court occurred at around the time that Thored disappears from the records. It seems that father and daughter – the king's wife, Ælfgifu – had been ousted, or at the very least eclipsed, by the queen mother.

Ælfthryth, presumably an elderly lady by this point, eventually retired to Wherwell dying on 17 November in either 1000, or 1001.[9] It is not known what happened to Ælfgifu and it is possible that she died at around the same time, for Æthelred married again in 1002. She might have been repudiated but, his first wife/wives having been completely overshadowed by his mother, it is probably no coincidence that he did not remarry until after Ælfthryth's death.

At such remove, we can do no more than guess at the circumstances between 984/5 and 1002. Clearly Ælfthryth was acting as some form of regent during her son's minority and took a back seat when Bishop Æthelwold died and/or her son married for the first time.[10] Was she initially content to live quietly, replaced in seniority by the mother of the king's sons? In which case, why was Ælfgifu not given more prominence at a time when the mothers of kings, or potential kings, were being accorded greater status? Even during Ælfthryth's absence she did not come to prominence. What happened to make her mother-in-law return to court and to politics? Was Thored enough of an influence at court to keep Ælfthryth away from his daughter? Why was Athelstan brought up by his grandmother rather than his mother? These and many more are questions which cannot fully be answered. We do not even know when the marriage ended. The possibility cannot be dismissed that Æthelred had two marriages before 1002 and that the atheling Athelstan was brought up by his grandmother after his mother died, but we have no evidence to be certain of this.

Widower or not, Æthelred was free from the influence of his mother when he married in 1002, a marriage which was a political one, designed to ensure support against the Viking Danes, with whom Æthelred had a more troubled relationship than his father Edgar had done. Æthelred's bride was Emma (she was given the English name, Ælfgifu, but to avoid confusion, I shall refer to her throughout as Emma), daughter of Richard, count of Rouen, and sister of Richard II, duke of Normandy. Ælfthryth was a strident mother prepared to go to great lengths for her son, and an indomitable dowager queen, but Emma, who did not arrive in England until after her mother-in-law's death, would outshine her on both counts.

Æthelred's reign differed in many ways from that of his father, Edgar. In particular it was afflicted by renewed Viking attacks, and these shaped his life and his actions. The raids began again in 980 and intensified in the 990s. They differed slightly from the attacks in the late ninth and earlier in the tenth centuries in that riches, rather than territorial gains, were uppermost in the raiders' minds. Various strategies against them were employed, from paying *gafol* (tribute) to the infamous incident in 1002 when the king ordered all the Danes in the country to be killed in what has become known as the St Brice's Day Massacre. The judgement and analysis of his reign is subject matter for another book, but it is clear that the Viking activity overshadowed Æthelred's rule every bit as much as it had Alfred the Great's, and probably more so. Despite payments, the Viking army which arrived in 991 remained largely in the British Isles, but in 1000 it went to Normandy before returning to England the following year. This then, is the background to the marriage to Emma.

It is not known precisely when Emma was born but, given that she was probably at least 12 when she arrived in England and that she had an infant child in 1023, we can perhaps suggest a birth date of around the year 990. Her mother was Danish and if Emma learned to speak the language, this would prove a great boon later in her career.[11] A brief search in the indexes of the reference books pertaining to Anglo-Saxon England yields more results for Emma than for any other woman of the period. Yet in the early years of her marriage, she made little impact. She appeared on the witness lists, unlike her husband's previous wife but, significantly, her first-born son, Edward, did not outrank his father's existing sons, as her mother-in-law Ælfthryth's baby boys had done.[12] A later source suggested that when Emma was pregnant with Edward (the Confessor), all the nobles swore an oath that should the child be a boy, then he would be declared king, but this was a *Life* commissioned by Edward's queen, Edith. It is not known precisely when Edward was born, but his birth must have occurred between 1002, the date of the marriage, and 1005, the date of his first appearance in the charter witness lists. Emma had at least two more children by Æthelred – there was another son, Alfred, and a daughter, Godgifu – but it was the atheling Athelstan, the eldest child from the first marriage, who retained precedence.[13]

Emma's significance during this, her first marriage, derived primarily from who she was, not whom she married. The *ASC* noted her arrival on English shores, calling her 'Richard's daughter' and in 1013 when she was forced to return to Normandy she is recorded as going across the sea 'to her brother Richard'. Her Norman credentials were important to the chroniclers, but she was also referred to as 'the queen'.[14] She was associated with an incident early on in her marriage, when Exeter was attacked by the Danes, an event which was blamed on Emma's reeve Hugh, a Frenchman. The attack was allegedly in retaliation for the St Brice's Day massacre but might also have been a response to the marriage which was part of an agreement to restrict Danish access to Norman harbours. Other than this incident, written from a later perspective, the early years of her marriage were marked only by the births of her children. Her story became much more prominent as Æthelred's reign dipped further towards disaster.

Æthelred, a young boy when he became king, was of necessity dependent on his advisers. His epithet, *Unræd*, means badly-counselled. Early in his reign the old order died off, with Ælfhere of Mercia dying the year before Bishop Æthelwold, and his successor in Mercia being banished in 985. No new ealdorman was appointed in Mercia until 1007. From 994 to 998 only five ealdormen witnessed the king's charters, one of whom was Ælfhelm of Northumbria, whose story is significant and whose subsequent murder had far-reaching repercussions, as we shall discover shortly.[15]

Perhaps the adviser most deserving of the accusation of supplying bad counsel was the new ealdorman of Mercia, Eadric Streona. Around the time that Eadric came to prominence at court, Ælfhelm of Northumbria was murdered and his sons were blinded. Eadric was blamed; John of Worcester accused him of luring the ealdorman to a feast and leading him into an ambush. King Æthelred might have been asserting his authority by making new appointments and gathering a new guard around him. He had run out of kin, so he made new kinships. He married his daughter Eadgyth to Eadric Streona, possibly around the time that Eadric became senior ealdorman in 1012[16] and a few years before this the king's daughter Ælfgifu was married to Uhtred of Northumbria, who had succeeded the murdered Ælfhelm. These marriages were clearly designed to bind the two powerful earls to the king, and these two daughters were but the latest in a long line of princesses married off for political purposes. The difference here was that the marriages were not to royals, but to non-royal ealdormen – and Eadric was said by at least one chronicler to have been of lowly birth – something which was unprecedented. To find a comparable scenario we must look to the marriage of Alfred's daughter

Æthelflæd to Æthelred of Mercia in the ninth century but, as we have seen, his status was quasi-royal.[17] In Uhtred's case the alliance seems to have held, and he fought alongside Æthelred's son, Edmund, against the Danish forces of Cnut, until he was killed, seemingly on Cnut's orders, in 1016. Eadric's career has been discussed at length elsewhere but suffice it to say here that his vacillations and murderous tendencies helped more than hindered the next crucial round of Danish attacks.[18]

In 1013 the enemy was led by Swein Forkbeard who succeeded in obtaining the submission of the north. When Swein received the submission of the Londoners, discretion became the better part of valour for the king and Emma and their sons were sent for safety to Normandy, where they were joined shortly afterwards by Æthelred. In 1014 Swein Forkbeard died and the royal family returned to England with Æthelred being urged by his councillors to 'govern them more justly than he did before.' Swein's son, Cnut, was put to flight. Yet the struggles continued, both with the invaders and within the royal family. This time the matter was not which sons were born from legitimate marriage, or even which marriage took precedence. The simple fact was that the sons of Æthelred's earlier marriage were adults, whilst Emma's were still children. Was she showing signs then of the ruthlessness that would drive her later actions, albeit championing different sons?

The eldest royal son, Athelstan, died and was replaced as atheling by his brother Edmund, later known as Ironside. Athelstan's will, previously mentioned, showed that the brothers had connections and alliances with the family of the murdered Ealdorman Ælfhelm.[19] In 1015 two members of this family, the thegns Sigeferth and Morcar, were murdered by Eadric Streona and their property seized by the king, who also imprisoned Sigeferth's widow. The atheling Edmund promptly released the widow from prison and married her. It is assumed that the lady's name was Ealdgyth, but we cannot be certain. Nowhere is it recorded how she felt about becoming Edmund's wife, but presumably this was preferable to being incarcerated. That Edmund, along with his brother Athelstan, had links with the family suggests the likelihood that she already knew him; perhaps even that they formed part of the same circle of young nobles and royals. It would be nice to think of Edmund, who was undoubtedly a brave warrior, rushing to rescue Ealdgyth in the mode of the later, chivalric knights. But we must remember, too, that he would have gained, if not her lands, then the loyalty of the men living on those estates.

Divisions were opening up; Edmund might have been making a bid for the throne. Perhaps he feared Emma's intentions now that her sons were reaching double figures in age. It had been Edward, not he, who had acted as Æthelred's envoy during the negotiations with the nobles of England to arrange the king's return in 1014.[20] The family of Ælfhelm of Northumbria was clearly considered disloyal, and perhaps Eadric, by killing Sigeferth and Morcar, was merely doing the king's bidding in removing the threat. It was not to prove so simple. Swein Forkbeard's son Cnut fully intended to carry on where his father had left off and he returned to England in August 1015. Divisions became even more complicated when Edmund found himself fighting Cnut whilst also, in a roundabout way, being related to him. Having married the widow of a leading thegn of the Danelaw, Edmund might have found his standing there compromised by another union of marriage, that of his enemy and the daughter of a different branch of that same family.[21] While Emma took a back seat, another woman and her powerful family moved to centre stage.

Ealdorman Ælfhelm of Northumbria, murdered in 1006, was in fact not a Northumbrian but a member of a powerful Midlands family. His brother, a wealthy thegn named Wulfric Spott, left a will which shows

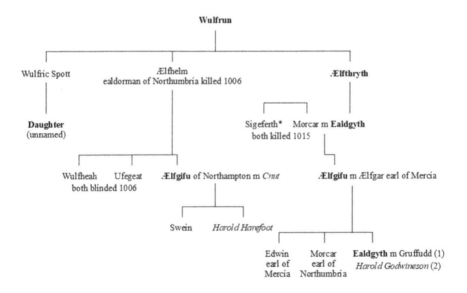

*his widow married *Edmund Ironside*

The Family of Wulfric Spott.

the extent of the landholdings of the family.[22] Wulfric was also known as the son of Wulfrun, a notable woman whom we will meet in Part VI. As mentioned above, when Ælfhelm was murdered, his sons Wulfheah and Ufegeat were blinded. They had a sister, Ælfgifu. She was related – possibly through her aunt – to the murdered thegns Morcar and Sigeferth, and thus to the widow of the latter, whom Edmund Ironside married. Her allegiance though, was not to Edmund and his father. This powerful and influential family was under suspicion, accused of encouraging or even facilitating the submission of the area to Swein. Indeed, it was around the time of that submission that Ælfgifu married Swein's son, Cnut.

She was later to be called a concubine, but the details of her life suggest that she was more to him than a mere sexual partner, even after Cnut remarried. Perhaps we can imagine how the two met. Swein based his operations in the north, camping at Gainsborough. It would have made perfect sense to strengthen the bonds with the northern families by marrying his son to the daughter of one of the most powerful among them. The union bears all the hallmarks of yet another political marriage, in which the wife's value rested solely on her bloodline. Yet Ælfgifu's later life and career show that she was anything but a timid maid given no responsibility other than to breed heirs. Had the couple met beforehand, when Swein was in the north and accompanied by his son? The wedding itself is not mentioned in the sources, but it is not impossible that her family had played host to Swein and his son at some point. However, by the time of the marriage – probably 1013 – her father was dead and her brothers had been effectively removed from political life. She must therefore have been living quietly on her estates.[23] Perhaps she was nursing her brothers? Blinding was a fairly common punishment yet nothing is recorded of the fate of those so afflicted. Her brothers were noblemen and would not starve, but life would have been difficult for them after they had been rendered ineffectual. However, the remnants of Ælfgifu's family were evidently still important enough for Swein to woo, and it is likely that the wedding took place while he was still alive, and before King Æthelred's return saw Cnut temporarily ousted.

Ælfgifu, known as Ælfgifu of Northampton, had two sons by Cnut, who were probably born early on in the marriage. (Cnut remarried in 1017, of which more in a moment.) They were named Swein and Harold, later known as Harold Harefoot, and the fact that they were given royal Danish names – after Cnut's father and grandfather respectively – suggests that they were considered legitimate children, regardless of the legal status of the union. The *ASC* was later to report that many considered that Harold was not Cnut's son, and John of Worcester remarked that some said he was the son of a cobbler. Slurs cast in a written work commissioned by Cnut's second wife suggested that the baby had been born to a servant and smuggled into the royal bedchamber.[24] Cnut remarried while Ælfgifu was still alive but she does not seem to have been repudiated in the way that earlier first wives of English kings had been, and it might be that the relationship was misunderstood by the English commentators. As has been observed by historian Timothy Bolton this was a union between the son of a Danish king and a daughter from an influential Danelaw family and may have resembled a Scandinavian model where aristocratic concubines often held high social status.[25]

There are many sources which document the years of Cnut's reign and its aftermath, not all of them without bias, but we do not know what happened to Ælfgifu when Cnut was forced to flee upon the return of King Æthelred. In 1015 when the thegns Sigeferth and Morcar were killed, if she had remained in England with one or both of her small sons, she must have feared for their lives, if not her own. Sources suggest that a woman of noble birth exhumed Swein Forkbeard's body and returned it to Denmark, but there is no solid evidence that this woman, even if the story is true, should be identified with Ælfgifu.[26] Historians differ as to her whereabouts at this point.[27] Although we know from later events that Cnut did not put her completely to one side, nevertheless she all but disappears from the records until the 1030s.[28] So what went on in the meantime?

In 1016 Edmund Ironside joined forces with Uhtred of Bamburgh, earl of Northumbria, while Cnut ravaged Mercia with Eadric Streona's help, and when he withdrew from Mercia it drew Uhtred of Bamburgh north, too. Uhtred submitted to Cnut, but was nevertheless killed on the orders of, according to the *ASC*, Eadric Streona. We are not told how the two men's wives, who were the royal daughters of King Æthelred and were full sisters, reacted to the news that one of their husbands had killed the other's. Those daughters also suffered bereavement with the loss of their father that same year. For Emma of Normandy and Ælfgifu of Northampton, the death, on 23 April, of King Æthelred II the 'Unready' meant that their two stories would henceforth be intertwined.

After Æthelred's death, his son Edmund fought five battles, at one point accepting the return of Eadric Streona to the English fold, only to have him change sides and leave the field of engagement at Ashingdon.

Cnut was victorious, but it was agreed that the kingdom should be divided, with Edmund succeeding to Wessex and Cnut to Mercia and presumably the rest of the north and east.[29] The battle of Ashingdon had taken place on 18 October; on 30 November, Edmund died. Cnut became king of England. It is possible that Edmund died from wounds received during the battle. Certain sources, however, accused the family of Eadric Streona of murder. Whatever the truth, Cnut was astute enough not to trust Eadric and ordered his death. Perhaps Ælfgifu of Northampton encouraged him in this, for she would certainly have felt no love for a man who had been implicated in the murder of her father and the blinding of her brothers, along with the killing of her kinsmen Sigeferth and Morcar.[30]

Whether or not she had personal influence, her usefulness politically had waned. Of the northerners who might have bound themselves to Cnut through association with her, most were dead by 1015 and Uhtred of Bamburgh, as we have seen, had allied himself with Edmund Ironside and continued to do so before then submitting and being killed. Cnut perhaps had less need of extra sureties in the north than his father had done.[31] Cnut set about neutralising any opposition threats. Eadric's was not the only killing; three other noblemen were executed, and Eadwig, seemingly the only surviving full brother of Edmund Ironside, was exiled and later killed. Edmund Ironside's young sons were also exiled. The only royal princes left, whose claims might be espoused by a rebellion, were those of Emma by Æthelred. To eliminate any threat from that quarter, Cnut married Emma.

Just as doubt remains over the whereabouts of Ælfgifu of Northampton at this time, so it is also unclear where Emma was during this period. Thietmar of Merseberg, an eleventh-century Continental Saxon chronicler, was sure that when the king, Æthelred, died in 1016, Emma and her sons were trapped in London, offered peace only if she would surrender her boys and pay a ransom although, according to this version, the boys managed to escape. The author of a work which she later commissioned, the *Encomium Emmæ Reginæ*, said that she was in Normandy when Cnut sought her out in order to marry her but, as we shall see, this was a panegyric which was highly biased and frequently inaccurate. The record in the *ASC* for the year 1017 says that Cnut ordered her 'to be fetched as his wife', which is ambiguous. Fetched from Normandy, or London? It should be noted that Thietmar's story was near-contemporary and based on a reliable witness account and that in the *Encomium* Emma did not acknowledge her first marriage and consequently would have wished the episode in London, if it happened, to be omitted.[32] With what we know of her later activities, it is not hard to believe that she would have been willing to give up her sons.

If she did indeed remain in London after Æthelred's death, her situation would have been unenviable. His successor in England at that point was Edmund Ironside, her stepson, who was married to a woman whose family would have few reasons to be sympathetic to Emma's plight. It was sensible for Edward to flee to Normandy, but it might be that Emma either could not, or would not, leave.[33] She might even have been prevented from doing so by Cnut himself, who would have been keen to keep her away from her sons and their cause. The *Encomium* reported a promise that any future child would be recognised as heir. Whether Emma was tempted, or whether she was presented with little choice, the marriage went ahead.[34] Cnut had been shrewd, offering the English continuity whilst neutralising the threat of the athelings.

A revised *ordo* was used for Emma's coronation and there are other indications that this marriage was a relatively equal partnership.[35] Charters show her name immediately after the king's, and there are examples where she was jointly associated with the king's grants.[36] Although we do not know her precise date of birth, she was much older than Cnut and perhaps this was a factor in the relationship. Certainly her status during her second marriage appears to have been higher than during her first. She was, despite her Norman blood, an English queen, one moreover who had already borne sons. The alliance was one between England and Denmark, rather than England and Normandy. She was lauded for her patronage of religious houses and the abbey of Ely recorded that when she married Cnut she adorned the church and 'made a pall of purpura, bordered all round with orphrey and decorated over all its parts with gold and precious gems, with wonderful artistry, in a sort of chequer design.'[37] An image of the royal couple survives, a symbol of their partnership: the frontispiece of the *Liber Vitae* of the New Minster, Winchester, shows Cnut and Emma together as they place a cross upon the altar. There were few hints during Cnut's reign of the storms to come after his death, but one thing of note was that Emma was given more prominence and status in her second marriage. Love might not have entered the equation, but her experience as a wife of Cnut might have coloured her actions as his widow.

She and Cnut had two children. Her son, Harthacnut, was born *c.* 1018 and his status was clear. A bloody episode in 1011 had resulted in the murder, by Cnut's troops, of the archbishop of Canterbury and in 1023 Emma attended the translation of the murdered Archbishop Ælfheah's bones with 'her royal child, Harthacnut'. A daughter, Gunnhild, was sent as a child to Germany where she became the wife of Henry III. Cnut visited Rome in 1027 and it might have been then that the marriage negotiations took place.[38] William of Malmesbury related that Gunnhild was accused of adultery and was defended in a trial by combat by 'a young lad of her brother's establishment' which perhaps denotes a page; other versions of the tale have it that he was a dwarf.[39] Emma was destined to be separated at various times from all her children.

Emma, with her credentials as an English queen, was no doubt important to Cnut, but so too was Ælfgifu of Northampton, and Cnut had a task for her to perform. Cnut had an empire to rule, and Harthacnut was in Denmark for some years before his father's death, ruling the country and minting coins in his own name.[40] Whether Emma was distressed by her son's absence, she must have been perturbed by the sending in 1030 of Ælfgifu and her son Swein to Norway, there to rule for Cnut.

The regency in Norway may have been hugely symbolic, but it was not a success. At the outset, it demonstrated the powerful status of the mothers of royal heirs. Swein would only have been around 15 and it is telling that the period was remembered in Scandinavian history as 'Ælfgifu's time'.[41] It was a rule noted for harsh taxation, but it has been argued that although the records do indeed indicate a heavy tax being raised during this time, it could not have been achieved without the cooperation of the majority of the nobles. It might also have been wrongly assumed to be an annual tax rather than a one-off payment.[42] Whatever the reason, the regency was not popular and in 1034 Ælfgifu and Swein were ousted and had to flee to Denmark. Swein died shortly afterwards, in 1035. The more significant death of that year, however, was that of Cnut, on 12 November. Now the battle between his two wives would really begin, as they revealed their aggressive determination to secure the kingdom of England for their sons.

The fight was on. Emma championed her son by Cnut, Harthacnut, whilst Ælfgifu was unsurprisingly batting for her surviving son, Harold Harefoot. When Cnut died, of the four of them only Emma was still in England. A letter written by a priest at the court of Henry III in Germany described how messengers brought news that a 'wretched and wicked stepmother' of Gunnhild's was trying to deprive Harthacnut of his throne by bribing the nobility so that they would swear oaths in support of Harold.[43] Harthacnut might have been Cnut's choice of heir, as promised to Emma upon their wedding, but the political situation in Denmark was too volatile to allow him to return to England, while Ælfgifu and Harold, on the other hand, were free to do so.

Ælfgifu's family connections proved to be advantageous. Cnut had ruled England with the help of ealdormen, some English, some Danish.[44] The leading earls in 1035 were the English earl of Mercia, Leofric, and Godwine, earl of Wessex. Godwine may have been the son of a man named Wulfnoth, a Sussex thegn who had been accused of treachery in the reign of Æthelred. Godwine rose to prominence during Cnut's reign and his family was to dominate English politics for nearly half a century. He married the king's sister-in-law, Gytha, but Leofric of Mercia might also have been related to Cnut; his son, Ælfgar, married a woman named Ælfgifu, who may have been the daughter of Ælfgifu of Northampton's cousin Ealdgyth and her husband Morcar, who had been killed alongside his brother Sigeferth. (See family tree for Wulfric Spott above, p. 103.) Related to Cnut, yes, but Leofric seems to have allied with this Northampton family.

Cnut had perhaps not helped matters regarding his successor. All of his sons were named after previous Danish rulers, which could be interpreted as recognition of their having claims. Initially, battle lines were drawn neatly. At a meeting in Oxford, the Mercians and the Northumbrians declared a desire for Harold Harefoot to rule as regent for himself and for Harthacnut. Godwine opposed this arrangement, championing Harthacnut's right as sole heir. Harthacnut had troubles in Denmark, fending off an invasion by Magnus of Norway. Emma, having had her treasures seized by Harold, had to sit by in Winchester and watch as Harold became more secure in England. The *Encomium* commissioned by Emma recorded that the archbishop of Canterbury had refused to consecrate Harold and the *ASC* cast doubt over his parentage. Although to begin with coins were being minted in both Harold's and Harthacnut's names, it was not long before the majority carried Harold's name.[45] Sir Frank Stenton was of the opinion that 'for part, if not the whole' of Harold's reign, 'his mother … was the real ruler of England.'[46] The *Encomium* is scathing about Ælfgifu, but the letter which Gunnhild saw revealed a woman whose ambition matched that of the queen. Emma needed to change tack.

The major stumbling block to her ambition for Harthacnut was his continued absence. Earl Godwine switched his allegiance to Harold, while Emma seems to have been reminded that she had other sons. If Godwine was the first to move, then Emma would have been left with little option but to send to her sons in Normandy. If, however, it was she who moved first, then Godwine, who owed his position to Cnut, would scarcely have expected to fare well under one of the sons of Æthelred.[47] Either way, self-preservation seems to have been the overriding factor.

Edward and his brother Alfred sailed from Normandy in 1036. In one version of events Edward arrived at Southampton with forty ships but was repulsed. One manuscript of the *ASC* carries a story that Alfred, attempting to visit his mother at Winchester, was captured by Godwine and blinded. Left to languish at Ely, he died. The incident was not universally recorded – one version of the *ASC* does not mention Alfred's death at all – but if, as some suggest, he was arrested by Godwine but handed over to Harold and Ælfgifu, then a chilling scenario unfolds. Ælfgifu of Northampton's brothers had been blinded on the orders of Æthelred II. It is not impossible that the same cruel punishment was meted out to Æthelred's son on the orders of a woman who had suffered the murder of her father and the blinding of her brothers and saw a chance for revenge.

With Edward repulsed, Alfred dead, and Harthacnut still in Denmark, Harold was chosen as full king of England and when Emma was driven overseas, Ælfgifu could finally enjoy supremacy as mother of the king of England. By now Harold was in his twenties and her influence might not have been strong, but the prestige was hers, especially as no wife of Harold was recorded. Alas, it was not to last. Harold died on 17 March 1040.[48] It is not known where Ælfgifu was immediately after Harold's death, but Emma's return to England in June 1040 makes it unlikely that she would have stayed for long after that. Harthacnut controlled Denmark, so that too seems an unlikely destination. There was one last possible 'sighting' of this once great lady of the Danelaw, in a twelfth-century cartulary from Aquitaine, which mentions a lady named Alveva who was related to a king named Heroldus. It is possible that these are Ælfgifu and her son Harold. This text mentions a grandson and given that Harold was only in his early twenties when he died, perhaps an infant son of his was given over to his mother who maybe took him with her to exile in southern France.[49]

Emma, having spent her exile not in Normandy but in Flanders, returned in triumph after Harold's death, and this time Harthacnut was with her. She had seen off her rival, Ælfgifu, and a charter of Harthacnut's reign (S 997), shows her exalted position: 'Writ of King Harthacnut and his mother Queen [Emma] declaring that they have given to the church of Ramsey land at Hemingford Grey, Hunts.' Nevertheless, her problems were far from over. Harthacnut's reign was not popular, and it was at this time that Emma commissioned the *Encomium*, an artful exercise in damage limitation and a wonderful example of 'spin'. The *Encomium*, written after Harthacnut's accession but before his death in 1042, begins with an account of the conquest by Swein Forkbeard and Cnut, and then goes on to describe the power struggle between 1035 and 1040. Much of it seems designed to cast slurs on Harold Harefoot, whilst exonerating Emma from any accusations of wrongdoing.

According to the encomiast, a letter was sent to Edward and Alfred in 1036, purportedly from Emma, urging one or other of her sons to come to England, but the letter was in fact forged by Harold Harefoot, who wanted to entice them into a fatal trap. Was the letter indeed a forgery, or was it written by Emma herself? If she had written the letter, which led to the mutilation and death of her son, Alfred, then the encomiast would have good cause to claim the letter was a forgery and lay the blame on Harold.[50] The *Encomium* was also the source for the story that Cnut swore never to set up the son of any wife other than Emma to rule after him, which was clearly designed to negate Harold's claim. The purpose of the document is to substantiate Emma's claims that Harthacnut was the rightful heir and to show Emma in a positive light. In the *Encomium*, she is a famous queen who negotiated her own marriage terms with Cnut, from her base in Normandy. Perhaps she had been stuck in London but did not wish to admit to such ignominy. With Harthacnut's reign proving unpopular, Emma's activities during the succession dispute might have been questioned and this could be why she decided to commission the account.

In the end, it did her little good, for Harthacnut reigned for just two years, dying in June 1042. The closeness of their relationship cannot be assessed. It is unlikely that Emma was especially close to any of her sons; she had been separated from Edward and Alfred since 1016, and Harthacnut had been sent to Denmark when he was still a small boy. She had proved herself to be a political animal and in 1042 she still had one son left, whose claim to the throne was strong. And yet, Emma was even accused of supporting the claims of Magnus of Norway over those of Edward. The story might have had its basis in the fact that on Harthacnut's death, Magnus attacked Denmark. His rival here was Swein, a nephew of Earl Godwine. Was Emma sufficiently embittered against Godwine's earlier defection that she would have supported a rival to his kinsman? Perhaps by the time of this accusation she was seen as primarily the wife and mother of Danish kings, rather than an English queen.[51] Nothing came of any claim by Magnus. But if the report of Emma's support for him was true, and her son Edward knew of it, it cannot have helped their relationship. She had already commissioned the *Encomium* which had completely neglected to mention her first marriage or the children thereof.

After an unpopular incident in which Harthacnut had ordered the ravaging of Worcestershire, he had invited Edward to share his rule; the *ASC* records that Edward was sworn in as king in 1041. Opinions differ as to the nature of Harthacnut's invitation, from brotherly love (the *Encomium*) to the notion that he knew he was dying (William of Poitiers). Brotherly love seems an unlikely motive, and it is certainly true that Harthacnut died the following year. Edward was crowned as sole king in April 1043. Later that year, he went to Winchester and deprived Emma of her treasures because, according to the *ASC*, she had 'formerly been very hard to the king, her son, in that she did less for him than he wished both before he became king and afterwards as well.' Emma was permitted to remain in Winchester and although she lived quietly, her reputation was such that her fame endured. A story circulated that she had conducted an affair with the bishop of Winchester between 1032 and 1047, and that she cleared herself of the charges by walking across hot ploughshares.[52]

When Edward went to Winchester to deprive his mother of her treasures, he was accompanied by his three leading earls, Siward of Northumbria, Leofric of Mercia, and Earl Godwine. By now in his late thirties, Edward, estranged from his mother for most of his life, would have had no desire to fall under her influence. His reign was dominated though, by the Godwine family and their fortunes. In 1043, Godwine was still holding sway, although whether Edward fully trusted him is another matter.

Emma's career was at an end. Her retirement however was not one in which she spent time with grandchildren, unlike her mother-in-law

Bamburgh Castle, Northumberland. Bamburgh was named after seventh-century Queen Bebba. (Image by Jonathan Cannon, sourced from Pixabay)

Whitby Abbey. The original abbey was founded by Hild and was the location of the Synod of Whitby in 664. (Photo courtesy of David Satterthwaite)

St Abb's Head, Berwickshire, looking across to Kirk Hill, possible site of St Æbbe's seventh-century monastery. (Author's own photo)

Coldingham Abbey, Berwickshire. The field in the foreground is the site of the recent excavation showing the site of an earlier Anglo-Saxon building. (Author's own photo)

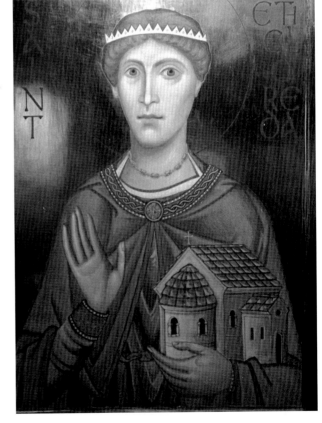

Above: Ely Abbey Seen from the Water. St Æthelthryth founded the original abbey and was buried there. (Photo courtesy of David Webster)

Right: Image of St Æthelthryth, Anglo-Saxon Exhibition, Hexham Abbey. (Author's own photo, by kind permission of Canon Dagmar Winter, Hexham Abbey)

Minster Abbey, Thanet, showing the original Saxon stonework. (Image kindly supplied by the community at Minster Abbey)

The Saxon Crypt at Minster Abbey. (Image kindly supplied by the community at Minster Abbey)

Above: Tapestry from Minster Abbey depicting the first three abbesses, Domneva, Mildrith and Eadburh. (Image kindly supplied by the community at Minster Abbey)

Below: The Cathedral Close, Chester, the site associated with St Werburg. (Author's own photo)

The cloister, Chester Cathedral. (Author's own photo)

Shop Parade at Chester, showing St Werburg's name and her continued association with the city. (Author's own photo)

Cynethryth coin, replica from author's own collection.

Above: Cynethryth coin reverse, replica from author's own collection.

Below: St Peter's, Winchcombe, Gloucestershire, near the site of the original abbey. (Author's own photo)

St Kenelm's Well, Winchcombe. It was said that the funeral procession paused here before taking Kenelm's body to Winchcombe Abbey for burial. (Author's own photo)

Above: Replica of Queen
Æthelswith's ring, from
author's own collection.

Right: Æthelflæd Statue at
Tamworth Castle. (Author's
own photo)

Above: St Oswald's Priory,
Gloucester, burial place of
Æthelflæd. (Author's own photo)

Left: The Cuthbert Maniple
commissioned by Queen Ælfflæd
for the bishop of Winchester.
(Drawing by Mia Pelletier)

Dunfermline Abbey. St Margaret's grave is said to be under the stone floor. (Author's own photo)

Above: St Margaret's
Shrine outside
Dunfermline Abbey.
(Author's own photo)

Left: Balthild's Seal
Matrix. (Image from
Portable Antiquities
Scheme, used under
Creative Commons
Licence 2.0)

Above: Replica of the Sutton Hoo
Grave Layout, Sutton Hoo, Suffolk.
(Author's own photo)

Right: Wulfrun Statue,
Wolverhampton. (Image by
Æthelred, used under Creative
Commons Attribution-Share Alike
4.0 International)

The Godiva Statue in Coventry (Author's own photo)

Ælfthryth. Only her daughters produced children, and they were abroad. Emma outlived Gunnhild, Alfred and Harthacnut, and possibly her daughter by Æthelred, Godgifu, too. A charter of 1045, if genuine, shows Emma alongside her daughter-in-law, and offers a tantalising scenario, in which the formidable old lady met her successor and attested a charter with her name appearing ahead of her daughter-in-law's.[53] Did it soothe her to think that she still held precedence? Or was it a moment where she thought of her mortality and all that had happened in her eventful life, and a reminder that she had been replaced? There might have been some contact between the two women in the crisis of 1051–1052, of which more in a moment, but the charter is probably spurious and in all likelihood Emma never ventured far from Winchester in the last few years of her remarkable life.

She died on 6 March 1052 – the very fact that her death was recorded indicating her importance – and she was buried alongside Cnut, her second husband. (During the writing of this book, news emerged from Winchester Cathedral that the bones of over twenty individuals found in mortuary chests might include the skeleton of Emma. Investigations are ongoing.) At around the same time, Edward's coinage changed, with his portrait becoming that of a warrior wearing a helmet. Perhaps it was to signify Edward's freedom from a mother about whom he must have had decidedly mixed feelings.[54]

It might be that Emma was genuinely torn by the various crises which beset the English crown during her adult life. She had to support one son over another, and perhaps there existed some genuine affection in her marriage to Cnut which prompted her to favour Harthacnut. Perhaps her dilemma would have garnered some sympathy were it not for the possibility that she then favoured Magnus of Norway over her own son, Edward. Was Edward simply a reminder of a terrible marriage? Both her husbands were capable of cruelty: Æthelred with the St Brice's Day massacre, Cnut with the savage killing of Archbishop Ælfheah. Because of the wealth of source material, we know a lot about Emma's life yet it is still hard to understand her. She and her rival, Ælfgifu of Northampton, were unwavering in their determination, prepared to go to extraordinary lengths to press the claims of their children, even if their motives might well have been simply to extend their own careers. Their ascendancy was assured by their having borne sons by kings. Emma's successor was not so secure in her role.

Edith married King Edward on 23 January 1045. She was the daughter of Earl Godwine and his Danish wife, Gytha. Less is known about her life than that of her famous mother-in-law, and the majority of that information comes from the *Life* of her husband, which she commissioned and which, like the *Encomium*, carries a fair amount of bias. Often Edith is referred to as the eldest child but this was not necessarily the case. It has been pointed out that Godwine and Gytha might have been expected, during Cnut's reign, to signal their loyalty by bestowing Danish names upon their offspring.[55] All the older sons had Danish names as did one of the daughters, Gunnhild.[56] Perhaps the naming of daughters was not so symbolic, or perhaps Edith was one of the younger of the couple's nine children. Her date of birth is unknown and could have been as early as 1020 or as late as 1030.

There is no doubt that it was a political marriage, but at first glance it seems an odd choice for Edward. Here was a half-Danish woman, whose father's career had burgeoned during service to the Danish king who had ousted Edward's father and was very possibly complicit in the murder of his brother. Yet it could be that Edward had little choice. Godwine was powerful and needed to be kept 'onside'. The marriage would, in theory, ensure this. Even if Edith had been one of the elder children, she was still considerably younger than Edward and it is hard to imagine that the match would have pleased her.

She grew up and received her education at Wilton Abbey where, according to the *Life* of King Edward, she developed artistic skill, particularly in embroidery. She was praised for her literary accomplishments, her piety and her beauty. William of Malmesbury said that, 'On seeing her, if you were amazed at her erudition, you must absolutely languish for the purity of her mind, and the beauty of her person.'[57] Edith never wielded the power of her predecessor, and her fate was tied utterly to that of her birth family. The marriage was childless, so she never enjoyed the elevated status of royal mother and, when her family fell from grace, so did she.

Much has been made of the childlessness of the marriage, with reasons varying from William of Malmesbury's assertion that Edward's hatred of Godwine resulted in an aversion to his daughter, to the suggestion that Edward was simply too saintly ever to consummate the marriage, an idea fostered by Edith herself in her commissioned history.

Edith received recognition as queen in charters for Winchester and Wilton, in the heart of her father's earldom, appearing alongside the king in the witness lists, as *conlaterana regis* (the king's wife), for example, S 1009 in 1045, a grant to her father. Like other queens before her, she ran her own household. A charter of Edward's shows the separate witness of the king's butler, the queen's butler, the king's steward, and the queen's steward.[58] Edith had a *femme de chambre*, a Frenchwoman named Matilda, who married a rich English thegn called Ælfweard and a picture emerges of a woman used to the sophistications of the Anglo-Danish court.[59] The difference in age might not have been the only gap between Edward and herself; perhaps there were cultural differences too. He had lived most of his life in Normandy, and the *Life* suggests that he took in little of his surroundings, walking at all times with eyes downcast.

At Wilton Edith replaced the wooden church with a new stone building and the *Life* says that her advice was much relied upon in court, where 'by God's grace she shone above all in counsel if she were heard.'[60] But we are led to believe that she was also full of humility: although by custom a royal throne was always prepared for her, the *Life* says that she preferred, 'except in church and at the royal table' to sit at the king's feet, 'unless perchance he should reach out his hand to her.'[61] The *Life* was begun as a history of Edith's husband, and of her family. The author was forced to change tack and Book II became a religious *Life* of King Edward, the other subjects being, in the main, dead by 1066. Whatever Edith's personal qualities – her piety and her wisdom – her fate and her reputation were tied to that of her father and brothers and there are hints that she had a determined, even ruthless, side to her personality.

Different tales emerge in sources other than the officially commissioned *Life*. Hugh Candidus of Peterborough said that his abbey was given a 'text of gospels beautifully adorned with gold, and ornaments worth three hundred pounds. All these things came to us … but Queen Edith took them away.' The monks of Evesham accused her of arranging to have all the relics of a number of monasteries assembled so that she could pick the best for herself. Apparently Evesham resisted by sending the relics not of St Ecgwine, as presumed, but of St Odulf, their patron saint, whom it was hoped would protect their relics from being appropriated by Edith for her house at Wilton. When the shrine was opened for the queen she was immediately struck blind, only having her sight restored after promising to bestow a pall on the shrine.[62]

In 1051 Godwine was still a dominant force. His son Swegn had broken away from the king and the rest of his family in the late 1040s, at one point even claiming that he was not Godwine's son, but Cnut's, thereby defaming his mother Gytha.[63] He had managed, however, with the help of the bishop of Worcester, to earn the king's pardon, although perhaps was never entirely forgiven by his family. It has been suggested that Edward, whilst not being especially comfortable about pardoning him, might have done it to spite the Godwines.[64] If Edward was looking for an excuse to break with the earl though, the opportunity came in 1051. His wife had not provided him with a son and, if the marriage had indeed been consummated, he might well have blamed her and been looking to repudiate her. We have two wildly differing versions of what happened to cause the earl's fall from grace.

The *ASC* notes that Eustace of Boulogne, a former brother-in-law of Edward, landed at Dover on an official visit to England. Godwine's son Tostig had married Judith, the half-sister of Eustace's rival, the count of Flanders, and Swegn Godwineson appears to have been embroiled in some animosity with the stepson of Eustace.[65] Whether or not this informed the incident at Dover, what occurred was that Eustace and his men were attacked, Edward ordered Godwine to ravage Dover in retaliation, and Godwine refused. Godwine and his sons Swegn and Harold came together, with the intention of going to the Council. Earls Leofric of Mercia and Siward of Northumbria joined Edward with their armed forces. Those on the king's side advised that hostages should be given and that they would meet again in London to consider the charges against Godwine. But the Godwines fled and Edward outlawed them.

The version of events depicted in the *Life* of Edward offers a completely different scenario. Here, the appointment of Robert of Jumièges as archbishop of Canterbury was in direct disregard of Godwine's choice of candidate. This erstwhile monk of Normandy then dripped poison in Edward's ear, saying that Godwine had despoiled Canterbury of certain estates, reminded the king that the earl was responsible for the death of Edward's brother Alfred, although the earl was 'guiltless' and, furthermore, that Godwine was now planning to bring about the death of Edward.

The chronicles differ, too, in the recording of the treatment of Edith. The *ASC* and the chronicle of John of Worcester state that she was deprived of her possessions and imprisoned at Wherwell Abbey where, according to John, she was sent without ceremony, with one waiting-woman, and was committed into the care of the abbess.[66] The *Life* of Edward on the other hand states that she was sent to Wilton, 'with royal honours and an imperial retinue'. We do not know whether Edward intended this to be a permanent separation and perhaps she went first to Wherwell and then to Wilton.[67] What is clear is that she was put away, whether as punishment for her childlessness, the sins of her father, or both. Equally clear is that she was reinstated when her family returned from exile in 1052.

Godwine had amassed a fleet and whilst Edward was prepared to challenge him, Earls Leofric and Siward were not. Peace – although it must have been an uneasy one – broke out, and Godwine and his family, including his daughter Edith, were restored. If she had, indeed, been confined at Wherwell, she might have welcomed a return to court life. If she had been sent with full retinue to Wilton, she could well have preferred to stay there. The *Life* informs us that she 'strongly' preferred the 'king's interest to powers and riches' when first at court but gives no information about how she felt upon being reunited with him in 1052. It is tempting to wonder, too, what the ageing Emma might have thought of the crisis of 1051, particularly the revisiting of the circumstances of Alfred's death, but alas we are not told. From 1055 onwards Edith attested charters regularly, her name appearing next to Edward's. Of the twenty-two surviving charters, Edith witnessed fourteen, and she issued a writ and land grants in her own name too.[68]

In 1053 her father, 'the earl of happy memory', had died, followed not long afterwards by Siward of Northumbria.[69] Siward's son, Waltheof, was too young to succeed him, and the earldom was given to Edith's brother Tostig after, according to the *Life* of Edward, the intercession of his brother Earl Harold and his sister, the queen. The details in the *Life* suggest a close relationship between Edith and Tostig who, it says, was a 'man of courage and endowed with great wisdom and shrewdness of mind.' It did not prove a popular appointment and the northern earls rebelled against him. John of Worcester recorded that they rose up in arms because they objected to a huge tribute which he had 'unjustly levied' on the whole of Northumbria but further, because of the killing of a number of Northumbrian thegns, including one Gospatric 'whom Queen Edith, on account of her brother Tostig, had ordered to be killed in the king's court on the fourth night of Christmas by treachery.'[70] Like the monks of Peterborough and Evesham, Worcester seemed prepared to believe the worst of Edith.

The rebels went to York where they seized two of Tostig's housecarls and killed them, before breaking open Tostig's treasury.[71] The following day they killed another 200 of Tostig's men. Leofric of Mercia had been succeeded by his son, Ælfgar, who in turn had been succeeded by his son, Edwin. The *ASC* recorded that the rebels called for Morcar, the younger brother of Edwin, to replace Tostig as earl of Northumbria. Once on the march, the rebels were joined by Morcar's brother Earl Edwin at Northampton, who had with him men from Wales as well as Mercia.

Discussions were held at Northampton and then at Oxford. The rebel demands were for the renewal of Cnut's law in the north, and the dismissal of Tostig. Tostig accused his brother Harold Godwineson of fomenting the rebellion against him and Harold had to swear an oath to clear himself of this charge. Edward wanted to use force to crush the rebellion, but his counsellors were against the idea, it was late in the year and so they gave in to the demands. Just before Christmas, Tostig and his wife Judith left for Flanders, where her half-brother Count Baldwin gave them welcome.

Harold's story, meanwhile, became linked to that of the Mercians. Earl Leofric of Mercia had died in the autumn of 1057. His son, Ælfgar, had been earl of East Anglia briefly, replacing Harold Godwineson when the Godwines were forced overseas in 1051 but he was displaced upon their return in 1052. In 1053 after Godwine died and Harold replaced him as earl of Wessex, Ælfgar was reinstated as earl of East Anglia. In 1055 he was outlawed.

The E version of the *ASC* recorded him admitting his guilt 'before all the men assembled'. We are not told the nature of his crimes, but it was at this same assembly that King Edward gave the earldom of Northumbria to Tostig. Perhaps Ælfgar wanted Northumbria for himself or was concerned that Tostig would then get the vacant East Anglian earldom and leave the Mercians isolated. Possibly it had simply been difficult for Ælfgar to establish himself in an area which would have been loyal to Harold Godwineson. At around this same time, Edward put another of Godwine's sons, Gyrth, in charge of Norfolk, a shire within Ælfgar's earldom. It could be that Ælfgar bridled against the appointments, or that the Godwinesons trumped up some charges to get rid of him. Either way, his reaction was spectacular. He went to Ireland, where he acquired eighteen pirate ships, and then approached Gruffudd of Wales for help. According to Roger of Wendover's account, the rebels advanced on Hereford and slew five hundred men before killing seven clergymen who were defending the doors of the cathedral, and then burning the town. Harold Godwineson was forced to make peace, and Ælfgar was re-established in East Anglia.

When his father, Leofric, died, Ælfgar would not have been King Edward's first choice as replacement for the earl of Mercia, but there was really no other suitable candidate. Queen Edith's brothers carved up the remaining territory; Gyrth took over in East Anglia and another brother, Leofwine, became responsible for the shires around the mouth of the Thames. Harold took Herefordshire, part of Gloucestershire and perhaps Shropshire.

It was probably around this time that Ælfgar's daughter Ealdgyth was married to Gruffudd of Wales. She had at least one child by him, a daughter named Nest. She was widowed when Harold led a force into Wales and seemingly engineered the death of Gruffudd. No doubt her marriage to Gruffudd was a political match, designed to seal the alliance between the Welsh king and the earl of Mercia. But relations between the Welsh and the Mercians were as often friendly as antagonistic – Penda of Mercia fought in alliance with Cadwallon in the seventh century and Ælfhere, earl of Mercia, had allied with the Welsh in the tenth – and it might be that Ealdgyth was happily married to this friend of the family. We cannot know. Nor can we know how she felt about subsequently being married to the man responsible for her first husband's murder.

It is unlikely that Ealdgyth had any say in this arrangement. The exact sequence of events is not clear, for the precise date of the marriage to Harold Godwineson was not recorded. Whether she was the price for the support of the brothers Edwin and Morcar for Harold's kingship after Edward's death, or whether marriage to her was a part of the deal which ensured Harold's support for Morcar's appointment to Northumbria, it is clear that Ealdgyth was a valuable commodity. Presumably there was also a desire on Harold's part for legitimate heirs. Her feelings were unlikely to have been considered. It must, however, have been doubly hard for her, because Harold, like Cnut, already had a woman whom he seems not to have repudiated.

It was probably during his time as earl of East Anglia that he formed a relationship with the woman who is usually referred to as Edith

Swanneck (*Swanneshals*). She has been identified with Eadgifu the Fair, named in the Domesday record as one of the largest landholders in the east of England, owning 270 hides of land. This Eadgifu held land in Harkstead, Suffolk, which was attached to a manor of Harold's. Her fate post-Conquest is not known, but she appears to have been deprived of her lands after 1066. Edith/Eadgifu appears to have borne Harold at least five children, named Godwin, Edmund, Magnus, Gytha and Gunnhild. According to later chroniclers there was another child, perhaps still born, who was buried in Canterbury next to the tomb of St Dunstan.[72]

Edith Swanneck is remembered in the story contained in the chronicle of Waltham Abbey – whose patron was Harold – as being the woman who identified King Harold's body in the aftermath of the battle of Hastings. This account suggests that she maintained a close relationship with him even after his marriage. Ealdgyth might well have been little more than a brood mare with the sole function of providing a legitimate heir. It is not even known if she was ever crowned as queen. She gave birth to at least one son, but not before Harold's death on the battlefield. Her son, also Harold, seems to have survived and was last heard of sailing with the king of Norway.[73] Ealdgyth was allegedly taken to safety by her brothers to Chester in 1066 but her fate after that is unknown. It is worth noting, though, that she had been, however briefly, married to kings of both England and Wales (Gruffudd was unusual in being a king rather than a prince of Wales). It is hard to imagine that this elevated and unique status brought her much happiness.

Edith Swanneck's sons by Harold, along with his mother, Gytha, retreated to the West Country, escaping from Exeter when it was besieged by the forces of William the Conqueror in 1068. Gytha had suffered the hurt of having her eldest son refute his parentage, the defection and death of Tostig and yet more of her sons dying at Hastings (Gyrth and Leofwine died alongside Harold). She had asked for the return of Harold's body in exchange for his weight in gold, but was refused. Her daughter Ælfgifu was also dead by this point.

What of Edith the queen? When Edward died in 1066 she might not, in fact, have supported her brother Harold in his bid for the throne. She was evidently devastated by the events which led to Tostig's departure from England, 'confounded by the quarrel of her brothers' and showing her 'foreboding of future evils by her tears'.[74] There may have followed a rift in the relationship between Edith and Harold, for the *Life* also reported that Harold had encouraged the northerners in their rebellion. The tone of the *Life* generally suggests that Tostig was Edith's favourite brother, which might have fuelled accusations of murder on Tostig's behalf, even if they were not true. William of Poitiers, a chaplain who wrote the *Life* of King William, went further, portraying Edith as hating Harold and working to ensure William of Normandy's succession. Edith was, according to Poitiers, 'so unlike [Harold] in morals, but unable to take up arms against him, fought him with prayers and counsel' and 'this woman of masculine wisdom ... wished William, who was wise, just and strong, to rule over the English.'[75] A work dedicated to William would hardly have said otherwise, but the *Life* of Edward also dismisses Harold's claim concerning Edward's deathbed wish that he succeed him and although Book II of the *Life* was written after 1066 it makes no mention of Harold's coronation or reign, although this omission would have been wise, perhaps.[76]

Edith does not emerge from the sources as a stupid woman and she must have been aware that a succession crisis was inevitable. She was clearly close to Tostig, so perhaps the murder accusation should not be entirely dismissed, although she could not possibly have foreseen the outcome. When Edward died, she was in a similar position to that which Emma had faced, except that she had no son to champion, or to support her.

The political events of 1066 have been well-documented elsewhere, and the bare bones are widely known: Harold Godwineson was elected king, ruled for a few short months, Earls Edwin and Morcar were defeated by the forces of Harald Hardrada (allied with the banished Tostig) at the battle of Fulford, and Harald was then defeated by Harold at Stamford Bridge where Tostig was killed. William of Normandy was then successful at Hastings and Anglo-Saxon rule came to an end.

Edith was a childless widow. But she was also a consecrated queen and, whether or not she had colluded with and/or supported William, she fared better than the rest of her family and she was able to retain a good proportion of her landholdings after the Conquest. She has been described as the 'true survivor' of Harold's family.[77] In 1071 she attended the consecration of Walcher, bishop of Durham. Walcher was later murdered and, according to William of Malmesbury, Edith had foretold the events: 'When she had seen Walcher being led to his consecration at Winchester, his milk-white curls, rosy cheeks and ample form prompted her to say, "A pretty martyr we have here".' William supposed it was a 'shrewd guess' at the ferocity of the Northumbrians, ferocity which of course Edith would have cause to remember.[78]

'There has never been such a powerful "instant aristocracy" established by a foreign king, which has wielded such massive power for a generation and then vanished from the scene.'[79] This is a succinct summing up of the Godwine family, but Edith at least survived the turmoil of 1066. She was not, however, immune to the fashion for accusing high-powered women of adultery. According to William of Malmesbury, she cleared herself of such charges on her deathbed, with echoes here of Emma's being similarly accused towards the end of her life. She died in 1075, and it was King William who arranged her burial. She might well have wished to be buried at Wilton, but perhaps William, however cordial their relationship had been, did not want a cult to grow up around her. She was, after all, not only Edward's widow but the sister of Harold Godwineson.[80]

For all that we have the *Life* of Edward to flesh out the bare facts of Edith's life and queenship, it is still difficult to sum her up and that summary largely depends on one's view of her family. She, perhaps more than any other women whose lives have been included in this book, remained a member of her birth family. She was a Godwine first, queen second. She did not have the security of children, so that it was easy for Edward to banish her. Her fate was linked to that of her family, and even when that family fractured, she was accused of going to extraordinary lengths to support one of her brothers over the other. She managed to survive the monumental upheaval of 1066 and was clearly well-treated by the new Norman king, who respected her status as former queen. She was not the last of the Anglo-Saxon women to become a queen, however.

When Edmund Ironside's sons, Edward and Edmund, were exiled by Cnut following their father's death in 1016 they went to Europe, being sheltered initially by the king of Sweden, then sent to Kiev and finally to Hungary. Edward married a lady named Agatha, whose parentage has been debated by historians.[81] They had three children – Edgar, Margaret and Christina – and in 1057 the family travelled to England. Edward, a contender as a successor to Edward the Confessor, being his half-nephew and a grandson of Æthelred II, died within a year of arriving in England. His son Edgar was named as atheling by Edward the Confessor, according to the *Leges Edwardi Confessoris* (Laws of Edward the Confessor) and we are told that while Edgar was groomed for the throne, his sisters were taught Latin and French, and were trained in needlework, while Edgar was introduced early to the martial arts.[82] But he must have been a young child, perhaps only about 14, in 1066. He was not the son of a king; neither was Harold Godwineson, but Harold had a powerful family to support his claims and Edgar did not. He did, however, become a rallying point for those Englishmen who continued to resist the new regime after Hastings. Initially making peace with William, Edgar appears to have been caught up in the rebellion of the north in 1068 and he and his mother and sisters fled to Scotland, although this might not have been their original intended destination. Ailred of Rievaulx believed that the family was trying to get back to Hungary.[83] Edgar continued his fight but, for his sister Margaret, Scotland was to become home.

Historians disagree as to whether Margaret was older or younger than Edgar, but clearly she was of marriageable age when, in either 1069 or 1070, she married King Malcolm III of Scotland, known as 'Canmore'. As with Emma and Edith, we have a document which gives very specific, if subjective, information about Margaret's life, commissioned by her daughter and written by Bishop Turgot, who had been Margaret's chaplain. Margaret seems to have wanted to live the religious life and was reluctant to marry Malcolm, but the family was dependent on his hospitality, and Edgar needed his support.

Walter Bower, in his fifteenth-century *Scotichronicon* (*A History for Scots*), wrote that Edgar and his sisters had attempted to return to the land where they were born but that God stirred up the sea and they were forced to land in Scotland, at a place which was thenceforth known as St Margaret's Bay, because the people believed that she came to that place by providence. As soon as the king saw Margaret, said Bower, and learned that she was of royal and imperial descent, 'he sought to have her as his wife and succeeded, with Edgar the Atheling her brother giving her away, more in accordance with the wishes of her people than her own desire, or rather at God's command.'[84]

If Margaret was reluctant to become a bride, she nevertheless played the role to perfection. A foreign queen, she won over the hearts of the Scots and made her marriage work. Turgot's *Life* makes it clear though that she was driven at all times to improve worship in Scotland. She was married at Holy Trinity in Dunfermline and she converted the church into a Benedictine priory. It was probably initially established as a daughter house of Canterbury and the monks were sent from England.[85] Queensferry in Fife is so named because she persuaded Malcolm to do away with the ferry charges for pilgrims crossing the Firth of Forth to visit St Andrews. Turgot said that her first language was in fact English, not French, and that her husband acted as interpreter for her, because he spoke English as well as Gaelic. Her good works were carried out with the indulgence of her husband and she not only appears to have made the best of her situation, but set about influencing Malcolm, too.

Turgot records how 'she made him most attentive to the works of justice, mercy, almsgiving and other virtues. From her he learned how to keep the vigils of the night in constant prayer.' If the king found that a book was a particular favourite of hers, he would examine it closely and hold it affectionately, sometimes commissioning a jewelled adornment for the volume.[86] Every so often, Margaret would help herself to an item of Malcolm's property, always to give to the poor. Malcolm took this 'pleasantly and in good part'. She pillaged some of his Maundy coins to give to a beggar and although the king was 'fully aware of the theft, he generally pretended to know nothing of it and felt much amused by it.'[87] Walter Bower said that the king and queen were 'both equal in works of charity, both outstanding in the pursuit of holiness.'[88]

Stories abound in Turgot's *Life* of Margaret feeding the poor, be it nine little orphans, twenty-four people, or even 300. She visited prisons and persuaded the Church in Scotland to fall into step with the Church of Rome, restoring the sanctity of the Sabbath and regulating the date of the start of Lent. The *ASC* recorded that she put down 'the evil customs which this nation practised.' She worked to help those Englishmen who had been reduced to poverty and even slavery by the English wars and paid their ransoms from her own pocket.

Her reforming zeal was perhaps the overriding feature of her life. Whilst certain of Turgot's remarks suggest playful exchanges between the king and queen, he also wrote that there was a 'gravity in her very joy, and ... with her, mirth never expressed itself in fits of laughter.'[89] Her noble ladies were employed in the embroidering of altar cloths, chasubles and other priestly vestments, no men were admitted among them, and no 'giddy pertness' was allowed. She had a similarly stern approach to raising her children, wishing them to be trained in virtue but believing that 'he that spareth the rod hateth the child' and it is clear that she had strict values when it came to all matters pertaining to family, prohibiting marriage between a man and his stepmother or between a brother and his deceased brother's widow.[90]

She might indeed have been a strict mother but she was a loving mother nonetheless. She bore Malcolm eight children; three of her sons became kings of Scotland, one of her daughters married Eustace III of Boulogne and the other daughter, Matilda, for whom Turgot wrote the *Life*, married Henry I of England, thereby bringing the Anglo-Saxon royal line back into that of the monarchy of England. Margaret's love for her family was demonstrated by the circumstances and manner of her death.

She was accustomed to undergoing prolonged periods of abstinence, surviving on a scanty diet which led her to suffer acute abdominal pain. A shoulder bone, alleged to be that of Margaret, is in the keeping of St Margaret's Catholic Church in Dunfermline. The bone indicates that the skeleton from which it came was small in stature. If it is indeed one of Margaret's bones, her lack of height might corroborate the suggestion of a life of fasting. Research is ongoing.[91] She was ill, according to Turgot, when Malcolm went to war in 1093 and she begged him not to go. Ignoring her pleas, he led a raid into Northumberland and he and their eldest son, Edward, were killed near Alnwick. Her son, Edgar, had the heart-breaking task of returning to his mother to inform her. Three days later, after hearing the news, evidently weakened by self-imposed under-nourishment, Margaret died, as Henry of Huntingdon reported, commending herself in prayer and giving up the ghost. A collection of miracles attributed to her survives in a manuscript in Madrid.[92]

She was remembered both in Scotland and by the Anglo-Norman chroniclers as a saintly woman, deeply religious and highly educated. She seems to have made a success of her marriage, going some way to reforming her warrior husband, and providing him with many 'heirs and spares'. The Anglo-Saxon monarchy's bloodline had not completely died out in 1066, and through her daughter's marriage, it was absorbed into the line of royalty descended from William the Conqueror. Yet it is not as a member of this ancient royal house or even as a mother of Scottish kings that she is chiefly remembered. Rather she is revered as a saint, and a woman who acted on her own initiative to work changes where she felt they were needed and to right social injustices wherever she found them. Fittingly, for the lady who comes last chronologically in this volume, she was able to wield power not through her husband, or her children, but through her own determination.

Part VI

On Foreign Soil: Travel, Widowhood and Living in Shadow

Emma and Margaret were not the first queens who spent their adult lives in kingdoms which were not their birth countries. In Part I we met Æthelburh 'Tate' of Kent, who married Edwin of Northumbria and it might be that her mother, Bertha, can be seen in the same light as her daughter, that of a queen-missionary. However, things are not so clear cut. It appears that these women had less influence on the religion of their husbands than is often supposed and, as already mentioned, it is even possible that Bertha was not, in fact, Tate's mother.

Bertha, like Queen Emma, was not born in England. She was the daughter of the Frankish king Charibert, and she married Æthelberht of Kent, but the dates surrounding her marriage and of her husband's reign are the subject of some debate. Gregory of Tours, writing around or before 580, said that she was the daughter of Charibert, Merovingian king of the Franks and his wife, Ingoberga and that she married a 'husband' in Kent.[1] Charibert died in 567 and Gregory said he 'thought' that Ingoberga was 69 when she died in 589, which would suggest that she was quite old when she had Bertha. Bertha must have been born no later than 568, and must have been married before 580, for Gregory to have recorded it. So perhaps a date of around 579 could be suggested for her wedding. The other problem with dating is Bede's assertion that Æthelberht of Kent, who died in 616, reigned for fifty-six years, while Gregory of Tours did not say that he was a king when he married Bertha. Fifty-six years seems an extraordinarily long reign, and this is not the only example of regnal lengths being confused.[2] If, however, Æthelberht was 56 when he died, then he would have been born around 560, and in which case would have been a similar age to Bertha and more likely to have still been a prince when they wed.

Bertha was, Bede tells us, married on condition that she be allowed the freedom to practise her religion and she brought with her from the Continent not a chaplain, but a bishop, named Liudhard.[3] It has been noted, however, that the marriage does not seem to have had any great significance to the Franks, for there was no shortage of Frankish princesses and that after Charibert's death his kingdom was 'dismembered'. It is unlikely, therefore, that Bertha had any wealth or influence.[4] Furthermore, although Bertha brought with her a bishop, and probably corresponded with her family – according to Gregory of Tours she was literate – there is no suggestion that the Kentish court mimicked the Merovingian court and no proof that Æthelberht even minted his own coins.[5] Most importantly, it seems that although Bertha came to England with the freedom to worship, she was not able to convert her husband. Bede does not say so, but presumably the intention was that conversion was a condition of the marriage. Yet it seems that Æthelberht did not wish to be tied too closely with Frankia and ensured his independence by receiving conversion through Rome.[6] This raises the question: why did the marriage take place at all, if not for religious purposes and not, it seems, for any perceived gain by either side? Perhaps, if Æthelberht was not yet king there might have been no guarantee that he would become so, and he needed Frankish support; the marriage would be the seal on a political alliance, but perhaps one in which Kent was the needier partner, that need diminishing once Æthelberht secured his throne.[7] Nevertheless, the expectation for Bertha to play her part in the mission was made clear in a papal letter of 601 in which she was exhorted to 'incline [her] husband's mind.' This is not mentioned by Bede and it might be that he deliberately ignored the information because it did not suit his narrative.[8]

Bertha might have had her work cut out. Conversion was not an overnight sensation and many kings, including her own son, apostatised. It is not entirely clear whether she was, indeed, the mother of Æthelburh 'Tate', whose own husband, Edwin of Northumbria, seems similarly to have weighed up the political considerations carefully before deciding to embrace the new religion. How much influence these women had is hard to gauge, and perhaps we should be wary of placing too much credit or, indeed, blame on these marriages. Bertha was unusual, but not unique, however, in being a foreign princess married to an English king.

Another was Judith of Flanders, who found herself caught up in the tussles between father and son in Wessex. Judith was the second wife of

King Æthelwulf, father of Alfred the Great (and we will meet his first wife in a moment.) She was the daughter of the Carolingian king Charles the Bald and, unlike Bertha's marriage, her wedding seems to have been an important event on the Continent. Æthelwulf had been on pilgrimage to Rome, hence his presence in Europe at that point; the ceremony took place in Verberie in 856 and the coronation *ordo* survives. Judith was probably no more than around twelve at the time of her marriage and she was crowned and anointed by Hincmar, who was archbishop of Rheims. The anointing was unusual – blessing her womb and conferring throne-worthiness upon her male offspring – and the inference must be that a son of this marriage was presumed destined to succeed to Wessex.[9] Asser reported that king's wives were not known as queens in Wessex, the blame for which, as we saw in Part III, having been placed squarely on Eadburh, accidental poisoner of King Beorhtric, so perhaps the Carolingians were anxious to ensure that Judith's status was recognised by her adoptive country.[10] Indeed, in a charter of 858 (S 1274) she attested as *regina*. Such pomp and ceremony might well have served to show how highly-prized Judith should be, but it stirred up resentment in Wessex.

Æthelwulf had five sons already, the youngest of whom, Alfred, was around 7 years of age when his father remarried. The eldest, Æthelbald, however, had been left as regent of Wessex while his father was abroad and evidently did not respond favourably to his return. Asser reported that the only way to avert civil war was to carve up the territories of Wessex, a settlement which saw Æthelwulf retaining the eastern half of the kingdom and Æthelbald the west.[11]

It is not surprising that Æthelbald did not take kindly to the idea of any future stepbrothers having a stronger claim to the throne than his own. In the end, no such thing came to pass for, just two years after his remarriage, King Æthelwulf was dead. Æthelbald succeeded him but, scandalously, and no doubt confirming Judith's high status, he married his father's widow. Asser proclaimed that it was 'against God's prohibition and Christian dignity'.[12] The aim must surely have been to maintain the alliance with the Franks, and to confer throne-worthiness on any future sons he might have had with Judith. Perhaps, and it is pure conjecture, they might even have formed a close bond while his father was alive. Such things are not recorded, but it is not impossible that Judith, a young woman, might have been more attracted to the son than the father.

Whatever the true nature of the relationship, dynastically it was doomed to failure. Æthelbald himself died in 860 and Judith, still only a teenager, returned to the Continent. She was said to have sold up her possessions and returned to her father who kept her under episcopal guardianship in his stronghold at Senlis.[13] She fled from there with the aid of Baldwin, count of Flanders and later married him. Again, it is hard to know how much she was a willing participant, but it seems she considered the marriage preferable to a cloistered life. She had two children by Baldwin and her son, Baldwin II, later married Ælfthryth, daughter of Alfred the Great. Judith's marriage, to Æthelbald, marked the last time before Emma that an English king married a non-English woman. Spirited though she clearly was – marrying her stepson and then eloping with her third husband – she did not play such a starring role in politics as Emma was destined to do.

Judith's namesake, who was the daughter of Baldwin IV, married Tostig Godwineson and was similarly embroiled in familial squabbling, fleeing to the Continent with her husband when Tostig was ousted from Northumberland as we saw in Part V. Overshadowed by her infamous husband, Judith is little mentioned in the narratives which framed the events of 1066. She remarried in 1071, becoming the wife of Welf I of Bavaria. She had a large collection of books and illuminated manuscripts and in 2018/19 her Gospels book was on display at the British Library. The front cover has a border of filigree metal, there are two depictions of Christ, and the whole is studded with brightly-coloured jewels.[14]

Though it was rare for princesses to come from the Continent to marry, many English princesses, as we have seen, were married off abroad. One lady, however, became a queen without having any royal blood. Her name was Balthild and her story is extraordinary. It should be noted at the outset that almost all of the information we have about Balthild comes from a *Life* which was written at the monastery she founded, with little outside corroboration, but it is a story worth including here.

From the *Life*, we learn that Balthild was an Anglo-Saxon, enslaved and taken across the sea to Frankia when she was still a child and bought by a man named Erchinoald, who was the mayor of the palace of the Merovingian kings. He was connected to the Kentish royal house, for his daughter married King Eadbald, son of Bertha and King Æthelberht. Balthild became his cup-bearer, and her duties included serving his important guests, taking off their boots and washing their feet. It is staggering to imagine, but when Erchinoald decided that he wished to remarry and take Balthild as his bride, this slave not only refused, but went further, saying that since she had rejected a king's servant, she would marry the king instead. In 648 she became the wife of King Clovis II who ruled the western part of Frankia known as Neustria (the eastern part being known as Austrasia).

Her marriage to Clovis and her subsequent career is not in dispute, but her lowly origins may be. As noted above, Erchinoald was no lowly servant himself and it is possible that it was he who arranged the marriage. Romantic as it sounds, it is unlikely that Clovis, a new king, chose a slave of lowly birth as his bride. There were many links between the Franks and the Anglo-Saxons at this time and it is feasible that Balthild was a noblewoman whose contacts might have helped strengthen his kingship.

According to the *Life*, Balthild was pious, generous, and just. She founded monasteries, including Chelles where she died, she gave gifts to other churches, and she ended the enslavement and exportation of Christians, freeing many already enslaved, especially those of her own country. She bore three children, the eldest of whom, Clothar, became king whilst still a minor and it seems that Balthild served in some capacity as regent.[15] However, whilst the *Life* remembers her in glowing terms, others did not record her actions so sympathetically.

According to the *Life* of Wilfrid, 'the wicked Queen Balthild was persecuting the Church just like Jezebel.' Eddius Stephanus, Wilfrid's hagiographer, continues: 'She spared priests and deacons but had nine bishops put to death.' Bede recorded the event and said that Wilfrid desired to perish with one of the bishops but the executioners, on discovering that Wilfrid was English, refused to put him to death.[16] Bede was repeating Eddius Stephanus' story and the latter was clearly biased towards his subject. It has been posited that the bishop might have been a victim of local factional conflict rather than Balthild's tendency to violence.[17]

When Clothar reached his majority, Balthild retired to Chelles. Her youngest son Childeric was, according to the *Life*, received in Austrasia as their king 'by the arrangement of Lady Balthild.' Clearly Balthild was from the same mould as other dowager queens who remained influential in the lives of their sons. A seal-matrix, dated to around 648 and believed to have been that of Balthild's, is housed in Norwich Castle Museum and Art Gallery. Examination found that 'one side of the seal had a face of a queen, with the word "Baldehilds" in Frankish lettering, and on the back two figures which seemed to be naked, seemingly in an erotic position beneath the cross.' It is not clear how the item found its way back to England.[18]

Her relics were preserved at Chelles and were rediscovered in 1983.[19] It seems that she was about five feet tall and she was buried wearing a cloak made of coloured silk. Most revealing of all was a plait of her hair, found among the clothing, showing that at one time she had been blonde, but that her hair had faded to grey. A chasuble, supposedly of Balthild's, is in the Musée de Chelles and consists of a piece of woven linen, decorated with embroidery. The embroidery is in a pattern of two necklaces, a pectoral cross and a deeper necklace with pendant medallions. It is said that St Eligius appeared three times to one of Balthild's courtiers and proclaimed that she should desist from wearing such rich trappings and that the tabard represents the shadow of the insignia, showing that she had eschewed the accoutrements of her wealthy life as an empress.[20] There are echoes here of St Æthelthryth who had admitted to the vanity of necklace-wearing in her earlier, secular days. Sketchy as our knowledge might be of Balthild, Bertha and Judith, it is detailed in comparison to some English queens who appear to have been strong, independent and wilful, and yet merit no more than a throwaway comment in the annals.

Bede tells us of the wife of Rædwald, king of East Anglia and *Bretwalda* in the seventh century who, when told of his conversion, 'seduced' him into returning to his heathen practices. She must have been persuasive indeed, if she managed to change his mind after his visit to the strongly Christian kingdom of Kent had convinced him of the benefits of conversion. She lost a son at the battle of the Idle in which her husband and Edwin of Deira overcame Æthelfrith of Bernicia. If it was her husband whose burial mound was unearthed at Sutton Hoo, and if she outlived him, we must assume that she had a significant role in the preparation of the burial ceremony and the laying out of the grave goods. Yet Bede does not even tell us her name.

All we know of the first wife of Æthelfrith, that seventh-century king of Bernicia, was that her name was Bebba, and that the mighty fortress of Bamburgh (*Bebbanburg*) was named after her. Why? Was she a rich princess who owned the land? If the *Historia Brittonum,* written by Nennius in the ninth century, is to be believed, it might have been a bride-gift (*morgengifu*) from Æthelfrith: '[He] gave to his wife, Bebba,

Dynguoaroy, which from her is called *Bebbanburg*.'[21] Did she defend it in time of war? Alas, Bede and Nennius, if they knew, declined to record it. It is not impossible though, for we do hear of other queens participating in skirmishes. Henry of Huntingdon puts some flesh on the bones of a statement in the *ASC* which says that in 722 a Queen Æthelburh 'demolished Taunton, which [King] Ine had built.' Henry tells us that 'Eadberht the Atheling' had obtained possession of the castle but that Ine's queen stormed it and razed it to the ground, compelling Eadberht to escape into Surrey.[22] Perhaps this was another situation where there was a succession dispute and Æthelburh might have been acting on behalf of a son who was still a minor, although Ine did not abdicate until 726. He was, however, succeeded by a man who was not closely, if at all, related to him. William of Malmesbury furnishes us with a little more information about this redoubtable lady. He recorded that she was a woman of 'royal race and noble disposition' and that she wished to persuade the king to think more of spiritual matters than earthly things. To that end, 'when they had been revelling at a country seat with more than usual riot and luxury' the next day, with her connivance, a servant 'defiled the palace in every possible manner, both with the excrement of cattle and heaps of filth'. The queen then enticed the king to return and, watching his dismay, reminded him that all such luxuries were transient, like 'smoke and vapour' and persuaded him to search beyond such earthly pursuits. William credits her with being thus instrumental in the king's abdication and pilgrimage to Rome.[23] This is all we know of the queen who torched a castle, but she was not the only such fearless consort.

Seaxburh of Wessex, in fact, was more than a consort and is the only woman to appear in an Anglo-Saxon regnal list. She was the wife of Cenwalh, king of the West Saxons, who had at one time been married to and repudiated the sister of Penda of Mercia, thereby provoking the latter's ire. Bede recorded that after Cenwalh's death there was a troubled period during which sub-kings 'took upon themselves the government of the kingdom, dividing it up and ruling for about ten years.'[24] The *ASC*, on the other hand, says that in 672, 'Cenwalh died and his queen Seaxburh reigned one year after him.' This succinct entry gives no hint about the circumstances. Was she, as would become more common, reigning on behalf of a son?

If we add to these two conflicting reports a third, that of Roger of Wendover, who said that Seaxburh ruled for one year in Cenwalh's stead, 'but was expelled [from] the kingdom by the indignant nobles, who would not go to war under the conduct of a woman,' a scenario begins to build in which Cenwalh died with no adult heir, and Seaxburh and the local nobility were in conflict over the succession. Clearly she was not able to win them over even if, as she surely must have done, she had some of the nobility fighting on her side. The chaos seems to have lasted more than a year, for the next king is not recorded as succeeding until 674. If she was fighting for her own right to the throne, and not on behalf of any sons, then she truly was a trail-blazer. We could infer as much from the stark entry in the *ASC*, but it was probably not so straightforward. The information we have on this pugilistic queen makes what we have on Æthelflæd, Lady of the Mercians, seem bounteous and extensive by comparison.

We do not know anything of Seaxburh's background, although she might have been a member of the East Saxon royal house, because her name has the element *Seax*, used more commonly among the East than the West Saxons.[25] The other element of her name, though, might be the more interesting. Many noblewomen had names ending in *burh* which of course means a fortified town. It has been suggested that it was symbolic of the duty expected of these women that they would defend the towns and fortresses.[26] Sometimes it was the other way round and monasteries were given the name *burh* after queens and princesses. Fladbury in Worcestershire might have been named after Ælfflæd, daughter of Oswiu of Northumbria, who as we saw in Part I was given to the Church when still an infant in return for Oswiu's success over Penda of Mercia. The suggestion is that after she received her education from her kinswoman, Hild, at Whitby, she went south when her sister, Osthryth, married Æthelred of Mercia, founding Fladbury before returning to help her mother Eanflæd with the running of Whitby when Hild died in 680. The theory goes that monastic life at Fladbury then collapsed, possibly because of the unpopularity of Osthryth who, it will be remembered, was murdered by the Mercians.[27]

Sometimes our information about a queen helps only to confirm political situations. A case in point is the seventh-century Queen Eafe who, according to Bede, was baptised in her own country, the kingdom of the *Hwicce*. We are told that she was the daughter of King Eanfrith, who was Christian, as were their people.[28] The *Hwicce*, as mentioned in

Part I, were at one time an independent people with their own kings, who then became relegated to the position of sub-kings of Mercia. Eafe was a member of their royal house, but it is clear that by her time, the kings of the *Hwicce* were subjects of greater Mercia. Her marriage to Æthelwalh of the South Saxons probably led to, or was conditional upon, her husband converting to Christianity. The baptism was at the 'suggestion and in the presence of' Wulfhere, king of Mercia. The implication is that the South Saxons and, indeed, the *Hwicce*, were subordinate to Mercia. Only in the context of Æthelwalh's conversion are we introduced to Eafe and there is nothing else of her in the records except the fact that she greeted the exiled Bishop Wilfrid when he sought refuge at the court of the South Saxons.[29]

Some queens slip between the pages of history with nothing to hint at their circumstances or personality. We know that King Wiglaf of Mercia reigned twice, and that he was married to a lady named Cynethryth. She attested two charters, in 831 and 836 and was styled *regina*, but all we really know of her is that she might have been the abbess of Winchcombe who is sometimes confused with Cynethryth, widow of Offa.[30] Her daughter-in-law, Ælfflæd, was, as we saw in Part III, the daughter, wife, and possibly mother of kings, yet is barely remembered.

Conversely, we learn a great deal about a certain group of pioneering women through their correspondence with a man, in this case St Boniface. Boniface was an Englishman, originally going by the name of Wynfrith. He was born around 675 and he is known mainly for his missionary work on the Continent. By his surviving letters we know of a number of women who either wrote to him, or travelled abroad to be involved in his mission, but identifying them is not always easy.

Boniface established religious houses and the heads of these new communities were predominantly English. While some were men, such as Wigbert, who became abbot of Fritzlar, others were women including Thecla, abbess of Kitzingen and Leoba, abbess of Tauberbischofsheim. Leoba wrote to Boniface on a number of occasions, at one point referring to her teacher, Eadburh, of whom more in a moment. It is clear that Leoba and Boniface had a close relationship. She asked him to pray for her mother who was beset with infirmities, and said that as he knew, she was an only child and she wished herself worthy enough to call him a brother. She sent him a gift, which she hoped would remind him of her though they were a long way apart. Leoba closes her letter to Boniface with a verse, perhaps the oldest extant verse written by an English woman:

> May the Omnipotent Judge, Sole creator of all,
> Ever resplendent with light in the father's heavenly kingdom,
> Where reigns the glory of Christ, amid splendour unfailing,
> Keep thee unharmed in His justice eternal.[31]

Sometime between 723 and 755 Boniface wrote to Leoba giving her permission to instruct a young girl and between 742 and 746 he wrote to her 'and all the dear sisters in Christ who live with you' and urged her to pray for his soul.[32] It is perhaps easy to underestimate the task facing Leoba, but it is clear that she undertook the journey, no small matter in those days, successfully established the abbey and earned the respect and love of her mentor Boniface. It is thought that an embroidered sacrament cloth sent from Boniface to another bishop in 735 was worked by women educated by Leoba.[33]

Another woman known from her correspondence – in this case only one letter – with Boniface, was Ecgburh. Here is where identification becomes difficult. She wrote to Boniface calling him 'holy father and true friend' and goes on to say how she drew strength from his teaching to help her cope with the death of her brother, Oshere, and talks of her dearest sister, Wethburh 'a new wound, a fresh grief – suddenly vanished from my sight.'[34] The letter includes a post script from a man who later added a similar post script to a letter by an abbot who attested a charter of the king of Mercia. This link with Mercia has led some to identify Ecgburh's dead brother Oshere as Oshere, king of the *Hwicce*. H.P.R. Finberg agreed with this identification and went further, suggesting that Oshere's tragic death was somehow connected to the death of Queen Osthryth of Mercia, whom we met in Part I, but it is not, as mentioned there, a universally supported theory. Patrick Sims-Williams pointed out that no sister of Oshere named Wethburh was ever recorded.[35] Ecgburh has sometimes been identified as Eadburh, abbess of Gloucester, possible widow of King Wulfhere of Mercia whom we met in Part III. As Sims-Williams observed, the two names are distinct, but the latter does appear as a corruption of the former in some cases. There was another lady named Ecgburh who was connected to the East Anglian royal family. However, she is mentioned in the *Life* of St Guthlac, which describes how Guthlac asked for his body to be wrapped in a cloth which Ecgburh had sent him, and this Ecgburh has in turn sometimes been confused with Eadburh, abbess of Thanet.[36]

Eadburh of Thanet was the recipient of the letter briefly mentioned in Part II in relation to a vision concerning King Ceolred of Mercia. She succeeded St Mildrith as abbess and she promoted the cult of her predecessor, of which more in the appendix. As we have just seen, Leoba mentioned that her teacher was named Eadburh but there is no evidence that Leoba ever went to Kent so it cannot be assumed that this was the same Eadburh. An abbess named Eadburh received three letters from Boniface; however, the recipient might not have been Eadburh of Thanet, but perhaps a West Saxon woman of the same name.[37] A diminutive form of the name Eadburh is Bugga, and there was a Kentish abbess of that name who corresponded with Boniface, but in this case her full name was Hæaburh.

Hæaburh was also the name of the daughter of a Kentish abbess named Eangyth who corresponded with Boniface but, again, we cannot be certain that the two Hæaburhs are one and the same. Eangyth's letter is revealing, as it tells of the pressures put on the religious houses to provide for the itinerant courts, especially those of proprietary churches. Eangyth wrote in detail of her woes in a tear-stained letter which described the loss of friends and family,[38] and her worries about external worldly affairs. She complained, too, that the *servitium* which she owed to the king, queen, bishop and prefect was adding to her troubles. King Æthelbald of Mercia promised in 749 to take monastic hospitality only when it was freely offered, which certainly implies that often it was not. Boniface also wrote of King Osred fornicating his way through the Northumbrian nunneries which gives a picture of some of the problems concomitant with the peripatetic court. The fact that many charters were issued from minsters suggests that when the kings visited, they stayed a while, so perhaps Eangyth's complaints were justified.[39]

The letters of Boniface are at once revealing and confusing. It is hard to identify his correspondents, but the letters themselves show that these women were highly motivated and literate. If we leave aside for a moment the problems of identification, and concentrate on the letters themselves, we can see that Ecgburh's letter is poetic in nature: 'Thy love is as a bond that holds me; since I tasted it in my inner being, like some honeysweet essence the sweetness of it fills my soul.' The letters emphasise that the correspondents felt that their work made them kin, with one religious woman who had lost her mother and sister addressing Boniface as a brother and others confiding in him about their personal sorrows.[40] Of the three letters sent to Eadburh – whoever she was – one is the description of the vision of the monk at Much Wenlock, in relation to King Ceolred, while another is a letter of thanks for the books which she has sent to Boniface. The third is one in which Boniface asks Eadburh to copy for him the Epistles of St Peter in letters of gold.[41] Whether this means that he wished Eadburh herself to do it, or whether it was a job which she would pass to one of the sisters, it is clear that the levels of skill – particularly of illumination – and literacy were high.

Three letters survive which were all written by a nun named Beorhtgyth. She writes to her brother, Balthard and the personal detail is poignant. The siblings had left England to live in Germany where they were in contact with Lull – their kinsman through their mother – a monk who had joined Boniface's mission. Beorhtgyth's letters date from around the 770s. Her first letter asks why Balthard has left it so long to visit her: 'Why do you not want to remember that I am alone on this earth and no other brother visits me, nor any family members will come to me?' In the second letter, she beseeches him once again to visit her, and tells him that 'sadness never recedes from my soul, nor can I rest my mind in sleep, because love is as strong as death.' In her third letter she mentions again that she is alone and abandoned, but it seems as though Balthard has at least replied to one of her earlier letters, and she thanks him for his words and gifts. Yet again, she pleads with him to visit her, and she encloses 'a little present, although small, still loaded with great love, which we send to you by the faithful messenger named Aldræd; that is a ribbon.' This snapshot of a woman's situation shows her desperately unhappy, and since no other correspondence between the pair survives, we cannot know whether she ever saw her brother again. Boniface's mission had been the first to include women, but the plaintive entreaties suggest that the missionary's life was not for everyone and Beorhtgyth's misery in her isolation speaks to us loud and clear, even from so many centuries ago.[42]

Aldhelm, the seventh-century abbot who as we saw in Part I dedicated his *De Virginitate* to Hildelith, presumed a certain level of literacy among the religious women for whom he was writing and asked if his writing style was pleasing to their intelligence. He thanked the nuns at

Barking for their letters and complimented their verbal eloquence. We have already seen, also in Part I, that Ælfflæd, abbess of Whitby, wrote a letter to the abbess of Pfalzel.

Female literacy was not confined to the religious, however, for as we have also seen, a letter survives which was sent by Queen Ælfthryth in her role as female advocate (above p. 93). Queen Edith was praised for her learning and some of her letters survive, although it may be presumed that she, and Ælfthryth before her, dictated rather than wrote the letters. Judith of Flanders married King Æthelwulf of Wessex and her marriage did nothing to help his relationship with his son. Æthelwulf's previous wife, however, seems to have led a somewhat calmer life and was also demonstrably literate. She was called Osburh and was the mother of his five sons, the youngest being Alfred the Great, as well as his daughter, Æthelswith, who as we saw in Part III was married to Burgred of Mercia. Like Alfred's wife, Osburh did not attest any charters and it is not clear whether, when Æthelwulf married Judith, Osburh was dead or had been repudiated. If she had been put aside, she might well have lived to see her son rebel against his father. Yet such things are not recorded and we would have to look to the career of Eleanor of Aquitaine in the twelfth century to find a high profile example of a queen witnessing her son in rebellion against her husband.

Osburh might have had links with the Isle of Wight, and her father was King Æthelwulf's butler, an indication of the high rank of such office.[43] Little else is known about her, but from Asser we learn that she taught her young son Alfred and his brothers to read. She showed them a book of poetry and told them she would give the book to whichever of them could memorise it the most quickly. Asser was no doubt recording the story to show how swiftly his subject, Alfred, could learn, but this episode illustrates that Osburh was herself literate, and able to educate her children.[44] The same must have been true of the majority of royal women; indeed the point has been made that the *Encomium* would have made an inadequate impression upon Queen Emma had she been unable to read it.[45]

Laywomen who were not royals were also influential and held land and property in their own right. We know about some of them because of their wills. Wulfwaru, a noblewoman whose will was drawn up somewhere between 984 and 1016, left jewellery, gold, and estates to her beneficiaries. She has not been otherwise identified, but she was evidently a wealthy woman, bequeathing an armlet consisting of sixty *mancuses* of gold, two gold crucifixes, and estates to an abbot, her son and her daughter – who received joint portions – her younger son, and her elder daughter, and a gold band and a wooden chest to her servants. Those who succeeded her were also to provide for twenty freed men and to furnish a food-rent for Bath Abbey every year for ever.[46]

Another interesting will comes from Wulfgyth, dated 1046, in which she leaves to her lord his 'due *heriot*'. This is an unusual bequest. *Heriot* was war gear, bestowed on men by their lord and returnable upon death. As historian Dorothy Whitelock pointed out in her notes to her collection of Anglo-Saxon wills, this is the only incidence of *heriot* being bequeathed by a woman.[47] It is frustrating, but we simply do not know why she had possession of this war gear, or whether she ever used it.

A woman named Silflæd made two wills, one of which mentions that she is going over the sea. Perhaps she made one before travelling – maybe fearing that she would not survive the journey – and another upon her arrival or return. She says in one that, 'If I come home, then I wish to occupy [that] estate for life.' She does not say where she is going, or why. She had a large amount of land, and one of her wills frees all her slaves, so she was a wealthy woman. It does not appear that she was going on a pilgrimage, and there is no indication of her age. She makes bequests to her brothers but does not name any children. We can only guess what sort of adventures she had while travelling.[48]

Ælfflæd – sister of Æthelflæd of Damerham, consort of King Edmund – was the wife of Byrhtnoth whose valour at the battle of Maldon was recorded in the famous poem of the same name. She bequeathed land to Queen Ælfthryth, who was at the time described as 'my lord's mother', so this would date the will to after King Æthelred II the 'Unready' acceded to the throne. Her will, like the pleas of Abbess Eangyth above, shows the problems relating to proprietary churches. She gifted land to friends and to relations with the obligation for them to be the church's protectors – 'that you will protect the holy foundation at Stoke [by-Nayland] … and the property … as an immune right of God' – but it seems that by 1066 there was no evidence that her church at Stoke had ever stood there.[49] Ælfflæd was clearly concerned about the future of Stoke-by-Nayland, her ancestral minster, but her will shows the ambivalence displayed by members of the laity to the Benedictine reform of the tenth century mentioned in Part IV, for her husband had been pro-monastic. Whether or not the monasteries were filled with married clerks or celibate monks seems not to have been a concern for the majority. Another lady, Æthelgifu, whose will we will examine in a moment, had left land to the reformed house of St Albans, but also bequests to her local minsters.[50]

The will of a lady named Leofgifu begins: 'Leofgifu greets her lady with God's greeting.' The lady in question is Queen Emma, and this will is the only surviving example of one which is addressed solely to the queen. It shows how families, rather than individuals, could be in the service of the monarchy. Leofgifu wishes that 'my kinsman, Ælfric' should receive an estate at Boreham. Ælfric administered estates for Queen Emma and it has been suggested that he entered her service because of Leofgifu.[51]

Leofgifu is not the only noblewoman to have had influence at court. Æthelgifu, a tenth-century noblewoman, asked in her will that her legatee, Leofsige, may be allowed to serve 'the atheling'.[52] This is usually taken to mean Athelstan, son of Æthelred II the 'Unready' – the fact that the testatrix addresses the queen suggests that the atheling is a minor and we know that Queen Ælfthryth was said by Athelstan to have brought him up – and he had estates in Hertfordshire close to where Æthelgifu held lands. She appeals to the queen, one influential woman to another, to watch over him, 'and let him serve the prince, and do not let anyone rob him of his lands.'[53] Another interesting feature of her will is that she makes provision for the freeing of a priest. One might assume that all priests were free men, but the unusual detail here could be simply the mention of his status; perhaps unfree priests were not uncommon. She makes more provision for this man, whose name is Edwin, than to her other three priests. 'Edwin the priest is to be freed, and he is to have the church for his lifetime on condition that he keep it in repair, and he is to be given a man.'[54]

Æthelgifu also freed three women, on the condition that each of them chanted four psalters a week for a month, and one a week for a year, after her death. It has been suggested that this shows lay as well as clerical participation in religious ritual.[55] It might be that Æthelgifu had established a small religious community among members of her household; the assumption must be that these women had a certain level of education. With laywomen in her household who were capable of chanting the psalter, it is possible that Æthelgifu was a widow who, rather than entering a nunnery, ran a religious house from her own home, like another widow whose will we shall examine below. This is not to say that her life was austere. Her will makes mention that her kinswoman is to be given 'a dish and a brooch and a wall-hanging and a seat-cover and all the best bedsteads'. She also bequeaths 'three purple kirtles' which are made from *godwebb*. *Godwebb* was a particularly fine silk cloth which was expensive, possibly akin to shot-silk taffeta.[56]

Extended families could engender fractious relationships. Æthelgifu was free to dispose of her husband's property as she wished, but her inheritance as his widow was nevertheless disputed. She had to appeal to the king to have land restored which her nephew had taken from her. None of her husband's kin can be identified with any certainty from her will, with the exception of his daughter, who receives only a small bequest. Apart from this all the other beneficiaries whose relationship to Æthelgifu is described are members of her own kin.

Wynflæd was another wealthy woman whose will survives, but all that we know of her comes from this one document. It has been argued that she might have been the mother of Ælfgifu, the first wife of King Edmund (see above p. 79), partly because the name Wynflæd is uncommon. Ælfgifu, it will be recalled, became known as Ælfgifu of Shaftesbury, and Wynflæd's will mentions Shaftesbury, but it does not include bequests to any members of the royal family, so it cannot be said conclusively that Wynflæd the testatrix was Edmund's mother-in-law.[57] She left her 'best dun tunic' to one beneficiary while another legatee has the pick of the 'black tunics'. It is the only occasion where tunics are referred to in the context of women's clothing and the fact that these tunics are dull-coloured suggests that they might have been religious garments.[58] She also left a 'holy veil'. Thus Wynflæd was probably another widow who was living the religious life in her home, rather than in a nunnery, one of a number of such women who did so without giving up their worldly goods. Her landholdings, furniture and wardrobe speak of a rich life, and of literacy. Among her bequests there are books, tapestries, a filigree brooch, an engraved bracelet, clothing chests, and she disposes of several estates in Hampshire, Berkshire, Wiltshire and Somerset. She also frees a number of slaves, although unlike in the will of Æthelgifu, there is no specific condition, only a request that she be remembered.[59]

The women who made these bequests all have a large number of woven and embroidered goods to disperse, and the furniture in which to store them; Wynflæd left two chests, for example, and in them a set of bedclothes and Æthelgifu mentions her 'best' wall-hanging and seat-cover, while Wulfwaru left bed linen, wall-hangings and table linen to her sons.[60] It is no great surprise that they concern themselves more with such matters than do the men who leave wills. The larger estate-owners would have prided themselves on the quality of the textile work produced in their households but how much of the work was done by the landowners is debateable and they might rather have supervised it. A lady by the name of Æthelswith is mentioned in the *Liber Eliensis* as having 'scorned alliance with a husband' and chosen the religious life. She was given Coveney, 'a place close to the monastery' (Ely) where she devoted her time to 'gold embroidery and tapestry-weaving', accompanied by her *puellulae* (maidens). It is then recorded that she made a white chasuble 'at her own expense and with her own hands, being very expert at this sort of craft.' This mention has been regarded as an indication that it was rare for noblewomen to engage in this work, yet the *Liber Eliensis* clearly states that she was an expert, so perhaps it was her especial skill which made her the rarity among her peers.[61]

The wills discussed here were made by widows, not surprisingly given that in such times, warfare would have left many women bereaved. Many of Wynflæd's bequests are to her female friends and are personal in nature. Her will speaks of her daughter, and of everyday household items and the document allows us to build up a picture of how she lived. She probably travelled between her various estates, and she enjoyed owning – and presumably wearing – jewellery. She was literate, and we need not assume that all her books were religious in nature. Wills such as hers show women able to dispose of their land and property as they wished, although of course she was a wealthy individual and therefore was not representative of all women. Nevertheless these extant wills give fascinating insights into the world of the Anglo-Saxon woman.[62] Wynflæd was clearly rich and well-connected, whether or not she was the king's mother-in-law.

Another well-to-do noblewoman with connections was one by the name of Ælfwynn, the wife of a powerful ealdorman whose epithet was 'Half-king' and was briefly mentioned in Part IV. Athelstan Half-king was ealdorman of East Anglia from 932 to 956. He had four sons, the eldest of whom was the first husband of Queen Ælfthryth, who later married King Edgar. The youngest of the Half-king's sons was

Æthelwine, who became ealdorman of East Anglia and was connected with the monastic reform movement. Æthelwine, known as *Dei amicus* (friend of God), donated some of the family lands at Ramsey for the foundation of Ramsey Abbey. These family lands, though, were inherited from his mother and it seems that she, rather than her husband, was local to the area. Ælfwynn came from a Huntingdonshire family and it was their estates which provided the land for Ramsey. We know very little else about her – some have connected her with Ælfwynn, daughter of the Lady of the Mercians, although this seems unlikely – but she was an important noblewoman, who evidently had outstanding qualities.

It will be recalled that King Edmund died while his sons were still infants. It is possible that Edmund's queen, Ælfgifu, died in childbirth, either in labour with her youngest son or perhaps a subsequent pregnancy. It is not known where the eldest boy, the rather unsuccessful Eadwig, was raised, but the younger, who grew up to become King Edgar, was fostered in East Anglia, under the care of Ælfwynn. The Half-king was powerful and served under successive kings – he might even have acted as regent during King Eadred's illness[63] – retiring either just after or just before Eadwig's ill-fated accession, but it was into his wife's care that the infant Edgar was entrusted. We have no further information than this, but it is not difficult to imagine that she and the queen were close friends. Such relationships would not have interested the chroniclers but, with her husband so involved in the government of the day, Ælfwynn would have been in a position to develop connections of her own to the royal family. We can suppose that men and women alike formed strong bonds which went far beyond the niceties required by diplomacy just as, similarly, we should not overlook simple personal antipathy as the reason for many disputes. It is difficult to know precisely what the 'fostering' entailed. The will of the atheling Athelstan mentions a foster mother, Ælfswith, but also speaks of his grandmother Ælfthryth who brought him up. Perhaps the former was a wet-nurse, while the latter raised him. Edgar was an infant when entrusted to Ælfwynn's care, but it seems more likely that she was a foster mother in the same sense as Ælfthryth, insofar as it was her house in which he was brought up.

Family relationships are not always completely ignored. Felix's *Life* of the seventh-century hermit St Guthlac of Crowland mentions Guthlac's sister, Pega, who received the message that her beloved brother was dead. Her reaction was severe: she 'fell down in a headlong fall, and as she lay upon the ground she withered away to the very marrow by the mighty affliction of her grief.' She managed to rouse herself, 'heaving deep sighs from the bottom of her heart' and fulfilled the commands to wrap the body and place it not in a coffin, but in a monument. The *Life* makes it clear that Guthlac placed great faith in his sister, insisting that his message be told only to her and to an anchorite and entrusting only her with the task of tending to his body.[64] A later chronicle has Pega living on the island of Crowland until the devil took on her appearance in order to tempt Guthlac to take food before sunset, contrary to his vow. To avoid further such incidents, Pega was banished and brother and sister never saw each other again. In this story the woman is, as so often, the instrument of the devil, whereas Felix's *Life* concentrates on the sibling relationship and the respect that Guthlac retains for his sister.

We are also told the name of Guthlac's mother. Guthlac was said to have been the son of a Mercian warrior named Penwalh – his name might suggest some connection with the Mercian royal family – whose wife was named Tette. She was 'from among the ranks of noble maidens and from her earliest days she had been zealous to live in maidenly modesty.'[65] The name is unusual although it is also the name of a sister of King Ine of Wessex. This Tette was abbess of Wimborne and was alive around 700. It is said that Tetbury in Gloucestershire was founded by Ine. Could it have been named after his sister, another '*burh*' named after a woman?[66]

We met the family of Wulfric Spott in Part V – in particular in relation to Ælfgifu of Northampton – but Wulfric's ancestry was equally interesting. An incident in 940, a year after King Athelstan's death, was recorded by the *ASC*, in which the Northumbrian Vikings were 'false to their pledges' and occupied Tamworth in Mercia, taking high-status hostages. One of these hostages was named: 'Wulfrun was taken captive in that raid.' The fact that Wulfrun was named by the *Chronicle* indicates that she was, indeed, of high status. There is evidence that she was the mother of Wulfric Spott. It has been proposed that Wulfric Spott was 'probably through his mother' related to the English royal line, so perhaps she was a member of a branch of the royal house.[67]

A charter of 995 (S 886) describes Wulfric as her son (*Wuifric Wulfrune suuu*) and one of the estates held by Wulfric and mentioned in his will had belonged to Wulfrun (S 878). It is possible that Wulfric's father was a man named Wulfsige, who had previously held the same estate, but what is interesting is that Wulfric is named not as Wulfsige's son, but as Wulfrun's. Either Wulfric's father died young, or was disgraced, or both. Wulfrun is thought to have founded Wolverhampton Priory, and is the person after whom the city of Wolverhampton is named. Once again, we have a glimpse of a woman who must have been rich and important – she was not only taken hostage but was named as such – and yet the *ASC* does not elaborate. The two things we do know about her, though, are very telling. She was significant enough to be taken hostage, and she founded an important monastery which led to a city being named after her. We can guess what kind of life she led as a member of the nobility but we are not told how well she was treated while a prisoner.

At least with Wulfrun we have two facts on which to pin our assumptions. All we know of her daughter-in-law, Wulfric's wife, is that her name was Ealhswith.[68] In his will he left provision for his 'poor daughter', presumably a widow, but she is not named. Men were clearly happy to leave property to their female as well as male kin, and Wulfric was obviously anxious to ensure his daughter's continued welfare. (Curiously, Wulfric left nothing to his mother's foundation at Wolverhampton.) Another member of the extended family barely emerges from the shadows, but when she does, it is to hint at a life of sadness.

It will be recalled that Wulfric Spott's brother, Ælfhelm, was murdered in 1006 and his sons – brothers of Ælfgifu of Northampton – were blinded. This was not the first of such incidents during the reign of Æthelred II the 'Unready', however. In 993 a man named Ælfgar was blinded on the orders of the king. Ælfgar held land in Moredon, Wiltshire, which he gave to his wife, yet another woman named Ælfgifu.[69] The 1006 incident in which Ælfhelm was murdered and his sons blinded, also involved another man, whose name was Wulfgeat. He was associated with the family and he was deprived of his property in 1006 when the others were either murdered or blinded. It is just possible that he is the same Wulfgeat who married this Ælfgifu, widow of Ælfgar, the victim of the previous blinding, because it seems his wife brought to her new marriage that land at Moredon. If this is the same woman then she had an unfortunate life indeed, her first husband being blinded and her second deprived of all his property.

Another widow whose plight warranted only the briefest of mentions is a lady named Eadflæd. We hear of her in charters *c.* 999 when King

Æthelred II the 'Unready' restores land which was taken from her: 'This estate had been usurped from a matron named Eadflæd by the ealdorman Ælfric, and forfeited by him, with his other possessions, when a council at Cirencester found him guilty of treason. It was then restored to Eadflæd.'[70] We know from the *ASC* that this ealdorman, known as Ælfric *cild*, was banished in 985. He was the successor of Ælfhere of Mercia, who was an ally of Queen Ælfthryth. One of the forfeited estates was Wormleighton, which had been granted to Ælfhere. It is supposition, but it is possible that Eadflæd was Ælfhere's widow, deprived of her lands after her husband's death by his unscrupulous successor. Trying as this might have been, she at least had recourse to the king in order to have her lands restored to her. Women, though perhaps only the wealthy ones, were not powerless in law.

A woman named Wynflæd – not the same woman who left the detailed will – was in dispute with a man named Leofwine about land in Berkshire. She claimed that the lands were given to her by his father – Leofwine being her stepson – and she made the claim before witnesses who included the king and the king's mother, Queen Ælfthryth. Having made her claim she was permitted to produce proof of ownership. In what would most closely resemble a modern-day 'out of court settlement' it was decided, probably because her case was so strong, to dispense with the oath and Leofwine surrendered the land and said that he would make no further claim on it.[71] Wynflæd was required to return to him all the gold and silver that had belonged to his father. Wynflæd had been able to petition for the return of her lands and had the documentation to prove her ownership. She and Eadflæd were not helpless widows.

Some women did not have the same control over their lives. Ecgfrida was the daughter of the powerful bishop of Durham and she was married off to Ealdorman Uhtred of Northumbria whom we met briefly in Part V; he subsequently married one of King Æthelred II's daughters. Ecgfrida brought to the marriage six valuable estates in Teesdale and she bore one son.[72] She was yet another wife who was put aside when her husband wished to marry again. If she retired to a nunnery one might suppose that she lived the rest of her life in peace. But nuns and especially abbesses were not always safe. St Æthelthryth, whom we met in Part I, managed, we are told, to preserve her virginity throughout two marriages. Others appear not to have been so fortunate.

It will be recalled that early on in his reign, Edward the Elder faced a rebellion from his cousin. This cousin was the son of Alfred the Great's elder brother, who had been king before Alfred. The cousin, whose name was Æthelwold, had been too young to rule when his father died, and so Alfred succeeded to the throne of Wessex. It was a different story, however, when Edward the Elder succeeded, for now Æthelwold was a grown man. His rebellion began when he went to Wimborne, a symbolic gesture because his father was buried at the minster there.[73] It seems he also took a hostage, 'without the king's permission and contrary to the bishops' orders, for she had been consecrated a nun.' We know that Wimborne had been built, even though as a double house, as two monasteries, each of which was surrounded by high walls, so it might have proved a good place for a rebel to defend. His own uncle's laws carried penalties for attacking a nun or removing her from a nunnery.[74]

It might be that the lady was in fact a nun from Wimborne; on the other hand, it has been suggested that she was none other than Alfred's daughter, Æthelgifu, who was abbess of Shaftesbury. Some historians think that Æthelwold married the captive lady, while others are not convinced. Her identity is not proven, nor is it established that a marriage took place, but whatever the truth, it seems that Æthelwold's actions were driven by a desire to strengthen his claim to the throne. This woman, whatever her identity, was clearly of high status and politically important. In the event, Æthelwold escaped in the night and went to join the Viking army in Northumbria, who swore allegiance to him as their king. (He was later killed at the battle of the Holme in 902.) The woman, according to the *ASC*, was 'seized' after Æthelwold's escape from Wimborne, but this is rather ambiguous. Was she taken from his clutches, or had she been complicit and was somehow arrested for her part in the revolt?

If the stories about King Edgar are true, then being a nun was a hazardous occupation, although as we saw in Part IV, it is unlikely that any of his wives/women were consecrated nuns. Not so in the case of Eadgifu, abbess of Leominster, who might also have been a less than unwilling captive.

In 1046, the first act of disobedience from within the ranks of the powerful Godwine family saw Swegn Godwineson teaming up with Gruffudd of Wales. According to the *ASC*, on his way back from Wales Swegn 'ordered the abbess of Leominster to be brought to him, and he kept her as long as he pleased, and then let her go home.' From John of Worcester: 'Meanwhile, Earl Swegn, son of Earl Godwine and Gytha who had left England earlier because he was not permitted to marry Eadgifu, abbess of the convent at Leominster, whom he had seduced, went to Denmark, and returned with eight ships, saying dishonestly that he would henceforth remain faithful to the king.'

What might we make of the statement in the *ASC* that he 'kept her as long as he pleased'? Was she kept against her will, or was she a willing concubine? As one historian put it, it may have been an 'act of unbridled passion', but marriage to Eadgifu would have given him control of a great estate in north Herefordshire.[75] It was, apparently, the threats of the archbishop of Canterbury and the bishop of Worcester which forced him to give her up and in revenge, Swegn deprived the Church of Worcester of Maesbrook, Hopton, North Cleobury and 'many other places in Shropshire'.[76]

According to one source, Eadgifu was with Swegn for about a year. A note in Domesday records that, 'The abbess holds Fencote. She held it herself before 1066.'[77] Fencote had belonged to the abbey of Leominster, so was Eadgifu given it? Perhaps we might imagine that she retired there and was still living there in 1086; if she had been a willing partner of Swegn's, how must she have taken the news of the family's fall from grace? If she had indeed been held against her will then twelve months would have seemed a very long time. It is clear that not all people revered abbesses and those who lived the religious life.

One abbess became the subject of a dispute, but in this case, after her death. She is another woman whose identity has been confused. According to William of Malmesbury, there was a place 'among the East Saxons in the diocese of London, called Chich by the heathens, which is the resting place of the blessed Osith, a virgin famous for her miracles.'[78] She – Osith, Osgyth or even Osyth – is an obscure figure, and really all that is known of her is that she founded a monastery at Chich. Her name was thought by H.P.R. Finberg to suggest that she came from the kingdom of the *Hwicce*, given that her name was so similar to those of the ruling family (Oshere, Osred, Osric), and that this scenario sat well with King Wulfhere's dealings with the South Saxons where, to consolidate conversion to Christianity, he had given to the newly-converted King Æthelwalh a wife chosen from the *Hwiccian* royal family, Eafe, who has been mentioned above.

Conversely, Osith was also said to be the daughter of a sub-king of Surrey, Frithuwald, and his wife Wilburh, sister of King Wulfhere of

Mercia. According to later, twelfth-century, stories she was brought up in Aylesbury in the nunnery of her aunt St Eadgyth.[79] On a journey to meet another aunt, St Eadburh, she drowned in the River Cherwell but was revived by the prayers of her aunts. She wanted to remain a virgin but was married off by her parents to King Sigehere of the East Saxons, but she avoided consummating the marriage, putting herself under the protection of a bishop name Beaduwine. Sigehere seems then to have accepted the situation and given her the land at Chich, where she built her abbey. She was apparently kidnapped by pirates and beheaded after refusing to renounce her faith. In one version of her story, she was buried at Aylesbury, while in another version she was buried at Chich, taken to Aylesbury for nearly fifty years, and then returned. If Osith was indeed the daughter of Wilburh, wife of Frithuwald, then a connection with Aylesbury, a probable royal minster, makes sense. Her story might have been confused with that of another lady of the same name, because there were two feast days and one explanation is that the temporary relocation of the relics from Chich to Aylesbury was an attempt to reconcile two separate cults.[80]

So we have yet another story of a kidnapped nun, although in Osith's case it might be no more than a later invention. There were, of course, other notable stories which left far more of an impression. No book about powerful Anglo-Saxon women would be complete without the inclusion of the woman who had such influence over her husband that she forced him to lower taxes by taking up his 'dare' that she ride naked through the streets of Coventry. The lady's name was Godgifu, and she is more commonly known as Godiva, but is the story true?

There is no doubt that Godiva was a wealthy woman and, typical of her time, she was generous to the Church. She was married to Earl Leofric of Mercia, who was a contemporary of Earl Godwine. Records show that she and her husband were benefactors of Coventry in particular. The impression of Leofric is that of a steady and sensible man, protective of his lands but lacking the overweening ambition displayed by his predecessor, Eadric Streona, and his rival, Godwine. He was himself the son of an ealdorman and was in power for over twenty years 'without violence or aggression'. Of his wife Godgifu, or Godiva, much has been written but little can be said with certainty.

The story goes that Leofric founded the monastery at Coventry on the advice of his wife. He endowed the foundation with so much land, woods and ornaments that 'there was not found in all England a monastery with such an abundance of gold and silver, gems and costly garments.' Godiva was keen to free the town of Coventry from financial burden and yet, when she spoke to her husband about it, he rebuked her, saying, 'Mount your horse, and ride naked, before all the people, through the market of the town, from one end to the other, and on your return you shall have your request.' Whereupon, she 'loosed her hair and let down her tresses, which covered the whole of her body like a veil, she rode through the market-place, without being seen, except her fair legs, and having completed the journey, returned with gladness to her astonished husband,' who then freed the town from the aforesaid service. He confirmed what he had done by charter.[81] Entries in the *ASC* of events of the eleventh century are full of detail yet there is nothing within its pages about this incident, or indeed anywhere else. Only Roger of Wendover has the story.

In fact it seems that the charters relating to Leofric's gift to Coventry are spurious; for example, S 1226 which records his granting land to Coventry in 1043, and S 1098, a writ of King Edward's declaring that he confirms the gifts made by Earl Leofric and Godiva to the abbot and brethren at Coventry Minster. S 1000, dated 1043 and showing King Edward confirming to Coventry Abbey privileges and land, as granted by Leofric, *dux*, is also considered to be of doubtful authenticity.

Since the charters relating to Leofric's foundation of Coventry are forgeries, can we be sure that he, or indeed Godiva, had any hand in the endowment of the monastery? Henry of Huntingdon said, when writing of the death of Leofric, that he was 'the renowned earl of Chester, whose wife Godiva, a name meriting endless fame, was of distinguished worth, and founded an abbey at Coventry, which she enriched with immense treasures of silver and gold.' Henry seems sure that the foundation of Coventry was attributable to the lady alone, and what of his comment that her name merited endless fame; was he hinting at that same story, of her ride through the town?

The monk known as Florence of Worcester, which is only just over forty miles from Coventry, writing before 1118, stated that Leofric and Godiva were jointly responsible, saying that Leofric 'was buried with all pomp at Coventry; which monastery, among the other good deeds of his life, he and his wife ... had founded.' Perhaps the truth is that Leofric made the grant, but that the land belonged to Godiva. With regard to the spurious charters, it might be that they were forged to suit the needs and claims of later priors of Coventry.[82]

It is safe to assume that Godiva was involved with the founding and endowment of Coventry, but with no other source to corroborate him, Roger of Wendover stands alone with his romantic tale of her naked journey through the streets of the town. Leofric comes across in the records as a staid man, unassuming and not given to impetuous behaviour. If his wife truly had behaved in such a shocking manner, it would have caused quite a stir and might have been more widely reported.

There is one other mention of Godiva, in relation to Hereward the Wake, the legendary figure who conducted a spirited rebellion against William the Conqueror. According to a fifteenth-century genealogy of the Wake family, setting out the descent of the Barony of Bourne, Hereward was the son of Earl Leofric and Lady Godiva. It has been put forward that this was either a guess by the compiler of the Wake genealogy or, more probably, it was an attempt to give Edmund Holland, earl of Kent, for whom the work was written, a more noble lineage.[83]

Little more is known of Godiva, except that she was possibly originally from northwest Mercia – she held lands in Leicestershire, Warwickshire, Staffordshire and Shropshire – and that she might still have been alive in 1066. If so, she would have seen the deaths of her husband, their son Ælfgar – who was banished twice because of his rivalry with the Godwine family (see above p. 118) – and the ill-fated last brave stand of her grandsons, the earls Edwin and Morcar, whose sister married Harold Godwineson. Whether or not she really did travel naked on horseback through Coventry, this doughty old lady saw the world around her change beyond all recognition and outlived her family, surely against all expectation. We do not know when she was married, but Leofric became ealdorman of Mercia in 1023. It is possible that they were married as early as 1010, and that she might have been born around 990.[84] If she died around 1066 or shortly afterwards then she might have been well into her seventies, having lived through the reigns of Æthelred II the 'Unready', Swein Forkbeard and Cnut, Harold Harefoot and Harthaknut, Edward the Confessor and Harold Godwineson, and lived to see William of Normandy crowned king of England.

Whatever the truth about Godiva's horse ride, we at least know for certain that she existed. Another noblewoman, whose story was pivotal to events in 1002, when Æthelred II the 'Unready' ordered the killing of all the Danes in England, is much more elusive. Her name was Gunnhild, and she was supposedly the sister of Swein Forkbeard. For her story, we must turn again to Roger of Wendover, who recounts the details of the St Brice's Day massacre when the Danes were 'shamefully slain, and their wives and little ones dashed against the posts of their houses.' King Swein, 'moved to tears thereat … called together all the nobles … whereupon they all with one acclamation determined that the blood of their kinsmen and friends should be revenged.' Roger continues: 'Their fury was increased by the death of Gunnhild, sister of King Swein, who was slain in England on this occasion. For this Gunnhild had been married to Earl Pallig, a Danish nobleman, and coming to England in former years with her husband, had there embraced the faith of Christ.'[85] According to Roger, Gunnhild had tried to act as a mediary and had offered herself as a hostage to King Æthelred, but was committed by the king to the custody of Eadric Streona, who ordered her husband and son to be murdered in her presence, and then for her to be beheaded.

This story adds piquancy to the subsequent invasion and conquest by Swein, but is it true? Henry of Huntingdon also chronicled the event, but implied that it was mainly the Danish men who were targeted. William of Jumièges talks of the slaughter of men, women and children, but it is only Roger of Wendover and William of Malmesbury who give the detail that Gunnhild, sister of Swein, was among the victims. Roger was known to have relied on other writers for earlier events so perhaps this story emanated from just one original source. William, for his part, conflates the tale with Swein's invasion of 1013, so there is definitely an amount of confusion over the details. It is hard, though, to justify the embroidery on the basis that Swein needed to be given some honourable motive for his invasion. William of Malmesbury says himself that Swein was 'naturally cruel' so there is no reason for him to excuse his behaviour by concocting a revenge story.[86] If she existed, then the woman who apparently did not 'pale or lose her beauty even in death' may well have had a part to play in the Danish conquest of England.

Some women are mentioned only in passing, but their very existence inspired moments in history. Matilda, abbess of Essen, was the woman to whom Æthelweard, the tenth-century chronicler, dedicated his history. The work was the first of its kind to be produced in England and written by a native Englishman.[87]

There are noblewomen about whom we suppose we know a great deal, while others remain in the shadows. Some of those who are familiar in fact did not have such exotic lives as the later chroniclers would have us believe, while others reveal their significance in just a few short sentences, demonstrating their wealth, or their influence, or both. One woman, however, was neither influential, nor well-known. Yet her story serves to show just how much remained unwritten about the fascinating lives of even the women of nobility in Anglo-Saxon England. If only the chroniclers had seen fit to give us more of these stories. The Gloucester Cartulary has details of a woman named Cyneburh, who, according to legend, was a Saxon princess who fled to Gloucester in order to avoid an arranged marriage. She took service with a baker, who was so impressed by her work that he adopted her as his daughter. This aroused the jealousy of the baker's wife, who murdered Cyneburh. She then disposed of the body by throwing it into a well, which was thereafter known as St Cyneburh's Well.[88] When the baker returned home and could not find Cyneburh, he began calling her name and she, though dead, answered him, thus revealing where her body was hidden. She was buried near the well, and a church was then built on the site. Thereafter miracles were recorded, with one woman being cured having lost the use of her muscles down one side of her body, another's withered hand was restored, while someone else was cured of dropsy.

It is hard to identify this woman, if indeed she ever existed. She is not Cyneburh daughter of Penda, for she married Alhfrith, son of Oswiu of Northumbria, as noted in Part I. Nor can she be identified with Cyneburh of the West Saxons, wife of Oswald of Northumbria, who was briefly mentioned on p. 9 and is generally assumed to have taken the veil at Gloucester and become abbess there. The Cyneburh who was murdered must either be a figment of the Gloucester chronicler's imagination or she is yet another woman of the shadows of whom only one detail was deemed relevant to be included in the narratives.

Yet, while some women remained in the shadows, and some had their reputations besmirched, others acted in a way that made it hard for the chroniclers to ignore them, and more still left us their own writings and commissioned works. We might need to shine a bright torch on them, but it is possible to see these women of the so-called Dark Ages, and to bring their stories out into the light.

Fair, but not Weak

The most written-about of the earliest royal women were those who were, perhaps surprisingly, respected members of the religious community, ruling monasteries as powerful abbesses, but who were also accepted as major players on the wider stage. Æbbe, Ælfflæd and Hild were all advisers, not only to the Church, but also to 'high council'. The first monasteries were founded by royal women who 'exercised an influence on the life of their time to which there is nothing parallel in later history.' The decline of the double houses and the Benedictine reform changed this and the later abbesses were 'shadowy figures in comparison … . No woman in the Middle Ages ever held a position comparable with that of Hild of Whitby.'[1] Hild was an educator, and Æbbe was able to have Wilfrid released from prison, as well as healing Queen Iurminburg. The royal abbesses were not considered in any way inferior but revered by men and in the eyes of God. However, even in the early days we see a marked difference in attitude towards those royal women who did not follow the religious path.

We have seen that women tended to remain part of their birth family and with that in mind, it would have been impolitic for kings to accept the customs of their wives for fear of signalling submission to their 'in-laws'. Edwin of Northumbria, for example, waited until Rædwald of East Anglia was dead and until he had inherited his status as *Bretwalda* before he agreed to conversion. Similarly, perhaps Asser's mindset was to smear rather than mimic Mercian practices, so that he spoke disparagingly about Mercian queens who came to Wessex; he disdained to name Alfred's wife and poured scorn on the notion of king's wives being queens. Yet we have some evidence that there were queen-making rituals.[2] Alfred's brother's wife was styled *regina* so it seems that there were political reasons for Asser's stance; Eadburh, the daughter of the Mercian king Offa, had propped up King Beorhtric's reign and needed to be diminished in the official record. Whether or not her husband was a West Saxon, her marriage to him did not make her any less Mercian.

Why were so many royal women accused of murder? It became something of a trope, and while many of the women were praised for their wisdom there seems to be a favouring of those royal ladies who took the religious life. We can see a different slant between the law codes and charters, and the hagiographies and religious tracts. Bede claimed that Peada of Mercia's apparently murderous wife played no part in his conversion because he said he would gladly become a Christian even if he were refused her hand.

The queens might not have been successful as peace-weavers, or even instrumental in the conversion process, but they too were influential. Those who came from Kent and East Anglia were married to some of the most powerful kings of the era: Æthelburh 'Tate' to Edwin, her daughter Eanflæd to Oswiu, and Eormenhild to Wulfhere of Mercia. Domneva proved to be a cunning negotiator, duping the king into giving her a large estate on which to build her monastery. Eanflæd and Æthelthryth were pivotal in the career of St Wilfrid and when Æthelthryth left the Northumbrian court, Wilfrid's power diminished. With Deiran blood, and the support of the Kentish royal family, Eanflæd exercised a great deal of influence.

Defining the status of these women is difficult. We have seen that in some instances it was the Mercian queens who exercised more power than their West Saxon or Northumbrian counterparts, yet one woman in Mercia who behaved like a queen, Æthelflæd, was never given that title. Many of these women used their influence in other ways, and in the later period their status was considerably advanced if they were mothers of kings. There was no parity, no equality of the sexes, but that is not to say that these women were powerless, nor that they were merely 'chattels'. We have notable cases where a quiet word whispered in the ear was effective in influencing policy and women did not have to wield swords to wield power. Rædwald of East Anglia was persuaded by his wife to renounce his new religion. Margaret wrought changes in the behaviour of her husband, Malcolm, who was keen to mimic many of her pious practices.

Yet royal wives were not necessarily safe from being discarded. The laws protected women, particularly those with children – seventh-century laws especially seem to place more value on women who were mothers – and those who were widowed, but royal women were different. Some exercised their right not to marry at all, but for those who did become wives, they had less choice about whom they married, for their unions were often the seal on a political alliance and while some went through amicable and mutual separation, like Cuthburh from Aldfrith for example, many first and even second wives were put aside. By the later part of the period the abbeys were perhaps less appealing, in that they were single houses and provided less social interaction but, as we have seen from the wills of wealthy widows, many were able to live at home, in charge of their estates, running quasi-religious communities from their own homes.

Widows lived comfortably on their estates, and not all queens retired to nunneries or if they did it was through choice. Emma lived on her estates in Winchester, whilst Ælfthryth chose to retire to Wherwell, but only at the very end of her life. There is no doubt that life was – to paraphrase Thomas Hobbes – nasty, brutish and short, but for these Anglo-Saxon women, it was comparatively easy. We should remember that they lived over 1000 years ago. In such a context, these women lived a relatively free and easy life. For those who were widowed but entered the nunneries, it was perhaps not a terrible fate. The wives who were repudiated might have been heartbroken, although we are not told, but we have seen that for those who lived in the nunneries, it was a comfortable retirement. No doubt their children would have visited them; it is recorded that King Edward the Elder visited his daughter Eadburh at Winchester.

There are high-profile cases of royal daughters like Eadburh being given to the Church, some at a very early age. But it seems that this was not in any way a reflection of how little they were valued; quite the contrary. They were precious gifts to God, in some cases given in expectation of, or in thanks for, momentous victories. Nunneries were not 'dumping grounds'.

Births were celebrated, even when they were girls. Edwin gave thanks for Eanflæd, and we know from both Bede and Asser that royal couples were not immune to the common loss of children at birth or in childhood. A daughter was not a burden; she was cherished. Of their childhood, we know little, unless they were dedicated to the Church from a young age, but we do know that Edith was educated at Wilton before she married Edward the Confessor. There is no reason to think that royal and noble women were not educated for, as we have seen, levels of literacy were reasonably high, and not just among the religious; Edward the Elder made sure that all his daughters were learned and skilled.

On the whole, and throughout society, mothers and daughters appear to have been more highly valued than wives. We hear of queens as mothers of kings, but often little about queens as partners of kings. We do not know why Edward the Elder put Ælfflæd aside, and when Eadwig was depicted 'wallowing like a pig in a sty' there was no mention of the fact that he was doing so with his queen. *Regina* was a title given to some, not to others, and clearly had a very loose definition. Formally married queens were also in danger of being put aside. Marriage was a source of power, but one that could be easily taken away, although the property settlements provided an element of security. In theory, widows had a claim on their husband's lands but often they had to resort to litigation to press those claims.[3]

Status was, to an extent, fluid and social mobility was possible. Royal daughters often made diplomatic foreign matches, be it from one English kingdom to another, or across the Channel, but the later English kings tended to marry noble, rather than royal, women. The most prominent of our eleventh-century women, Emma and Edith, were not born into royal families but were remembered as queens. They are often remembered together, but there are also strong parallels between Emma and her mother-in-law, Ælfthryth.

The later queens endowed monasteries and many retired to such establishments, but they also had involvement in secular affairs. Ælfthryth acted as regent for her son, often present at meetings, and Emma had a degree of control over the distribution of royal lands.[4] We have also seen though that in both these cases, the queens' careers were as mothers, rather than as wives.

To be a royal mother was to wield power. Seaxburh ruled as regent for her son; Ælfthryth, anointed queen, was never as powerful as Eadgifu, widowed mother of kings but, like Eadgifu, she continued to be influential even when her son Æthelred had not only reached maturity but taken a wife. Ælfgifu of Northampton, never a queen, was able to influence policy and was appointed regent of another country. Another who was never a queen was Æthelflæd, whose achievements apparently warranted so little mention that in some sense there must have been a tacit acceptance that a woman was able to rule a country, and in a time of war, too. Anglo-Saxon noblewomen were far from helpless. They were playing a secondary role to men, yes, but they were still to an extent the power behind the throne. They were not equal, but different. Their strategies were not those of men, and their wars were not won and lost on the battlefields. They knew the game, and they played to win.

Times change, and the Norman Conquest brought sweeping changes to England. Women's roles and their rights altered. Nowadays the 'Dark Ages' tends to be referred to as the 'Early Medieval' period, but for the women of power in Anglo-Saxon England, life was neither dark, nor typically medieval. They had rights, they were able to influence events and mindsets, and although they took up little of the scribes' time and attention, they nevertheless left their mark, enough at least for us to find them.

Appendix

The Saints' Cults

Queens, princesses and sometimes kings from the royal houses of Northumbria, Kent, Mercia and East Anglia were venerated as saints from early on in the Anglo-Saxon period. It was a way in which the Church could offer examples of holy living and the royal families could increase their prestige. Royal cults tended to flourish not in episcopal churches but in the double monasteries; those abbeys ruled by the royal women. From the late seventh century we know of a number of cases where the founder saints of minsters were honoured by having their bodies placed in coffins or shrines above ground.[1]

By the ninth century the great royal nunneries were on the wane – Abbess Cwoenthryth in Mercia was opposed by Wulfred, who managed to take Minster-in-Thanet from her control – and many were lost when the Vikings came. The emergence of Wessex as the most powerful kingdom might also have had something to do with the process. Very few comparable monasteries had been established there, Wimborne being a notable example, but as has been pointed out Wimborne was founded by Cuthburh, who had been married to a Northumbrian king (Aldfrith) and she perhaps brought northern traditions back to Wessex.[2] Only one house in Wessex contained the tomb of a king, at Wareham where Beorhtric was buried, but as discussed in Part III, he might well have been a Mercian. Most West Saxon royal burials were in the cathedral church at Winchester. In later years, burials took place in the New Minster, completed by Edward the Elder, but no saint was enshrined there. Over the course of the tenth century the situation changed, with a keenness for relic-collection and cults growing up around the family of Edward, and perhaps influenced by Mercia, with Edward's sister and son having spent substantial amounts of time there.

The value of a royal saint was that they brought prestige to those still ruling on earth. Such things became especially important when there had

159

been a change in the ruling dynasty and when Cnut – according to Goscelin – venerated St Edith, it was to the extent that he became 'more West Saxon than the West Saxons'. Possession of relics symbolised continuity, but also indicated possession of the land itself and signified proprietorship. In venerating the saints, the monks of those establishments who held them were also publicising their right to the land and property associated with the saint.[3]

Here then are a few additional brief details of some of the female saints featured in this book; of their cults, and miracles associated with them.

From Part I

St Æbbe: The miracles attributed to Æbbe number forty-three, and the majority of those healed were female. The afflictions cured included paralysis, dumbness, blindness, swellings and insanity. Some of those cured were of the nobility, but most were poor. The majority were young so it appears that her shrine attracted young, impoverished females. There were three centres to the cult: her tomb and shrine in the priory church at Coldingham, the oratory on St Abb's Head (mentioned above in Part I) and two springs where the drinking water was said to heal. In the twelfth century her cult attracted pilgrims, but it seems that because her miracles were mostly associated with the young and the poor, it was hard to promote her cult, people being less inclined to believe their stories because they were 'poor and unknown'.[4]

St Æthelthryth: Æthelthryth, who died in 679, was said to have preserved her virginity throughout two marriages. Her cult was established when her remains were translated by her sister Seaxburh sixteen years after her death, in 695, and her body was found to be undecayed. Her cult was fostered in eighth-century Ely, where she had been buried and where her original coffin and grave clothes were also said to have worked miracles. The monastery came into the Mercian orbit when Seaxburh's daughter Eormenhild married King Wulfhere and according to the *Liber Eliensis*, two churches were founded in Lindsey – an area under Mercian control – and dedicated to St Æthelthryth. St Werburg, Eormenhild's daughter, might well have been the one who promoted the cult.

Meanwhile at Ely, her community continued until it was attacked by the Vikings late in the ninth century, but the shrine survived and by the middle of the tenth century there was a community of married priests back at Ely and promoting her cult. Bishop Æthelwold, champion of the monastic reform in the tenth century, refounded Ely *c.* 970 and the married clerics were replaced with Benedictine monks who placed the shrine next to the recently translated remains of St Seaxburh, her sister.

Those involved in the rebellion of Hereward the Wake, centred around Ely and resisting the Norman invasion, viewed St Æthelthryth as their patron and swore oaths of loyalty on her relics. Early in the twelfth century the relics of all four saints were moved to new shrines within the abbey church, with Æthelthryth's being placed east of the high altar in a position of honour. Her cult continued to be promoted, with the fair on her feast day giving rise to the development of the word 'tawdry' as mentioned in Part I.[5] Her feast day was 23 June.

St Æthelburh: According to the *Life* of St Wilfrid, she accompanied Abbess Ælfflæd (654–714) of Whitby to King Aldfrith's deathbed. In Part I we discovered that there was a cell of Whitby Abbey at a place named Hackness. She is mentioned in a twelfth-century resting-place list – '*in Hacannessa sancta Ethelburga*' – but in Hackness Church there is more tangible surviving evidence in the form of fragments of an eighth- or ninth-century memorial cross. The inscription includes the phrase 'Blessed Æthelburh, always … your community/devotees are always mindful of you … . Most loving mother'. It has been suggested that this speaks not of commemoration, but that for the local community at least, Æthelburh was venerated as a saint.[6]

St Eanflæd: This saint, the former queen who died after 685, is not known to have been the object of a pre-Conquest cult. In the twelfth century her name was engraved on one of the monuments that stood near the church at Glastonbury. According to William of Malmesbury, her remains had been translated there. Given that she was known to have retired to Whitby, this might seem unlikely; however the same was said to have occurred with her kinswoman Hild, too. Some calendars have her feast day as 24 November.

St Hild: The relics of Hild (614–680) were translated from Whitby to Glastonbury, perhaps as early as the eighth century, but more probably in the reign of Edmund I. By the twelfth century they had been placed in a monument by the high altar. But as mentioned in Note 64 Part I p. 172, there is some evidence that Whitby never relinquished her bones. Hild was patron saint of over a dozen medieval churches, eight of which were in North Yorkshire. St Hilda's College, Oxford, is named for her.

St Hildelith: Bede describes a miracle associated with her: she had decided that since space at the monastery (Barking) was limited, all the bones of the servants and handmaidens of Christ should be transferred to the church and buried in one place. A heavenly light was often seen at this single tomb and a sweet fragrance was also noted. A local nobleman's wife was afflicted by blindness so he arranged for her women to take her to the monastery where she prayed at length on bended knee, and her sight was restored before she had even left the site.[7]

From Part II

St Mildburg: Her cult appears in the earliest list of saints' resting places where she was said to lie at Wenlock 'beside the River Severn'. In 901 the Lord and Lady of the Mercians gave a golden chalice of 30 *mancuses* to the church in her honour. The original double house of Wenlock became a college of priests and when the lord and lady made their gift it was ruled by a male superior rather than an abbess. Mildburg's feast day was 23 February. Her remains were said to have lain hidden in the disused abbey church, along with a collection of ancient documents and were rediscovered when the abbey was refounded as a Cluniac priory in 1079.

St Mildrith: Her cult developed after her death, and texts refer to the translation of her remains by her successor, Eadburh. The *Gotha* text of the Mildrith Legend expressed the claims of St Gregory's, Canterbury, and included an account of the foundation of Minster-in-Thanet, the career of Mildrith and the treatment of her relics by Eadburh. Goscelin wrote in opposition to the claims of St Gregory's to possess them. Mildrith's feast day was 13 July. Few churches were dedicated to her.

Minster abbey, despite being destroyed by the Vikings, was rebuilt before being sold into private hands during Henry VIII's dissolution of the monasteries in the sixteenth century. The community returned, only to be evacuated during the Second World War. Despite all this, the religious community of Benedictine nuns is still there, on the same site where Domneva, Mildrith and Eadburh once lived and worshipped, a fitting post-script to the perseverance and fortitude of those pioneering women.

St Werburg: Her cult seems to have been promoted by Mercian kings in their own kingdom and in Kent; by the eighth century Mercian rulers were encouraging the devotion to their own kin. She died somewhere between 700 and 707 and was venerated at Ely where her *Life* was composed. In the tenth century, though, the main focus of her cult was Chester, where her remains were enshrined probably at the command of Æthelflæd, Lady of the Mercians, at a minster which became known as St Werburgh's. There is evidence to show that her cult retained its royal associations with the existence of a royal vill named *Werberging wic*. Goscelin recorded that miracles were wrought: people called upon the virgin as they walked past the monastery and were cured from pain and malady.[8] The cult was active in the twelfth century after the minster had been refounded as a Benedictine monastery. In the fourteenth century her remains were housed in a new shrine, and in the sixteenth a monk of Chester, named Henry Bradshaw, composed her *Life* in verse.[9] Over a dozen parish churches were dedicated to her. During the Reformation, St Werburgh's Abbey became the cathedral of the new see of Chester.

From Part III

St Ælfgifu of Shaftesbury: Her cult was established at Shaftesbury by about the last decade of the tenth century and was flourishing around Winchester in the early eleventh. Æthelweard's tenth-century chronicle mentions it: 'She was held to be a saint, and at her tomb … many miracles take place.' Therefore the cult must have begun no later than his death in *c.* 1000. She was the first saint to be enshrined there and her mother, Wynflæd, was said to have been a lay member of the community there. She was mentioned in the *ASC*, described there as a saint, and William of Malmesbury recorded that she gave clothing to the poor and endured lengthy illness.[10] She had the gift of prophesy, too. Her name appears in a later list of saints' resting places and in a number of pre-Conquest calendars.

From Part IV

St Eadburh: Eadburh of Winchester was one of Edward the Elder's daughters. The earliest full-length version of her legend was written by Osbert de Clare in the twelfth century. She was buried at Nunnaminster, first outside and later in a tomb by the high altar, at which time her body was found to be undecayed. Bishop Æthelwold promoted her cult but it is likely that so too did the royal family of Wessex. According to Osbert's *Life*, she was translated three times, first by the community at Nunnaminster, then by Æthelwold, and then in the late tenth century by a nobleman connected with Pershore Abbey and from then on the two houses shared her. It is by no means clear that she was ever abbess, and even Osbert does not name her as such, even though it seems he was more knowledgeable about Nunnaminster than he was about Pershore.[11]

St Edith of Polesworth: Another daughter of Edward the Elder's, her name is included in the list of saints' resting places and her identity has been confused but it is most likely that she was the sister of Athelstan, and that she founded Polesworth. If she was the subject of a cult, it did not survive. Her feast day was 15 July but barely included in any calendars. Her mother being Ecgwynn who was possibly Mercian, and her burial place being beyond the Wessex heartlands, might have been the reasons for her obscurity.

St Edith of Wilton: She became the patron saint of Wilton although her cult was not local and monastic but promoted by the royal family. She appeared in a vision to her half-brother Æthelred II the 'Unready' and to Dunstan, reminding him that she had prophesied that her body would remain uncorrupted. According to Goscelin, Dunstan went to Wilton and arranged her translation, seemingly on behalf of the king. Cnut also promoted her cult and Goscelin said that he prayed to St Edith when he was in danger at sea and gave the community a shrine in which to house her relics. Queen Emma, too, prayed to the saint.

Edith's seal-matrix was in use at the abbey until the dissolution of the monasteries in 1536.

St Wulfthryth: She promoted the cult of her own daughter, Edith, who was translated between 997 and 1000. The translation is the last dateable part of Wulfthryth's life; she died at Wilton we are told, on 21 September, but not in which year, although possibly *c.* 1000. She was buried in front of the main altar of the abbey church at Wilton, and Goscelin referred to her as the 'hidden treasure' of the community. She is recorded as having performed miracles in her lifetime, as well as after her death, but her cult never became widely established, especially compared with that of her daughter, Edith.

From Part V

St Margaret: Margaret died in 1093 on 16 November, which became her feast day and there were many reports of miracles at her grave. There is one account of the translation of her relics in 1180 which describes how an artist named Ralph was commissioned by the monks of Dunfermline to make a reliquary which was covered in gold leaf and decorated with carved images, and during this translation her remains were moved to the north side of the altar. In 1199 William the Lion, king of Scotland, was persuaded against an invasion of England by a vision he experienced when spending the night at the tomb of Margaret, his great-grandmother. Miracles were associated with a well which can still be seen underneath the old Dunfermline abbey. Her grandson, King Alexander II, asked the pope for her to be included in the catalogue of saints, but she was only canonised in the middle of the thirteenth century. In 1250 her bones, laid in a silver chest which was decorated with gemstones, were said to have emitted an aroma of spring flowers. Fourteenth-century relic lists include the flesh and hair of St Margaret, her cross and her chemise. During the Reformation, 'heretics stole into the kingdome ... and seized the sacred movables' of Dunfermline Church. Margaret's head was said to have been taken to Edinburgh during Mary Queen of Scots' residence and after she fled to England Margaret's and Malcolm's remains were translated by King Philip II of Spain to a chapel in Madrid. In 1673 she was officially named patroness of Scotland by Pope Clement X. The collection of her miracles survives in one manuscript in Madrid. Miracles attributed to Margaret are cures for paralysis, insanity, dumbness, toothache, blindness and there are two cases of cures for swallowing lizards. It has been noted that in contrast to the much earlier St Æbbe, the cult of Margaret in the twelfth and thirteenth centuries was more dominated by men. Although her help was sought by pregnant women, the majority of those recorded as being cured are male.[12]

Notes

Introduction

1. Stenton, *The English Woman in History*, p. 348.
2. Fell, *Women in Anglo-Saxon England*, p. 16.
3. For more on the find, see telegraph.co.uk/science/2018/11/27/anglo-saxon-burial-site-shows-dark-ages-enlightened-times.
4. There was a woman referred to in a charter of 996, who reputedly killed a king's thegn and fifteen others. She was a widow attempting to retain possession of disputed land: Hollis, *Anglo-Saxon Women and the Church*, p. 87.
5. Wallace-Hadrill, cited in Ridyard, *The Royal Saints of Anglo-Saxon England*, p. 76.
6. Two later chroniclers do have a story of one of King Æthelred of Mercia's sisters refusing to marry King Offa of the East Saxons: William of Malmesbury, *Gesta Pontificum Anglorum*, p. 214, although he erroneously says Offa is king of the East Angles; Roger of Wendover, *Flowers of History*, p. 126.
7. Finberg, *Early Charters of the West Midlands* (*ECWM*), pp. 197-8.
8. Blair, *The Church in Anglo-Saxon Society*, p. 212.
9. Ibid., p. 125, n. 208.
10. The term Viking is problematic, sometimes referring to Danish invaders, and sometimes Norse, and sometimes not being technically correct as a term in itself, but to ease confusion, it is the term I shall use throughout the book to describe the Scandinavian invaders, unless there is a need to specify their particular country of origin.
11. It has been suggested that levels of literacy were in fact higher among women than among men: Hough, 'Women', *The Blackwell Encyclopaedia of Anglo-Saxon England*.

Part I

1. Williams, Smyth & Kirby, *Biographical Dictionary of Dark Age Britain*, p. 117.
2. *Historia Ecclesiastica, (HE)*, iii, 6, 16; *Historia Brittonum (HB)* in Whitelock, *English Historical Documents Vol I, (EHD)*, p. 237.
3. HE, iii, 1.
4. Ibid., iii, 6.
5. Ibid., ii, 9.
6. See Kirby, *The Earliest English Kings*, p. 58.
7. The people of Elmet were referred to by the tribal name of *Loides*.
8. Bede named her as Cwenburh, daughter of Ceorl. Henry of Huntingdon adds that he was king of the Mercians. See Whitehead, *Mercia: The Rise and Fall of a Kingdom*, pp. 28-9 for discussion of Ceorl. As Nicholas Brooks pointed out, Ceorl can hardly have been subject to the Northumbrian Æthelfrith when he allowed his daughter to marry Edwin, Æthelfrith's enemy. Brooks, 'The Formation of the Mercian Kingdom', in Bassett, *The Origins of Anglo-Saxon Kingdoms*, p. 166.
9. *HE,* ii, 9; Klein, *Ruling Women*, p. 21: 'Throughout the *HE*, the reception of royal women is figured as contingent on a heathen king's agreement either to convert to Christianity or to tolerate Christian worship within his kingdom. Queens are thus acquired through bargains waged … and as the *HE* progresses, the price of queens grows ever steeper.' Klein notes that the Frankish princess Bertha was given to Æthelberht of Kent conditional upon her being allowed to practise her faith unhindered, but Edwin could not marry Æthelberht's daughter until he promised not only to tolerate Christianity, but also to consider accepting it himself, while Peada was granted Alhflæd on the strictest conditions of all: that he and his nation accepted the Christian faith and baptism. *HE*, i, 25; iii, 21. For more on Bertha, see Part VI.
10. *HE,* ii, 9.
11. *Bretwalda* was a term applied to an overking. At various times, kings of certain Anglo-Saxon realms had supremacy over others, and Bede listed seven of them. Later kings of Mercia and Wessex can be included in this list.
12. Kirby, *The Earliest English Kings*, pp. 24-5. The twelfth-century chronicle attributed to Florence of Worcester does not even mention

her by name, initially, just whose daughter and sister she is, although she is mentioned on the occasion of her flight back to Kent. He says on p. 443 that she was the daughter of Æthelberht *and* Bertha.

13. See Klein, *Ruling Women*, pp. 31-5.
14. Whitehead, *Mercia: The Rise and Fall,* pp. 24-5.
15. See Kirby, *The Earliest English Kings*, p. 51: 'Probably inspired by the continuing prestige of Eadbald and a desire to secure the best access to the more sophisticated economic and political world of the south-east and beyond'. He also points out on p. 65 that most kings were not Christian at this stage. His wife's connections were important and her religion gave Edwin access to Rome.
16. *HE,* ii, 9.
17. A difficult term to define, but either a minor landowner or a royal servant with a specific job.
18. The pope's name was Boniface; *HE,* ii, 9-10 and p. 379: the letters necessarily predate the death of Pope Boniface in 625, so the marriage must have taken place before this date.
19. For more on this see Kirby, *The Earliest English Kings*, pp. 32-5. Kirby concludes that Bede's narrative is wrong and that Eadbald's pagan reaction lasted more than a single year, more likely somewhere between five and eight years.
20. S. E. Kelly was unable to coerce the East Saxons into once more accepting Christianity. See Kelly, 'Eadbald', *Oxford Dictionary of National Biography (ODNB)*.
21. Ibid.; Kirby, *The Earliest English Kings*, p. 35; Yorke, *Kings and Kingdoms of Early Anglo-Saxon England*, p. 29.
22. 'The marriage ... was not only important for the spread of Christianity, but also sealed an alliance between the two kingdoms which was advantageous to Kent when Northumbria became militarily eminent ... One thing which distinguishes Kent from other Anglo-Saxon kingdoms is the strength of its Frankish connections.' This would be a vital lifeline for Tate when she was widowed; it is also possible that Edwin deliberately waited until after the death of the *Bretwalda* Rædwald before entering into negotiations with Kent. Once Edwin was supreme, his contract with Kent would seem less like a submission to the powerful southern Christian kingdom. Yorke, *Kings and Kingdoms of Early Anglo-Saxon England*, pp. 36, n. 92 and 39. Also see *HE*, ii, 9.

23. See Klein, *Ruling Women*, pp. 30-5 for a discussion of Bede's portrayal of royal women and their influence.

24. See Hollis, *Anglo-Saxon Women and the Church*, p. 221 and Klein, *Ruling Women*, p. 30.

25. *HE*, ii, 14.

26. Ibid., ii, 20; iii, 1.

27. Kirby, *The Earliest English Kings*, p. 75.

28. *HE*, ii, 20.

29. Rollason, *The Mildrith Legend*, p. 9; At the time of writing, excavation is underway at Lyminge and the fabric of the original Anglo-Saxon building is being unearthed. See more at lymingearchaelogy.org

30. A son of Oswald's, Œthelwald, was fighting on Penda's side at the battle of Winwæd in 655, and thus would have been too old, probably, to have been the son of Cyneburh; See Finberg, *ECWM*, pp. 164-5 and p. 176 for discussion on this.

31. 'It may have taken [Oswiu] some time to establish himself; it was a year before he was able to retrieve his brother's dismembered remains from the battlefield. The resurgence of the Deiran line must have been a factor in Oswiu's choice of Eanflaed, Edwin's daughter, as his second wife. The marriage was solemnised in 644 but not until *c.* 650 did Oswiu feel strong enough to challenge [Edwin's kinsman] Oswine directly.' Williams, *Kingship and Government in Pre-Conquest England*, p. 18.

32. *HE*, iii, 14.

33. *Florence of Worcester*, pp. 18-19.

34. 'Although Oswiu had attempted to make himself more acceptable to the Deirans by marrying Edwin of Deira's daughter Eanflaed, he did not take direct control of Deira on Oswine's death and it was ruled instead by Œthelwald.' As noted above, Œthelwald was Oswald's son and was probably the product of a first marriage for he was too old to have been the son of Cyneburh. Yorke, *Kings and Kingdoms of Early Anglo-Saxon England*, p. 78.

35. Miller, 'Dates of Deira', in Clemoes, *Anglo-Saxon England Volume 8* pp. 42-43; Bartlett, *The Miracles of St Æbbe of Coldingham and St Margaret of Scotland*, p. xiii and n. 7.

36. 'Oswiu's murder of Oswine was obviously a potential threat to such harmony; Oswine was Eanflaed's second cousin and she was in that unenviable position that so interested the writers of Germanic verse of only being able to revenge her relative by attacking her husband.

However, Eanflaed was also in the position to end the potential feud by accepting compensation for the murder and this she did in the form of an estate based on Gilling where Oswine had been killed and which was used to found a monastery.' Yorke, *Kings and Kingdoms of Early Anglo-Saxon England*, p. 80.

37. Eddius Stephanus, *Life of Wilfrid*, Ch 3.

38. Thomas Charles-Edwards, 'Early Medieval Kingships in the British Isles', in Bassett, *The Origins of Anglo-Saxon Kingdoms*, p. 31; Fisher, *The Anglo-Saxon Age*, p. 83.

39. *HE*, iii, 24.

40. Whitehead, *Mercia: The Rise and Fall*, p. 25.

41. See Charles-Edwards, 'Early Medieval Kingships', in Bassett, *The Origins of Anglo-Saxon Kingdoms*, p. 32; Dumville, 'The Origins of Northumbria' in Bassett, *The Origins of Anglo-Saxon Kingdoms*, p. 220; 'Alhfrith and Alhflæd must have been born no later than 635, since both were adults in 653; their mother was probably Rhianfellt. Aldfrith, son of an Irish princess of the Ui Neill, was probably born after Oswiu's marriage to Eanflaed.' Williams, *Kingship and Government*, p. 161; 'It may have been in the early 630s, when Oswiu was in his late teens, that he married Rhianfellt, granddaughter of Rhun [*HB,* Ch 57], for he had a son, Alhfrith and a daughter, Alhflæd, old enough to be married *c.* 650.' Kirby, *The Earliest English Kings*, p. 75. See *HE*, iii, 21.

42. Whitehead, *Mercia: The Rise and Fall*, p. 31; Rowley, *The Old English Version of Bede's Historia Ecclesiastica*, pp. 119-20; *HE*, iii, 21.

43. Hugh Candidus was a monk at Peterborough in the twelfth century and wrote the Peterborough Chronicle; 'Cyneburh: – also recorded as a patron of the monastery of Peterborough in the spurious 664 charter (Laud MS of *ASC* and other copies)', *HE*, notes p. 394; 'For these men [Peada, Wulfhere and Æthelred] with their holy sisters Cyneburh and Cyneswith, who now rest there, and with King Oswiu, built this monastery from its foundations'. Mellows & Mellows, *The Peterborough Chronicle of Hugh Candidus* p. 3; Williams, *Kingship and Government*, p. 163 citing Rollason, *Saints and Relics in Anglo-Saxon England* (Oxford, 1989), pp. 119, 202-03.

44. Rowley, *The Old English Version of Bede's Historia Ecclesiastica* pp. 119-20: Bede does not specifically say that the marriage ever took place; he concentrates on the baptism of Peada. Peada returns

home with four priests, rather than a bride, although Alhflæd did go home with him. Rowley's contention is that Bede mentions little else about the marriage because of the subsequent murder.

45. *The Chronicle of Henry of Huntingdon,* p. 117; Whitehead, *Mercia: The Rise and Fall*, pp. 67-8; Finberg *ECWM*, pp. 170, 176-8; Sims-Williams, *Religion and Literature in Western England*, p. 222 discusses this.

46. Yorke, *Kings and Kingdoms of Early Anglo-Saxon England*, p. 110; *HE*, iii, 11.; See Kelly, 'Osthryth', *ODNB*.

47. See Hollis, *Anglo-Saxon Women and the Church*, p. 214.

48. See Kelly, 'Osthryth', *ODNB*.

49. See Whitehead, *Mercia: The Rise and Fall,* p. 67; Florence of Worcester and Roger of Wendover suggest that she was married at the time of the battle of the Trent. *Florence of Worcester*, p. 27, Roger of Wendover, *Flowers of History*, p. 106; 'Though married to Osthryth, sister of King Ecgfrith, in 679 or 680 Æthelred fought against the northern Anglian king.' Kirby, *The Earliest English Kings*, p. 98.

50. In his translation of Byrhtferth of Ramsey, Lapidge notes that: 'Only one son of King Æthelred and his wife Osthryth is known to history, namely Coelred, who was king of Mercia 709-716.' Conversely, Kirby points out that he was said not to have been her son. Lapidge, *Byrhtferth's Life of St Oswald*, p. 239, n. 6 and Kirby, *The Earliest English Kings*, p. 108 (citing Thomas de Marelberge, *Chronicon Abbatiae de Evesham*, p. 73).

51. Kirby, *The Earliest English Kings*, p. 119.

52. 'The first West Saxon nunneries were founded during [Ine's] reign by his sister Cuthburh (at Wimborne) and his kinswoman Bugga, daughter of King Centwine.' Yorke, *Kings and Kingdoms of Early Anglo-Saxon England*, p. 139.

53. Kylie, *English Correspondence of Boniface*, XIII, p. 78; *HE*, iv, 10; See Sims-Williams, *Religion and Literature in Western England*, p. 179; Aldhelm, *The Prose Works*, p. 52; Yorke, 'Cuthburh', *ODNB*.

54. Kirby, *The Earliest English Kings*, p. 88.

55. *HE*, iv, 23.

56. 'She married Æthelric if the ninth-century genealogy of the East Anglian kings in MS BL Cotton Vespasian B 6 be believed'. *HE*, notes p. 407.

57. 'Aidan, bishop of Lindisfarne, to Hild. The place of one *familia* on the north bank of the River Wear, for a monastery'. Hart, *Early Charters of Northern England and the North Midlands (ECNENM)*, #138 647 x 652, p. 131; *HE* iv 23; But see Thacker for the argument that there might also have been a house at Strensall near York. Thacker, 'Hild', *ODNB*.

58. But see Thacker ibid. for query over dates.

59. 'Though no identifiable books from Whitby have survived, the work of Abbess Hild suggests that she had assembled a useful library, an assumption confirmed from the compilation there, between 704 and 710, of the earliest biography of Pope Gregory.' Fisher, *The Anglo-Saxon Age*, p. 156. 'As well as the *Vita* of Gregory, a letter survives, written in the early eighth century by Hild's successor, Ælfflæd.' Sims-Williams, *Religion and Literature in Western England*, p. 185; *Epistolæ*. For more on the blue-toothed nun, see digventures.com/2019/01/medieval-skeleton-with-blue-teeth-shows-women-illuminated-manuscripts-too.

60. historicengland.org.uk/research/support-and-collaboration/research-and-english-heritage-trust/Whitby-Abbey. 'Many double monasteries must also have been places of considerable ostentation, as Aldhelm's vivid invective against the aristocratic taste in clothing cultivated by some nuns attests' and the 'wealth of personal knick-knacks from the Whitby excavations shows that Aldhelm was not merely following a literary convention.' Sims-Williams, *Religion and Literature in Western England*, p. 208.

61. Alhfrith wanted Wilfrid to be bishop of Deira (York) which caused conflict, as did his father's refusing permission for him to go on pilgrimage; Alhfrith may have been apprehensive because Ecgfrith, his young half-brother, had been married to Æthelthryth in 660 and was perhaps clearly being groomed for the kingship. Kirby, *The Earliest English Kings*, p. 89.

62. William of Malmesbury, *Gesta Pontificum Anglorum*, p. 159; Wilfrid had a troubled and chequered career; for more on his life see Eddius Stephanus *Life of Wilfrid*. For proceedings of the synod of Whitby, see *HE,* iii, 25 and *Life of Wilfrid,* Ch 10.

63. *HE*, iv, 23 (21).

64. William of Malmesbury, *Gesta Pontificum Anglorum*, p. 132; Thacker says there is some evidence that Whitby never relinquished its claim to her bones. Thacker, 'Hild', *ODNB*.

65. *Florence of Worcester*, p. 28.

66. *Liber Eliensis (LE)*, ii, 21.

67. 'Dr Colgrave may have been right to suggest that the two royal princesses, Eanflaed and Ælfflæd, joint abbesses of Whitby, hoped that the remains of their relative [Edwin] would do for Whitby what King Oswald's relics were doing for the not far-distant house of Bardney.' Wallace-Hadrill, *Early Germanic Kingship*, p. 82; Ecgfrith, too, might have been buried at Whitby. Simeon of Durham reported that he was buried on Iona, but with his mother and sister there, Whitby remains a possibility, although so does his widow Iurminburg's abbey.

68. For full transcript and translation of the letter see epistolae.ctl. columbia.edu/letter/338.html.

69. Bede's *Life of Cuthbert,* Ch 23.

70. Kirby, *The Earliest English Kings*, p. 92 (Although his arguments are predicated on those involved viewing themselves as Bernician, whereas in fact they had Deiran blood too; however in the case of Æbbe this would only be true if Acha had, indeed, been her mother.)

71. Bede's *Life of Cuthbert*, Ch 87.

72. William of Malmesbury, *Gesta Pontificum Anglorum*, p. 160.

73. In Ch 59 of the *Life* of Wilfrid he is quoted as saying 'my successor, whoever he may be' but in Ch 60 he specifies 'bid my son and heir' [to come to terms with Wilfrid].

74. *Life of Wilfrid*, Ch 60; See Kirby, *The Earliest English Kings*, pp. 119-20.

75. Although Yorke points out that the murder of the young king in 716 was an indication that the family of Æthelfrith of Bernicia [Osred's great-grandfather] were not going to be able to dominate eighth-century Northumbria in the same way as during the seventh. Yorke, *Kings and Kingdoms of Early Anglo-Saxon England*, p. 88.

76. Thacker, 'Æthelthryth', *ODNB*; Whitehead, *Mercia: The Rise and Fall,* Ch 2; As this book was going through edits and proofs, news came to light that the site of St Æthelthryth's abbey at Ely has been found. Excavations are ongoing.

77. Yorke, *Kings and Kingdoms of Early Anglo-Saxon England*, p. 70.

78. *LE*, i, 7; *HE*, iv, 23 and note p. 407.

79. Hollis, *Anglo-Saxon Women and the Church*, p. 68.

80. *HE*, iv, 3.

81. *Life of Wilfrid*, Ch 19.

82. *HE*, iv, 19 (17); Ridyard, *The Royal Saints of Anglo-Saxon England*, p. 178.
83. See Hollis, *Anglo-Saxon Women and the Church*, p. 166.
84. *LE*, i, 11.
85. Reginald of Durham – See Thacker, 'Æbbe', *ODNB*; *Life* of Cuthbert, Ch 10.
86. *HE*, iv, 25.
87. Wallace-Hadrill, *Early Germanic Kingship*, p. 63; *Life of Wilfrid*, Ch 22.
88. *Life of Wilfrid*, Ch 39.
89. See Whitehead *Mercia: The Rise and Fall*, p. 63; Brooks, 'The Creation and Early Structure of the Kingdom of Kent', in Bassett, *Origins of Anglo-Saxon-Kingdoms*, p. 64; *Life of Wilfrid*, Ch 24.
90. William of Malmesbury, *Gesta Pontificum Anglorum*, p. 146.
91. *Life* of Cuthbert, Ch 27.
92. Kirby, *The Earliest English Kings*, p. 92.
93. Hollis, *Anglo-Saxon Women and the Church*, pp. 69-70.
94. Roger of Wendover, *Flowers of History*, pp. 191-2.
95. See digventures.com/coldingham-priory/timeline/diary/the-radiocarbon-dates-are-in.
96. Ridyard, *The Royal Saints of Anglo-Saxon England*, p. 3.
97. *LE*, i, 35.

Part II

1. William of Malmesbury, *Gesta Pontificum Anglorum*, p. 218.
2. *HE*, iii, 8; She should not be confused with another Æthelburh, who was the first abbess of Barking, and sister of Eorcenwald, bishop of London. See Bailey, 'The Middle Saxons', in Bassett, *The Origins of Anglo-Saxon Kingdoms*, p. 113: Eorcenwald was probably a member of the Kentish royal house, because of the alliterative name which seems confined to Kent. He was active in the London area, and established minsters at Chertsey in the 660s and at Barking for his sister. For signs that this foundation indicates an extension of Kentish influence into the territory of the East Saxons see Kirby, *The Earliest English Kings*, p. 83.
3. Ridyard, *The Royal Saints of Anglo-Saxon England*, pp. 59, 180-1; Yorke, *Kings and Kingdoms of Early Anglo-Saxon England*, p. 70, n. 106; *LE*, ii, 53; Rollason, *Legend of Mildrith*, pp. 82-7.

4. Stenton, 'The East Anglian Kings of the Seventh Century', in Clemoes (ed), *The Anglo-Saxons: Studies in Some Aspects of their History and Culture Presented to Bruce Dickins*, p. 45, n. 1 citing *Liber Vitae: Register and Martyrology of New Minster and Hyde Abbey* ed. Birch 1892 p. 85; *ASC,* F Chronicle 798.

5. Ridyard, *The Royal Saints of Anglo-Saxon England*, pp. 51-2, 179-96. See Stenton in Clemoes (ed), *The Anglo-Saxons,* pp. 46-9 for more on the difficulties of identifying members of this royal family.

6. *LE*, i, 18; *HE*, iii, 8; Goscelin of Saint-Bertin said that she founded Minster-in-Sheppey, a fact which Bede failed to record. See Love, *Goscelin of Saint-Bertin: The Hagiography of the Female Saints of Ely*, p. xxxi.

7. Roger of Wendover, *Flowers of History*, p. 84.

8. *LE*, i, 35.

9. See Rollason, 'Seaxburh [St Seaxburh, Sexburga]', *ODNB* for more on this text which is not wholly reliable.

10. Rollason, *The Mildrith Legend*, p. 34.

11. *HE*, iv, 22; *LE*, i, 23.

12. Ridyard, *The Royal Saints of Anglo-Saxon England*, p. 180 suggests that she was perhaps constrained by political circumstance and worked not as a founder of religious institutions but as a consolidator. On the other hand, 'Seaxburh, prior to her departure for Ely, had played in Kent a role closely analogous to that of Æthelthryth in the Fens. She had been married to Eorcenberht, described by Bede as the "first English king to order idols to be abandoned" and according to her *Vita* had given vital support to his work of Christianisation.' (See her n. 22).

13. Kirby, *The Earliest English Kings*, p. 95.

14. Sims-Williams, *Religion and Literature in Western England*, p. 123; Finberg, *ECWM*, pp. 160, 166.

15. See Love, *Goscelin: Female Saints of Ely*, p. xv.

16. Section 25 of *þa halgan*, see Rollason, *Legend of Mildrith*, p. 28.

17. Love, *Goscelin: Saints of Ely*, p. 13.

18. Ibid., p. 15.

19. *LE* Prologue, Book One; S (Sawyer Charter number) 20; *On the Feast of St Eormenhild*, Love, *Goscelin: Female Saints of Ely* p. 17.

20. Dugdale, *Monasticon Anglicanum, or the History of the Ancient Abbies, and other Monasteries, Hospitals, Cathedral and Collegiate*

Churches in England and Wales, p. 143; see Whitehead, *Mercia: The Rise and Fall,* p. 60, for the doubtful veracity of the story.

21. William of Malmesbury, *Gesta Pontificum Anglorum*, p. 239.

22. Dugdale, *Monasticon Anglicanum*, p. 20; *LE*, i, 17.

23. Æthelred was married to Osthryth, mentioned in Part I; While the *LE* indicates that Werburg was 'in charge', i.e. was the abbess, the *Vita Werburgæ* says only that she was a nun there.

24. Thacker, *Kings, Saints and Monasteries in Pre-Viking Mercia*; Rollason, *The Mildrith Legend*, pp. 25, 26, 28; Love, *Goscelin: Female Saints of Ely*, p. lxxvi.

25. Outside Chester, which probably ensures that the whole story is erroneous, given that there is no record of her having lived there, other than Dugdale's questionable record. William of Malmesbury, *Gesta Pontificum Anglorum*, pp. 208-9.

26. Sims-Williams, *Religion and Literature in Western England*, p. 49 and n. 169.

27. S 20: 'The most famous abbesses being present, that is Eormenhild, Eormenburg, Æbbe and Nerienda.'; Rollason, *Legend of Mildrith*, pp. 39, 153, n. 39. Eormenburg has also sometimes been confused with Iurminburg, second wife of Ecgfrith of Northumbria, mentioned in Part I.

28. See Whitehead, *Mercia: The Rise and Fall*, Ch 3.

29. Finberg, *ECWM*, pp. 205, 217.

30. Ibid., p. 218 said they separated no later than 673; Sims-Williams says that she separated from her husband by 678. Sims-Williams, *Religion and Literature in Western England*, p. 49.

31. In red ink, and probably added in Canterbury in the eleventh century; See Rollason, *The Mildrith Legend*, pp. 38, 39 for analysis of William of Malmesbury's version of events.

32. Rollason, *The Mildrith Legend,* p. 39.

33. A hide being usually a portion of land deemed sufficient to support one family.

34. Kirby, *The Earliest English Kings*, p. 103; Rollason, *The Mildrith Legend*, p. 39; CS 177; Finberg, *ECWM*, p. 220.

35. Finberg, *ECWM*, p. 220.

36. *Vita Mildburgæ*; Rollason, *Legend of Mildrith*, p. 34; Stenton, *Anglo-Saxon England*, p. 47; Sims-Williams called her one of the 'shadowy children'. Sims-Williams, *Religion and Literature in Western England*, p. 49.

37. Finberg thought that Mildburg might also have been sent there at some point. *ECWM*, p. 220.

38. Assuming that Domneva is correctly identified as Æbbe, first abbess there and not Eormenburg; Yorke says that Æbbe was succeeded by Mildrith but calls her niece, rather than daughter. Yorke, *Kings and Kingdoms of Early Anglo-Saxon England*, p. 38.

39. S 22; S 1180; Rollason, 'Mildrith', *ODNB*; Rollason, *The Mildrith Legend*, p. 16 (although as already mentioned on p. 40, Æthelred might have been laid to rest at Leominster).

40. Sims-Williams, *Religion and Literature in Western England*, pp. 50, 110; Finberg, *ECWM*, pp. 202, 208-09.

41. The *Wreoconsæte* were a Mercian tribe, based around the area of the Wrekin in modern-day Shropshire; Sims-Williams, *Religion and Literature in Western England*, pp. 60, 98; Pretty, 'Defining the Magonsæte', in Bassett, *The Origins of Anglo-Saxon Kingdoms*, p. 177.

42. Finberg, *ECWM*, pp. 209-10; Pretty, 'Defining the Magonsæte', p. 177.

43. See Whitehead, *Mercia: The Rise and Fall*, pp. 47-50 for more on Merewalh.

44. Finberg, *ECWM*, p. 211.

45. Whitelock, *English Historical Documents, Volume I, c. 500–1042 (EHD)*, 177 p. 755.

46. Finberg pointed out that Aldhelm addresses Hildelith with the same phrase with which the preamble of the *Testament* addresses Mildburg. *ECWM*, pp. 215-16.

47. Kylie, *Correspondence of Boniface*, Letter XIII, p. 78.

48. William of Malmesbury, *Gesta Pontificum Anglorum*, p. 207.

49. Rollason, *The Mildrith Legend*, p. 41.

Part III

1. SE Kelly, 'Cynethryth', *ODNB*.

2. Kessler and Dawson, 'Mercia's British Alliance', historyfiles.co.uk/FeaturesBritain/EnglandMercia01.htm.

3. Cynethryth and Offa were both named in a privilege of Pope Hadrian I which granted control of the monasteries which they had either

built or acquired and were dedicated to St Peter. See Hollis, *Anglo-Saxon Women and the Church*, p. 213.

4. S 59 dated 770: *Ego Cyneðryð regina Merciorum consensi ei subscripsi. + Ego Ecgferð filius amborum consensi et subscripsi.*

5. *Atheling* was the term used for those, usually sons of kings, who were considered throne-worthy i.e. potential royal heirs.

6. Williams, *Kingship and Government*, p. 57.

7. A Northumbrian who went abroad to serve in Charlemagne's court and wrote many letters to royalty and former pupils.

8. Stephen Allott, *Alcuin of York*, letters 35, 36, pp. 48-9; Pauline Stafford, 'Political Women in Mercia, Eighth to early Tenth Centuries', in Brown & Farr, *Mercia: The Rise and Fall* p. 39, n. 2: this is not confined to her appearances with Ecgfrith; Wormald makes the point that Alcuin, like Bede, was an important witness 'from without'. Wormald, 'The Age of Offa and Alcuin', in Campbell, *The Anglo-Saxons*, p. 110.

9. S 1258: A.D. 798 (*Clofesho*) 'Æthelheard, archbishop of Canterbury, to Cynethryth, abbess, grant of the minsters at Cookham, Berks., and at Pectanege, in exchange for 60 hides at Fleet, 30 at Teynham and 20 at the source of the Cray, Kent.'

10. 'The Winchcombe abbess may, however, be another Cynethryth, recorded as the queen of [King] Wiglaf in the 830s.' Sims-Williams, *Religion and Literature in Western England*, p. 160 and n. 107 for details; also see Part VI of this book.

11. Levison, *England and the Continent in the Eighth century: The Ford Lectures*, p. 251 and n. 1, 2, quoting S 127. However, this charter is deemed to be spurious. Sims-Williams says Abbess Æthelburh was leased the monastery at Fladbury by her kinsman Ealdred who was a sub-king of the *Hwicce*, and that she should be identified with Æthelburh, daughter of the thegn Ælfred (S 1255). Sims-Williams, *Religion and Literature in Western England*, pp. 37-8; Finberg, *ECWM*, p. 178: Ealdred granted a life-interest in the estate at Fladbury to Æthelburh, 'almost certainly the same abbess' i.e. the daughter of Ælfred.

12. Kirby, *The Earliest English Kings*, p. 146.

13. Roger of Wendover, *Flowers of History*, p. 158-9; Thacker, *Kings, Saints and Monasteries*, p. 15.

14. Rollason, 'The Cults of Murdered Royal Saints', in Clemoes (ed), *Anglo-Saxon England, Volume 11*, p. 21.

15. The two women are listed separately in *PASE* (Prosopography of Anglo-Saxon England): Æthelburh 7 is abbess of Fladbury *fl.* 774–777 x 780, daughter of Alfred (S 1255 and S 62) and sister of Ealdred. Æthelburh 8 in *PASE* is the daughter of Offa and recipient of Alcuin's letters.

16. Although Allott also mistakenly says that this Æthelburh was abbess of Fladbury. Allott, *Alcuin of York*, letter 42, p. 55.

17. The sheltering of Ecgberht in Frankia did not help relations between Offa and the emperor; *ASC* 839.

18. Asser's *Life of Alfred*, in Keynes, *Alfred the Great*, Chs 13-15.

19. Janet Nelson, 'Eadburh [Eadburga] Queen of the West Saxons', *ODNB*.

20. Kirby, *The Earliest English Kings*, p. 152.

21. Williams, *Kingship and Government*, p. 28, n. 55 citing Barbara Yorke, *Wessex in the Early Middle Ages*, p. 63.

22. S 268: *Ego Beorhtricus rex tradendo et confirmando signum crucis aravi. + Ego Eadburg regina consensi et subscripsi. + Ego Wor princeps subscripsi.*

23. S 156; Whitehead, *Mercia: The Rise and Fall*, p. 106.

24. S 165: *Ego Quoenðryð filia regis consensi et subscripsi.*

25. Levison discussed in some detail the veracity of the foundation charter of Winchcombe and concluded that although the foundation charter was a forgery, it might have been based on a synodal charter of 811. Levison, *England and the Continent*, p. 249*ff.*

26. J. Stevinson and J. Stevinson, *Qwenfryth, Abbess of Winchcombe*, citing Brooks and Cubitt.

27. Unidentified; Cwoenthryth and Wulfred are said to have met in 825 at *Oslafeshlau*, which could have been a public meeting place, see Finberg, *ECWM*, p. 169: this might have been the place which was later changed to Oswaldslow in Edgar's reign (959–975).

28. S 1434: A.D. 824 (*Clofesho*). Record of the recovery by Archbishop Wulfred of land at Easole, Kent, granted to him by Ealdberht, *comes*, and Selethryth, his sister, but fraudulently acquired by Cwoenthryth, abbess of Minster-in-Thanet. S 1436: A.D. 825 for c. 827 (*Clofesho*). Record of a dispute between Archbishop Wulfred and Coenwulf, king of Mercia, and his heir Cwoenthryth, abbess, concerning the minsters of Reculver and Minster-in-Thanet.

29. She was required to give up all claims to hereditary privilege in relation to the lands; See Levison, *England and the Continent*, p. 252.

30. *Florence of Worcester*.

31. William of Malmesbury, *Gesta Pontificum Anglorum*, pp. 189-99. Roger of Wendover says the dove's letter translated thus: 'In Clent the cow pasture, Kenelm, king's child, lieth under a thorn, bereaved of his head.' Roger of Wendover, *Flowers of History*, p. 174; Thacker, *Kings, Saints and Monasteries*, n. 55.

32. Kirby, *The Earliest English Kings*, p. 160; Yorke, *Kings and Kingdoms of Early Anglo-Saxon England*, p. 120.

33. Wigstan became another murdered royal saint, and the crypt at Repton where he is said to have been buried – or at least his bones laid to rest – still exists and can be visited.

34. See Whitehead, *Mercia: The Rise and Fall*, pp. 126-7 for more about Ceolwulf II.

35. Asser's *Life of Alfred*, Ch 9.

36. S 206-211, S 214; S 1201. It has been suggested by Barbara Yorke, among others, that part of the marriage agreement was that Berkshire should become part of Wessex: Yorke, *Early Kings and Kingdoms of Anglo-Saxon England*, p. 122 and see Whitehead, *Mercia: The Rise and Fall* for discussion about Berkshire pp. 122-4.

37. Asser's *Life of Alfred*, Ch 46; *PASE*: 'Beocca 2 taking of alms to Rome: On 888 prince Beocca 2 carried to Rome the alms of King Alfred 8. On that journey died Æthelswith 1, the sister of the same king, and was buried in Pavia.: NorthernAnnals.SecondSet 80 (888)'; It has been argued, however, that the marriage was uncanonical, and that Burgred gave up his throne to go on pilgrimage to atone, and separated from Æthelswith before doing so. Woolf, 'View from the West: An Irish Perspective on West Saxon Dynastic Practice', in Higham & Hill (eds), *Edward the Elder*, p. 98. This, however, does not take into account the very real presence of the Vikings, and of Ceolwulf II, in Mercia.

38. S 340: *Ego Wulfðryd Regina*; S 1274: *Iudith regina*; Barbara Yorke suggests that Asser's assertion about there being no West Saxon queens was a tactic to undermine the throne-worthiness of Alfred's nephews, one of whom mounted a rebellion after Alfred's death. Yorke, 'Edward as Ætheling', in Higham & Hill (eds), *Edward the Elder*, p. 3.

39. Asser's *Life of Alfred*, Ch 29; Yorke suggests that Alfred's and Ealhswith's son, Edward the Elder, was named after his maternal grandmother, Eadburh. 'Neither element of Edward's name is

known to have been used before by members of the West Saxon house.' Yorke, 'Edward as Ætheling', p. 25.

40. S 340: A.D. 868 (Dorchester, Dorset). Æthelred, king of Wessex, to Hunsige, his minister, grant of 5 hides at Martyr Worthy, Hants. *Ego Mucel minister*; S 1201: A.D. 868. Æthelswith, queen of Mercia, to Cuthwulf, minister, grant of 15 hides at Lockinge, Berks. *Ego Mucel dux consensi et subscripsi.*

41. S 346. Perhaps Ealhswith was simply a timid person, or of nervous disposition. This is how I portrayed her in my novel about her daughter, as a way of explaining her absence in recorded history.

42. Æthelgifu became abbess of Shaftesbury (Asser, Ch 98); Ælfthryth married a count of Flanders related to Judith for whose career, see Part VI.

43. Ibid., Ch 75 and Keynes, *Alfred the Great*, p. 256, n. 144.

44. *HE*, ii, 14 and see Part I of this book.

45. S 340, S 1201 and S 1203; For Alfred's mother, see Part VI of this book; Keynes, *Alfred the Great*, p. 322 n. 79.

46. Asser's *Life of Alfred,* Ch 75.

47. For example, S 375: 909 *Ego Æðelweard frater regis*; Will of Alfred the Great S 1507 & Whitelock, *EHD Vol I,* p. 493: The list of land bequeathed to Æthelweard names eighteen places.

48. Keynes, 'Edward, King of the Saxons' in Higham & Hill (eds), *Edward the Elder*, p. 60: the calendar is preserved in the Athelstan Psalter BL Cotton Galba A xviii.

49. Asser's *Life of Alfred*, Ch 83.

50. Alex Woolf ('View from the West', p. 98) suggests that Æthelred was the son of Æthelswith, sister of Alfred and wife of Burgred, and thus that Æthelflæd was his first cousin. But Barbara Yorke at the Æthelflæd 1100 Conference in June 2018 postulated that he was descended from the ealdorman Æthelmund of the *Hwicce* who was killed in 802 fighting at Kempsford. See more about Æthelmund in Whitehead, *Mercia: The Rise and Fall*, pp. 46, 104 and Sims-Williams, *Religion and Literature in Western England*, pp. 123, 174-5. It is unlikely that the marriage of first cousins would have been allowed.

51. Æthelweard the Chronicler, a member of the West Saxon royal house, writing in the tenth century.

52. And see Stafford, 'The Annals of Æthelflæd', in Barrow & Wareham (eds), *Myth, Rulership, Church and Charters: Essays in*

Honour of Nicholas Brooks, p. 103 who points out: 'The entries do not, however, begin sharply at the point when she took over from her husband in 911 ... . Between the death of Ealhswith in 902 and this annal, three years are blank, two contain brief entries on astronomical events, two record the renewal of Chester's defences (907) and the translation of the bones of Oswald from Bardney to Mercia (909). The annals for 902, 907, and 909 may be argued as connected to Æthelflæd and her later activity.'

53. Ibid., p. 108.
54. Michael John Key has helpfully laid out the list of fortifications by brother and sister in his book on Edward the Elder, pp. 164-5.
55. The five main towns of Danish Mercia: Derby, Leicester, Lincoln, Nottingham and Stamford.
56. See Timmer, *Judith*, pp. 6-10.
57. See Whitehead, *Mercia: The Rise and Fall*, p. 136 and n. 16, p. 257.
58. S 224: 914 Æthelflæd, lady of the Mercians, to Ealhhelm, grant of 2 hides at Stantun (? Stanton by Newhall, Derbys.), in return for 60 swine and 300 solidi; S 225 915 (*Weardburg*, 16 Sept.). Æthelflæd, ruler of the Mercians, to Eadric, minister, grant of permission to acquire 10 hides at Farnborough (Warwicks. or Berks.), bought from Wulflaf. The original landbook, granted by King Offa to Bynna, Wulflaf's great-great-grandfather, had been destroyed in a fire.
59. See Blair, *The Church in Anglo-Saxon Society*, p. 306 and S 1446.
60. See note 52 above.
61. William of Malmesbury, *Chronicle of the Kings of England*, p. 123.
62. S 225, S 367 and S 1280.
63. Woolf, 'View from the West', p. 99.
64. Stafford, *Queen Emma and Queen Edith*, p. 93; But the same would have been true of Athelstan – his mother is assumed to have been Mercian – see Part IV of this book.
65. See Whitehead, 'Rioting in the Harlot's Embrace', in Jones, *Sexuality and its Impact on History*, p. 24.

Part IV

1. 'The near-contemporary Hrotsvitha of Gandersheim notes that Ecgwynn's status was lower than that of one of Edward's later wives,

but as she was praising the child of one of these later wives this is inconclusive.' Sean Miller, 'Edward [called Edward the Elder]', *ODNB*.

2. William of Malmesbury, *Chronicle of the Kings of England*, p. 139.

3. Ibid., pp. 124, 131; See also Yorke who points out that Ecgwynn was possibly related to the future Archbishop Dunstan. Yorke, 'Edward as Ætheling', p. 33.

4. Roger of Wendover, *Flowers of History*, p. 245; *ASC*, 926 (925); 'William of Malmesbury, who, although he does not name the princess, says that she was the daughter of Edward and Ecgwynn, and hence Athelstan's full sister. That, perhaps, carries especial weight, since, as Michael Wood has recently argued [1983], William seems to have had access to a reliable source about Athelstan.' Thacker, 'Dynastic Monasteries and Family Cults', in Higham & Hill (eds), *Edward the Elder*, p. 257.

5. S 366; Interestingly, though, when Ælfweard died prematurely, it was his half-brother Athelstan, and not his full brother Edwin, who was chosen to succeed him in Wessex. See Keynes, 'Edward, King of the Anglo-Saxons', pp. 50-1.

6. See Nelson, 'The First Use of the Second Anglo-Saxon *Ordo*', in Barrow & Wareham (eds), *Myth, Rulership, Church and Charters: Essays in Honour of Nicholas Brooks*, pp. 117, 122, 124 for more about the Second *Ordo*.

7. Sharp, 'The West Saxon Tradition of Dynastic Marriage', in Higham & Hill (eds), *Edward the Elder*, p. 82; Stafford, *Queen Emma and Queen Edith*, p. 129, n. 164.

8. S 340. Interestingly her name appears with a man, Wulfhere, who may well have been her brother and who defected to the Vikings (see S 362). This would, as pointed out by Yorke, give a different perspective to Æthelwold's rebellion. Yorke, 'Edward as Ætheling', p. 35.

9. For more on this, see Stafford, *Queen Emma and Queen Edith*, p. 57.

10. Yorke, 'Edward as Ætheling', p. 34.

11. Bailey, 'Ælfwynn, Second Lady of the Mercians', in Higham & Hill (eds), *Edward the Elder*, p. 114.

12. 'William of Malmesbury's *De antiquitate Glastonie ecclesiae* … the work contains many historical errors [and] cannot be relied upon.' Sean Miller, 'Edward [called Edward the Elder]', *ODNB*.

13. In 922 Charles was deposed and Eadgifu returned to England with her son, Louis and it was his opponent, Hugh the Great, who

approached Athelstan seeking a similar marriage alliance. Fletcher, *Roman Britain & Anglo-Saxon England*, p. 150. According to the *Liber Monasterii de Hyda* Edward and Ælfflæd had another daughter, also named Ælfflæd. Stafford, *Queen Emma and Queen Edith*, p. 90, n. 110.

14. Æthelweard the Chronicler; Michael Wood in The Guardian, 17 June 2010. For more on this, see Foot, *Athelstan*, pp. 50-1.

15. www.bris.ac.uk/news/2010/7073.html.

16. blogs.bl.uk/digitisedmanuscripts/2016/03/coronation-gospels-in-edinburgh.html.

17. Bailey, 'Ælfwynn, Second Lady of the Mercians', p. 123 and Stafford, *Queen Emma and Queen Edith*, pp. 95, 258 both suggest Wilton. However, Thacker says that she was 'probably' buried in the New Minster, Winchester. 'Dynastic Monasteries and Family Cults', p. 254.

18. S 363: *Eadward rex + Ealhswið mater regis + Elffled coniunx regis.*

19. See Coatsworth, 'The Embroideries from the Tomb of St Cuthbert', in Higham & Hill (eds), *Edward the Elder*, p. 296.

20. Eadgifu's father died in 902, so she must have been born no later than nine months after that and therefore was at least seventeen or eighteen when she married Edward.

21. Fell, *Women in Anglo-Saxon England*, p. 75. Although see Part V where barrenness might have been used by Edward the Confessor as an excuse to banish Edith.

22. See Sharp, 'The West Saxon Tradition of Dynastic Marriage', p. 82; Yorke, 'Edward as Ætheling', p. 32; Stafford, *Queen Emma and Queen Edith*, p. 134.

23. Ridyard, *The Royal Saints of Anglo-Saxon England*, pp. 96-103.

24. William of Malmesbury, *Gesta Pontificum Anglorum*, pp. 115-16, 202.

25. See Ridyard, *The Royal Saints of Anglo-Saxon England*, p. 136.

26. William of Malmesbury, *Chronicle of the Kings of England*, p. 125.

27. S 744; See Part VI of this book for discussion about Wynflæd's will.

28. William of Malmesbury, *Gesta Pontificum Anglorum*, p. 124.

29. Hart suggested that she may have died at Edgar's birth. Certainly she cannot have remained married to Edmund for much time after Edgar's birth if Edmund had time to remarry before his own death in 946. Hart, *ECNENM*, p. 309.

30. A charter, S 513, dated between 944 and 946 shows Edmund granting her, for life, 100 hides at Damerham in Hampshire; *LE*, ii, 64; Stafford, *Queen Emma and Queen Edith*, p. 134, n. 200.
31. S 514: Eadgifu is third on the list, Ælfgifu is twelfth, after the bishops.
32. See Stafford, 'Eadgifu Queen of the Anglo-Saxons, Consort of Edward the Elder', *ODNB* for more on these landholdings; it has been noted that sixty percent of her witnesses in the reign of Eadred related to land in Kent and Sussex and that, unlike in Edmund's reign, she appeared in a greater number of grants to lay people as opposed to ecclesiastics. Stafford, *Queen Emma and Queen Edith*, p. 60.
33. Possibly Crohn's Disease. Williams, *Kingship and Government*, p. 91; S 1515: Will of King Eadred, including bequests of land at Downton, Wilts., Damerham, Hants. (formerly Wilts.) and Calne, Wilts., to Old Minster, Winchester; at Wherwell, Andover and Kingsclere, Hants., to New Minster, Winchester; at Shalbourne, Wilts., Thatcham, Berks., and Bradford (? -on-Avon, Wilts.), to Nunnaminster, Winchester; at Amesbury, Wilts., Wantage, Berks., and Basing, Hants., with land in Sussex, Surrey and Kent to his mother.
34. *Life of Dunstan*, Whitelock, *EHD* 234, p. 830.
35. Whitehead, 'Rioting in the Harlot's Embrace', p. 21.
36. Æthelweard called Eadwig 'all-fair' (*Pankalus*) on account of his personal beauty and said that he was much beloved by the people.
37. The ealdorman of East Anglia, known as Athelstan Half-king, was the grandson of Æthelwulf of the Mercian *Gaini*, brother of Ealhswith, wife of Alfred the Great. It is possible that Ælfgifu the 'harlot''s mother was his relative.
38. S 1211 sets out the history of her estate at Cooling and the difficulties she encountered: 'When Eadred died and Eadgifu was deprived of all her property, then two of Goda's sons, Leofstan and Leofric, took from Eadgifu the two afore-mentioned estates at Cooling and Osterland, and said to the young prince Eadwig who was then chosen [king] that they had more right to them than she. That then remained so until Edgar came of age and he [and] his *witan* (council) judged that they had done criminal robbery, and they adjudged and restored the property to her.'

39. S 745: *Ego Eadgifu predicti regis aua hoc opus egregium crucis taumate consolidaui.*
40. Bailey cites her patronage of Ælfwynn of Mercia in S 535, if the religious woman named Ælfwynn in that charter can be identified with her (see Part III in this book regarding the identity of the religious woman), but even if it was not the same woman it still suggests a possible link to Wilton. Bailey, 'Ælfwynn Second Lady of the Mercians', p. 125. Stafford says she might have been buried in the Old Minster. Stafford, *Queen Emma and Queen Edith*, p. 95, n. 124.
41. S 737 and S 738.
42. The level of his dependence on the Mercians has been oft-debated. See Lesley Abrams, 'King Edgar and the Men of the Danelaw', in Scragg, *Edgar King of the English*, p. 171 *ff* but his law code, known as Edgar IV or the *Wihtbordesstan* Code, does seem to suggest his acknowledgement of their support.
43. S 1292.
44. *LE*, ii, 47 – land at Marsworth.
45. Although Stafford thought this unlikely and that the old Minster referred to might in fact be Dorchester. Stafford, *Queen Emma and Queen Edith*, p. 95, n. 124.
46. In my novel, *Alvar the Kingmaker*, which records these events, I hinted that Eadwig may even have been the victim of an assassination.
47. See Fell, *Women in Anglo-Saxon England*, p. 96; Whitelock, *Anglo-Saxon Wills*, p. 119.
48. *Chronicle of John of Worcester*, p. 416; Hart, *ECNENM*, pp. 331, 334.
49. *LE*, ii, 7; Whitehead, 'Rioting in the Harlot's Embrace', p. 30.
50. Whitelock, *Wills*, p. 15. It has been suggested that Wynflæd might have been Edgar's maternal grandmother, but there is still nothing in the will to connect Æthelflæd the White with the supposed first wife of Edgar.
51. Turner, Muir, & Bernard, *Eadmer of Canterbury, The Lives of Saints Oda, Dunstan & Oswald*, p. 135.
52. Yorke, 'Wulfthryth', *ODNB*, quoting Wilmart 31; Love, *Goscelin: Saints of Ely*, p. cix.
53. William of Malmesbury, *Chronicle of the Kings*, p. 160; William of Malmesbury, *Gesta Pontificum Anglorum*, p. 127.

54. See Ridyard, *The Royal Saints of Anglo-Saxon England*, p. 42 for a succinct summing up of William's stories versus Goscelin's.

55. See Williams, *Æthelred the Unready: The Ill-Counselled King*, pp. 5-6.

56. S 799; in a charter of 968 (S 766) she is not described as abbess so she must have ascended to the role later.

57. Yorke, 'Wulfthryth', *ODNB*; Ridyard, *The Royal Saints of Anglo-Saxon England*, p. 145.

58. Ridyard, *The Royal Saints of Anglo-Saxon England*, p. 143.

59. William of Malmesbury, *Gesta Pontificum Anglorum*, p. 126.

60. See Ridyard, *The Royal Saints of Anglo-Saxon England*, p. 39.

61. With one possible exception, that being Seaxburh of Wessex but she, apparently, was exiled because the men would not accept her command. See Part VI of this book.

62. Fell, *Women in Anglo-Saxon England*, p. 126.

63. To see photographic images of her seal-matrix: blogs.bl.uk/digitisedmanuscripts/2017/06/making-a-good-impression.html.

64. See Whitehead, 'Rioting in the Harlot's Embrace', pp. 24-8 for discussion of the division of the kingdom.

65. *Lestorie des Engles Solum la Translacion Maistre Geffrei Gaimar*, Line 3624.

66. William of Malmesbury, *Chronicle of the Kings*, pp. 159-64.

67. Stafford, 'Ælfthryth', *ODNB*; Williams, Smyth & Kirby, *Biographical Dictionary of Dark Age Britain*, p. 14; it is impossible to discover the fate of individuals but we do know that there was a plague followed by a fire in London around the time that he died, facts which allowed me to give him a dramatic death in my novel *Alvar the Kingmaker*.

68. S 904; S 731.

69. *Peterborough Chronicle of Hugh Candidus,* p. 25.

70. Bishop Oswald was given jurisdiction over three hundred hides of land in the heart of the territory presided over by the ealdorman of Mercia.

71. See Whitehead, 'Rioting in the Harlot's Embrace', p. 39.

72. Lapidge, *Byrhtferth's Life of St Oswald*, p. 111.

73. S 1242, S 1457, and S 1511. Also see Andrew Rabin, 'Female Advocacy and Royal Protection in Tenth-Century England: The Legal Career of Queen Ælfthryth'.

74. See Fell, *Women in Anglo-Saxon England*, p. 106.
75. *LE*, ii, 56; ii 37.
76. Fisher, *The Anglo-Saxon Age*, p. 299.
77. Lapidge, *Byrhtferth's Life of St Oswald*, p. 137.
78. Williams, *The Ill-Counselled King*, p. 9.
79. Stafford, *Queen Emma and Queen Edith*, p. 221.
80. *Peterborough Chronicle of Hugh Candidus* p. 16; Stafford, 'Ælfthryth Queen of England, Consort of King Edgar', *ODNB*; Stafford says that he was a 'palace bishop'. It was Ælfthryth who persuaded the bishop to move his monastery to Peterborough. Stafford, *Queen Emma and Queen Edith*, p. 136; Williams, *The Ill-Counselled King*, p. 8.
81. William of Malmesbury, *Chronicle of the Kings*, pp. 163-4. His body was later translated to Shaftesbury.
82. Stafford, *Queen Emma and Queen Edith*, p. 166; Perhaps the surprise lies in the list of those who championed Edward, given that he was not deemed legitimate and had what these days would be termed anger-management issues. Hart noted that the monastic party never forgave her for fostering the claims of her son, hence the later accusations. Hart, *ECNENM*, p. 274.

Part V

1. S 837 shows her as *regina* and attesting after the bishops; S 838 shows her as *mater regis* and her name comes between those of the archbishops; in one, she was even styled *mater basilei* (mother of the emperor). See Stafford, *Queen Emma and Queen Edith*, p. 200.
2. 'Edmund was not begotten of Emma the Norman, but a woman of low birth.' Roger of Wendover, *Flowers of History*, p. 286.
3. Williams, *The Ill-Counselled King*, p. 24.
4. Alternatively, the argument is made that if there was a second marriage it probably took place *c.* 990, was probably a legitimate union and 'its ending and the marriage to Emma a result of death rather than repudiation.' Stafford, *Queen Emma and Queen Edith*, p. 72.
5. See Part VI of this book for more on the will of Æthelgifu.
6. Whitelock, *Wills*, XXI p. 63; Whitelock argued that the friendship of the two eldest sons, Athelstan and Edmund, with the northern thegns, supports the idea of their mother's having had northern heritage.

On the other hand, if Æthelred married two women, the death of Athelstan's mother would explain why he was brought up by his grandmother Ælfthryth. Whitelock, *The Will of Æthelgifu*, p. 23.

7. Stafford, *Queen Emma and Queen Edith*, p. 216, n. 40.

8. See Williams, *The Ill-Counselled King*, p. 23.

9. In *Queen Emma and Queen Edith* (p. 216) Stafford says 1000 or 1001, but in 'Ælfthryth Queen of England, Consort of King Edgar', *ODNB*, suggests it could even have been 999.

10. '984 marked the beginning of his 'irresponsible phase' which ended in 993.' Miller, Anglo-Saxons.net. (timeline 978-1016). Was this what prompted the return of his mother?

11. Stafford, *Queen Emma and Queen Edith*, pp. 211, 214.

12. S 910: 1005 *Ego Æðelredus totius Brittanie monarchus mee largitatis donum agie Crucis taumate roboraui. + Ego Æðelstanus eiusdem regis filius plaudens consensi. + Ego Ecgbriht clito testis fui. + Ego Eadmund clito testimonium adhibui. + Ego Eadric clito non abnui. + Ego Eadwig clito non rennui. + Ego Eadgar clito non negaui. + Ego Eadweard clito faui. + Ego Ælfgyfu regina stabilitatem testimonii confirmaui.* (Ælfgyfu here is Emma, Ælfgifu being her given English name.)

13. Barlow, *The Life of King Edward the Confessor*, pp. 7-8; A charter of 1004, S 907, shows him as the only atheling on the witness list.

14. She was never named; For the significance of her status at the time, as an English queen, widow of a king and wife of a conqueror see Stafford, *Queen Emma and Queen Edith*, pp. 7-8.

15. Ibid., pp. 218-19. She makes the point that those who 'fell' at around the time of the marriage to Emma were those nobles associated with Ælfthryth.

16. Fletcher in *Bloodfeud* (p. 77) says the marriage took place in 1006 but Williams in *The Ill-Counselled King* disputes this (p. 196, n. 52).

17. Williams, *The Ill-Counselled King*, p. 75.

18. Whitehead, *Mercia: The Rise and Fall*, pp. 188-96; Keynes, Eadric [Edric] Streona', *ODNB*.

19. Whitehead, *Mercia: The Rise and Fall*, p. 191.

20. Williams, *Kingship and Government*, p. 100.

21. Edmund's standing in the Five Boroughs was presumably compromised by the fact that Ælfgifu of Northampton had the same status there as his own spouse, the widow of Sigeferth. Williams, *The Ill-Counselled King*, p. 139.

22. For more on this family, see Whitehead, *Mercia: The Rise and Fall*, pp. 183-9.

23. Hart stated that she was allowed to inherit the bulk of her father's estates. Hart, *ECNENM*, p. 259.

24. *Chronicle of John of Worcester*, p. 521; *Encomium Emmæ Reginæ*, p. 41.

25. Bolton, 'Ælfgifu of Northampton: Cnut the Great's "Other Woman"', in Jones (ed), *Nottingham Medieval Studies Vol LI*, pp. 256-8.

26. For example, Thietmar of Merseburg and *Encomium Emmæ Reginæ.*

27. Lawson suggests that she was provided with 'an establishment in her own part of the world, perhaps Northampton' while Bolton suggests that she went to Scandinavia before Cnut's remarriage. Lawson, *Cnut: England's Viking King*, p. 131 and Bolton 'Ælfgifu of Northampton', p. 260.

28. Bolton tentatively suggests that S 1423 might refer to her rather than Emma. Bolton, 'Ælfgifu of Northampton' p. 259

29. Miller, Anglo-Saxons.net (timeline 978–1016).

30. Lawson, *Cnut*, p. 83.

31. Bolton says her status as set-aside concubine gave her continued rights and she probably went abroad at this point. Bolton, 'Ælfgifu of Northampton', pp. 261-2.

32. See Williams, *The Ill-Counselled King*, p. 118.

33. It is not clear at what point his siblings joined him, but they were all there after 1016. Miller, Anglo-Saxons.net (timeline 983–1066).

34. Stafford points out that her Norman family may not have welcomed the union and William of Jumièges presented it as a 'marriage of capture'. Stafford, *Queen Emma and Queen Edith*, p. 228.

35. Ibid., p. 231.

36. S 972: *Ego Cnut rex Anglorum cum regina mea Ælfgyfu propriam donationem regali stabilimento confirmo.*

37. *LE*, ii, 79.

38. Stafford, *Queen Emma and Queen Edith*, p. 235.

39. William of Malmesbury, *Chronicle of the Kings*, p. 208.

40. Lawson, 'Harthacnut', *ODNB*.

41. Stafford, 'Ælfgifu [Ælfgifu of Northampton]', *ODNB*.

42. Bolton, 'Ælfgifu of Northampton', p. 264.

43. Immo to Bishop Azeko of Worms, Bolton, 'Ælfgifu of Northampton', p. 265. Miller, Anglo-Saxons.net (timeline 983–1066).

44. For more on how Cnut established his rule, see Whitehead: anniewhitehead2.blogspot.com/2018/11/how-cnut-established-himself-as-full.html.
45. Bolton, 'Ælfgifu of Northampton', p. 265.
46. Stenton, *Anglo-Saxon England*, p. 421.
47. Keynes says Godwine defected first while Miller says Godwine moved after Emma invited her sons from Normandy. Keynes, 'Emma [Ælfgifu]', *ODNB*, Miller, Anglo-Saxons.net (timeline 983–1066).
48. S 1467 might be an authentic description of him on his deathbed.
49. See Bolton, 'Ælfgifu of Northampton', p. 267.
50. Stafford: 'That they were summoned to England by a letter in their mother's name is clear.' She disputes Keynes's suggestion that the letter was forged. Stafford, *Queen Emma and Queen Edith*, pp. 241-2, n. 136.
51. Ibid., p. 251.
52. Keynes, citing *Annales monasterii de Wintonia,* 'Emma [*Ælfgifu*]', *ODNB*.
53. S 1011. Stafford: 'The document is extremely suspect.' Stafford, *Queen Emma and Queen Edith*, p. 254. Keynes, however, says the witness list may come from a reliable document of the same year. http://www.esawyer.org.uk/charter/1011.html.
54. 'An unusually virile design'. Barlow, *The Godwins*, p. 62.
55. Stafford, *Queen Emma and Queen Edith*, p. 257.
56. Stafford says of Gytha's marriage to Godwine that it was part of a process of cementing loyalties to the new regime and Gytha, like Emma, was a 'kind of hostage'. Stafford, *Queen Emma and Queen Edith*, p. 256.
57. William of Malmesbury, *Chronicle of the Kings,* p. 216. Alternatively, Barlow's translation in the *Life* of Edward has: 'On seeing her, you would have been amazed at her education, you would certainly also have been attracted by her intellectual modesty and the beauty of her body.' Barlow, *Life of Edward the Confessor*, p. 14.
58. S 1035: *Ego Wigodus regis pincerna. + Ego Herdingus reginae pincerna. + Ego Adzurus regis dapifer. + Ego Yfingus regis dapifer. + Ego Godwinus reginae dapifer. (pincerna*: butler, *dapifer*: steward.) The charter is not universally regarded as authentic, however.
59. Hearne, *Hemingi chartularium ecclesiæ Wigorniensis, descripsit ediditque Volume 2,* i, 253.

60. Barlow, *Life of Edward the Confessor*, pp. 3-4, 42, 46-8, 53-4.
61. Ibid., p. 42.
62. *Peterborough Chronicle of Hugh Candidus*, p. 37; Williams, 'Edith [Eadgyth]', *ODNB* and Barlow, *The Godwins*, p. 107.
63. See Part VI of this book for his abduction of the abbess Eadgifu.
64. Barlow, *The Godwins*, p. 55.
65. For a little more on Judith, see Part VI of this book.
66. *Chronicle of John of Worcester*, p. 563.
67. Stafford suggests that she went to Wherwell as a punishment, then to Wilton when it became clear that Godwine's return was likely. Stafford, *Queen Emma and Queen Edith*, p. 265.
68. Ibid., p. 267.
69. Barlow, *Life of Edward the Confessor*, Ch V p. 30.
70. *Chronicle of John of Worcester*, p. 599.
71. Another difficult term to define, but essentially the king's or nobleman's personal guard.
72. For more connections, see Williams, 'Eadgifu [Eddeua] the Fair [the Rich]', *ODNB*; Osbert and Eadmer; see Barlow, *The Godwins*, p. 78.
73. See Whitehead, *Mercia: The Rise and Fall*, p. 215.
74. Barlow, *Life of Edward the Confessor*, pp. 52-4.
75. *The Gesta Guillelmi of William of Poitiers,* p. 115.
76. See John, 'The End of Anglo-Saxon England', in Campbell, *The Anglo-Saxons*, pp. 233, and 221-4 for examination of the sources.
77. Barlow, *The Godwins*, p. 160.
78. William of Malmesbury, *Gesta Pontificum Anglorum*, pp. 182-3.
79. Humble, *The Fall of Saxon England*, p. 198.
80. Thanks to Marie Hilder for this insight.
81. For more on her see Ronay, *The Lost King of England*, pp. 111-12.
82. See *ASC, The Ecclesiastical History of Orderic Vitalis: Volume II: Books III & IV: Bks.3 & 4 Vol 2*, i, 24 and Bartlett, *The Miracles of St Æbbe of Coldingham*, p. xxx.
83. See also Ronay, *The Lost King of England*, p. 164.
84. Watt, *A History Book for Scots: Selections from Scotichronicon by Walter Bower*, p. 57.
85. Bartlett, *The Miracles of St Æbbe of Coldingham*, p. xxx.
86. Turgot, *Life of St Margaret*, pp. 38-40.
87. Ibid., p. 56.

88. Bower, *Scotichronicon*, p. 60.
89. Turgot, *Life of St Margaret*, p. 32.
90. Ibid., p. 33.
91. thecourier.co.uk/fp/news/local/fife/847074/3d-scan-in-dunfermline-searches-for-secrets-of-st-margaret-the-forgotten-queen-of-scotland/.
92. Henry of Huntingdon, p. 225; Bartlett, *The Miracles of St Æbbe of Coldingham*, p. xxxi and see appendix of this book.

Part VI

1. Gregory of Tours' History of the Franks, Book IV 26, https://sourcebooks.fordham.edu/basis/gregory-hist.asp#book4. In simple terms, the Merovingians were the earlier rulers of the kingdom of the Franks, overthrown by the dynasty known as the Carolingians in 751.
2. See Whitehead, *Mercia: The Rise and Fall*, p. 20 on the length of Penda's reign. Some chroniclers suggested that Penda was eighty when he rode into battle in 655!
3. *HE*, i, 25.
4. Brooks, 'The Formation of the Mercian Kingdom', p. 66; Yorke, *Kings and Kingdoms of Early Anglo-Saxon England*, p. 28: Bertha was not a 'prestigious' princess. For suggestion that Ingoberga was not her mother see Kirby, *The Earliest English Kings*, p. 26.
5. See Wallace-Hadrill, *Early Germanic Kingship*, p. 26 for discussion of Merovingian influence. For examination of whether Frankish chancery customs were introduced to the Kentish government via Liudhard, see Levison, *England and the Continent*, pp. 174, 225*ff*.
6. See Yorke, *Kings and Kingdoms of Early Anglo-Saxon England*, p. 29.
7. See Wallace-Hadrill, *Early Germanic Kingship*, p. 24 for a detailed discussion of the possible reasons why the marriage might have taken place.
8. Nelson, 'Bertha', *ODNB*; See also Klein, *Ruling Women*, pp. 18-43 for discussion on Bede's attitude to women and the conversion.
9. See Kirby, *The Earliest English Kings*, pp. 165, 235, n. 92.
10. Carolingian princesses were rarely sent abroad. See Sharp, 'The West Saxon Tradition of Dynastic Marriage', p. 80 who cites Charlemagne's reluctance to do so (Einhard, Bk iii).

11. Although Kirby disputed this, quoting Frankish annals and the *ASC*, and pointed out that Asser himself admitted that Æthelwulf was able to insist that Judith sit beside him as queen. Kirby, *The Earliest English Kings*, p. 166.

12. Asser Ch 17, but the Frankish annals do not echo the sentiment and it might be that as a dowager queen Judith retained her husband's status and thus upon remarrying conferred that status to her new husband. See Nelson, 'Æthelwulf', *ODNB*.

13. *Annals of St Bertin.* See Nelson, 'Æthelwulf', *ODNB*.

14. An image of the Gospels of Judith can be seen here: themorgan.org/collection/gospel-book/119042.

15. Nelson, 'Balthild [St Balthild, Balthilda]', *ODNB* cites the *Liber historiae Francorum.*

16. *Life of Wilfrid,* Ch 6; *HE*, v, 19.

17. Nelson, 'Balthild [St Balthild, Balthilda]', *ODNB*.

18. cityofstories.co.uk/the-seal-matrix-an-ancient-tale-of-romance

19. 'Balthild's relics came to the royal nunnery of Romsey' and 'She was there by 1013 x *c.* 1030 when the list of saints' resting places was compiled.' Stafford, *Queen Emma and Queen Edith*, p. 171 and n. 46.

20. To view a photograph of the tabard, see: kornbluthphoto.com/images/Balthild7.jpg.

21. *HB,* Ch 63 in Whitelock, *EHD* p. 237.

22. Henry of Huntingdon, p. 120.

23. William of Malmesbury, *Chronicle of the Kings of England*, p. 36.

24. *HE*, iv, 12.

25. Yorke, 'Seaxburh [Sexburga] Queen of the Gewisse', *ODNB*.

26. Yorke, Æthelflæd 1100 Conference, Tamworth 2018.

27. See Sims-Williams, *Religion and Literature in Western England*, pp. 92-3.

28. *HE*, iv, 13; Finberg said that Eanfrith was 'probably' a king. *ECWM*, p. 171.

29. *HE*, iv, 13. See also Finberg, *ECWM*, p. 179 for Eafe's family tree.

30. S 188 and S 190.

31. Kylie, *Correspondence of Boniface*, Letter XXIII, p 110.

32. Ibid., XXVIII, p. 130.

33. Ibid., 'Introduction', p. 14.

34. Ibid., Letter VII, p. 57; Sims-Williams says this sister was imprisoned in Rome. Sims-Williams, 'Ecgburh', *ODNB*.

35. See Sims-Williams, *Religion and Literature in Western England*, p. 223 and see pp. 224-5 for argument that she came from the west.

36. Colgrave, *Felix's Life of Guthlac,* p. 147 and see p. 191 for Ecgburh's gifts.

37. Yorke, Eadburh [St Eadburh, Eadburga], *ODNB*.

38. Kylie, *Correspondence of Boniface*, Letter VIII, p. 61; It seems that she and her daughter were somehow related to the royal house and that her kinsmen had been forced into exile; See Yorke, *Kings and Kingdoms of Early Anglo-Saxon England*, p. 36.

39. Blair, *The Church in Anglo-Saxon Society,* p. 283; Kylie, *Correspondence of Boniface,* Letter XL, p. 160; S 34, S 148, S 256 and S 152.

40. Kylie, *Correspondence of Boniface,* Letter VII, p. 57.

41. Ibid., XIII, XV, XIV, pp. 78, 92 and 90.

42. For full transcripts and translations of the letters, see *Epistolae,* epistolae.ctl.columbia.edu/woman/26090.html.

43. See Nelson, 'Osburh', *ODNB* and Sharp, 'The West Saxon Tradition of Dynastic Marriage', p. 79.

44. Asser's *Life of Alfred*, Ch 23.

45. Fell, *Women in Anglo-Saxon England*, p. 103.

46. Whitelock, *Wills*, XXI p. 62.

47. See Ibid., XXXII p. 85 and note on p. 100.

48. Ibid., XXXVII; XXXVIII pp. 92-5.

49. See Ibid., XV p. 39, also Thompson, *Dying and Death in Later Anglo-Saxon England*, p. 24.

50. Blair, *The Church in Anglo-Saxon Society*, pp. 354-5.

51. Whitelock, *Wills*, XXIX, p. 77; Stafford, *Queen Emma and Queen Edith*, p. 112.

52. See above Part V and the discussion of Æthelred the Unready's wives and the death of the atheling Athelstan.

53. See Whitelock, *The Will of Æthelgifu*, p. 23 and see Fell, *Women in Anglo-Saxon England*, p. 76 for the suggestion that Leofsige was also a minor when the will was drawn up.

54. See Blair, *The Church in Anglo-Saxon Society*, pp. 407-09 on how these small private churches became of interest to the Domesday Book commissioners.

55. Thompson, *Dying and Death in Later Anglo-Saxon England*, p. 64, n. 29.

56. Ibid., p. 109: Thompson points out that clearly this was not reserved for the clergy and see Gale Owen-Crocker, *Dress in Anglo-Saxon England*, pp. 211, 334.

57. Williams, *Wills in Pre-conquest England*, p. 10; Owen, 'Wynflæd's Wardrobe' in Clemoes (ed), *Anglo-Saxon England Volume 8*, p. 197.

58. Owen, 'Wynflæd's Wardrobe', p. 203.

59. Whitelock, *Wills*, III p. 10; Williams, *Names, Status and Service in the Will of Wynflæd*; S 1539.

60. Fell, *Women in Anglo-Saxon England*, p. 45 remarked that these items were made by the women of the household and thought of as 'female' property, but it should be remembered that these testatrixes were widows and therefore all items were their property.

61. *LE*, ii, 88; Fell, *Women in Anglo-Saxon England*, p. 41.

62. For an imagining of Wynflæd's world, see Michael Wood's article in *History Today* November 2018.

63. See Stafford, *Queen Emma and Queen Edith*, p. 187.

64. Felix's *Life of Guthlac*, pp. 156-9.

65. Ibid., pp. 73-5.

66. It is likely that Tetbury was named after a woman called Tette, but Ine's sister, according to Sims-Williams, flourished too late. Sims-Williams, *Religion and Literature in Western England*, p. 92.

67. Hart, *ECNENM*, p. 373, although Hart did not specify how they were related.

68. Ibid.

69. Williams, *The Ill-Counselled King*, p. 26, n. 44 (S 876 and S 918).

70. Finberg, *ECWM*, pp. 64-5, Whitelock, *EHD,* 123, pp. 537-9, and Hart, *ECNENM*, p. 84.

71. S 1454 990 x 992; See Williams, *Kingship and Government*, p. 112 – if the oath had been sworn then Leofwine would have been convicted as a thief.

72. See Fletcher, *Bloodfeud*, p. 129*ff* for their importance.

73. This might be another reason why Edward later placed such significance on Winchester, to establish a royal family mausoleum with no reference to Wimborne.

74. *Laws of Alfred*, #8, Whitelock, *EHD*, p. 375.

75. Williams, *Kingship and Government*, p. 104.

76. Barlow, *The Godwins*, p. 53 and n. 23.
77. Ruth Richardson, 'Scandal in the Nunnery', in *Absolute Herefordshire*. blancheparry.co.uk/articles/ruth_out_about/absolute_hereford/2012/absolute_hereford_october/absolute_hereford_october.pdf.
78. William of Malmesbury, *Gesta Pontificum Anglorum*, p. 95.
79. Thacker, *Kings, Saints and Monasteries*, p. 7 says that the granddaughter of Penda i.e. the daughter of Wilburh, 'has not been disentangled from that of her more famous namesake at Chich.'
80. See Blair, 'Osgyth [St Osgyth, Osyth, Osith]', *ODNB* and Blair, 'Frithuwald's Kingdom and the Origins of Surrey', in Bassett, *The Origins of Anglo-Saxon Kingdoms*, p. 106; and *ECWM*, pp. 182-3.
81. Roger of Wendover, *Flowers of History*, pp. 314-15.
82. See Lancaster, *The Forged Charters of Coventry*, especially p. 122.
83. Roffe, *Hereward and the Barony of Bourne*, n. 13: Michel, *Chroniques Anglo-Normandes Rouen*.
84. Williams, 'Godgifu [Godiva]', *ODNB*.
85. Roger of Wendover, *Flowers of History*, pp. 282-3.
86. Williams, *The Ill-Counselled King*, p. 54 for more details; William of Malmesbury, *Chronicle of the Kings of England*, p. 185.
87. Williams, *The Ill-Counselled King*, p. 40 who points out that the *Encomium*, for example, was commissioned abroad.
88. Hart, *Historia et cartularium Monasterii Sancti Petri Gloucestriae: Volume 1*, p. lxvi.

Fair, but not Weak

1. Stenton, *Anglo-Saxon England*, p. 162.
2. Hollis, *Anglo-Saxon Women and the Church*, p. 215, n. 46 citing J.L. Nelson.
3. Women were 'oath-worthy' and could defend themselves on oath; conversely they were also held legally accountable: S 926 documents that a woman named Æthelflæd forfeited land in Huntingdonshire because she had aided her exiled brother.
4. Klein, *Ruling Women*, p. 170, n. 20, citing *Encomium* and Keynes, *Diplomas of Æthelred the Unready*.

Appendix

1. 'The cases which Bede has made famous are Æthelthryth at Ely (in 695), but we also know that the relics of two abbesses of Minster-in-Thanet, Mildrith and Eadburh, had been translated into different churches, presumably for special veneration, by 748 and 804 respectively.' Blair, *The Church in Anglo-Saxon Society*, p. 145 (n. 36 *HE*, iv, 19 and *HE*, iv, 30, S 91 and S 160); Hollis, *Anglo-Saxon Women and the Church*, pp. 59-61.

2. Thacker, 'Dynastic Monasteries and Family Cults', p. 250.

3. Ridyard, *The Royal Saints of Anglo-Saxon England*, p. 195.

4. Bartlett, *The Miracles of St Æbbe of Coldingham*, p. xxvii.

5. For an in-depth examination of the royal cults of Ely, see Ridyard, *The Royal Saints of Anglo-Saxon England*, p. 176*ff.*

6. Blair, *The Church in Anglo-Saxon Society*, p. 146, n. 39; *Life of Wilfrid*, Ch 59; *HE*, iv, 23; *Peterborough Chronicle of Hugh Candidus*, p. 64.

7. *HE*, iv, 10; Hollis, *Anglo-Saxon Women and the Church*, pp. 109-112.

8. See Thacker, *Kings, Saints and Monasteries*, n. 22 for discussion on possible location of *Werberging wic*; Bradshaw, *Goscelin, The Life of Werburge*, Line 937, p. 163.

9. See Ward, 'Edward the Elder and the Re-establishment of Chester', in Higham & Hill (eds), *Edward the Elder*, pp. 164-5 and 169.

10. This might suggest that she did not, in fact, die in childbirth but was repudiated and lived for some time after her marriage had been dissolved – see Part IV.

11. Ridyard, *The Royal Saints of Anglo-Saxon England*, pp. 25-35.

12. Bartlett, *The Miracles of St Æbbe of Coldingham*, p. xxxviii.

Bibliography

Abrams, Lesley, 'King Edgar and the Men of the Danelaw' from Donal Scragg (ed), *Edgar King of the English 959–975,* (Boydell Press, Woodbridge, 2008)

Allott, Stephen, *Alcuin of York,* (Ebor Press, York, 1974)

Backhouse, J., D.H. Turner and Leslie Webster (eds), *The Golden Age of Anglo-Saxon Art 966–1066*, (British Museum Publications, London, 1984)

Bailey, Keith, 'The Middle Saxons' from Steven Bassett, *The Origins of the Anglo-Saxon Kingdoms*, (Leicester University Press, Leicester, 1989)

Bailey, Maggie, 'Ælfwynn, Second Lady of the Mercians' from N.J. Higham and D.H. Hill (eds) *Edward the Elder,* (Routledge, Abingdon, 2001)

Barlow, Frank, *The Life of King Edward the Confessor*, (Thomas Nelson & Sons, London & Edinburgh, 1962)

Barlow, Frank, *The Feudal Kingdom of England 1042–1216,* (Longman Group Ltd., London, 1980)

Barlow, Frank, *The Godwins,* (Routledge, Abingdon, 2002)

Bartlett, Robert, *The Miracles of St Æbbe of Coldingham and St Margaret of Scotland*, (Clarendon Press, Oxford, 2003)

Bassett, Steven, 'In Search of the Origins of Anglo-Saxon Kingdoms' from Steven Bassett (ed), *The Origins of the Anglo-Saxon Kingdoms*, (Leicester University Press, Leicester, 1989)

Baxter, Stephen, *The Earls of Mercia: Lordship and Power in Later Anglo-Saxon England,* (Oxford University Press, Oxford, 2007)

Blair, John, 'Frithuwald's Kingdom and the Origins of Surrey' from Steven Bassett (ed), *The Origins of the Anglo-Saxon Kingdoms,* (Leicester University Press, Leicester, 1989)

Blair, John, *The Church in Anglo-Saxon Society*, (Oxford University Press, Oxford, 2005)

Bolton, Timothy, 'Ælfgifu of Northampton: Cnut the Great's "Other Woman"' from Michael Jones (ed), *Nottingham Medieval Studies Vol LI*, (Nottingham University Press, Nottingham, 2007)

Brooks, Nicholas, 'The Formation of the Mercian Kingdom' from Steven Bassett (ed), *The Origins of the Anglo-Saxon Kingdoms,* (Leicester University Press, Leicester, 1989)

Cambell, Alistair and Simon Keynes (eds), *Encomium Emmæ Reginæ*, (Cambridge University Press, Cambridge, 1998)

Charles-Edwards, Thomas, 'Early Medieval Kingships in the British Isles' from Steven Bassett (ed), *The Origins of the Anglo-Saxon Kingdoms,* (Leicester University Press, Leicester, 1989)

Chibnall, Marjorie (ed & trans), *The Gesta Guillelmi of William of Poitiers,* (Oxford University Press, Oxford, 1998)

Chibnall, Marjorie (ed & trans), *The Ecclesiastical History of Orderic Vitalis: Volume II: Books III & IV: Bks.3 & 4 Vol 2,* (Oxford University Press, Oxford, 1969/1999)

Coatsworth, Elizabeth, 'The Embroideries from the Tomb of St Cuthbert' from N.J. Higham and D.H. Hill (eds), *Edward the Elder*, (Routledge, Abingdon, 2001)

Colgrave, Bertram (trans), *Felix's Life of St Guthlac,* (Cambridge University Press, Cambridge, 1985)

Crossley-Holland, Kevin, *The Anglo-Saxon World,* (Boydell Press, Woodbridge, 1982/2002)

Darlington, R.R. and P. McGurk (eds), Jennifer Bray (trans), *The Chronicle of John of Worcester,* (Clarendon Press, Oxford, 1995)

Duffus Hardy, Thomas and Charles Martin Trice (eds), *Lestorie des Engles Solum la Translacion Maistre Geffrei Gaimar Vol 2 Translation,* (Cambridge University Press, Cambridge, 1889/2012)

Dugdale, William, *Monasticon Anglicanum, or the History of the Ancient Abbies, and other Monasteries, Hospitals, Cathedral and Collegiate Churches in England and Wales,* (Keble, 1693/Forgotten Books, London, 2015)

Dumville, David, 'The Anglian Collection of Royal Genealogies and Regnal Lists' from Peter Clemoes (ed), *Anglo-Saxon England Volume 5,* (Cambridge University Press, Cambridge, 1976)

Dumville, David, 'The Origins of Northumbria: Some Aspects of the British Background' from Steven Bassett (ed), *The Origins of the Anglo-Saxon Kingdoms,* (Leicester University Press, Leicester, 1989)

Fairweather, Janet (trans), *Liber Eliensis,* (Boydell Press, Woodbridge, 2005)

Fell, Christine, *Women in Anglo-Saxon England*, (Colonnade/British Museum Publications, London, 1984)

Finberg, H.P.R., *The Early Charters of the West Midlands,* (Leicester University Press, Leicester, 1972)

Fisher, D.J.V., *The Anglo-Saxon Age,* (Longman, Harlow, 1973)

Fletcher, Richard, *Roman Britain & Anglo-Saxon England 55BC–AD1066,* (Stackpole, Mechanicsburg, 1989)

Fletcher, Richard, *Bloodfeud: Murder and Revenge in Anglo-Saxon England,* (BCA by arrangement with Allen Lane, Penguin Press, London, 2002)

Foot, Sarah, *Athelstan, The First King of England,* (Yale University Press, New Haven, 2012)

Forester, Thomas (trans & ed) *The Chronicle of Henry of Huntingdon,* (Bohn, London, 1853/Nabu Public Domain Reprints)

Garmonsway, G.N. (trans), *The Anglo-Saxon Chronicle,* (JM. Dent & Sons, London, 1984)

Giles, J.A. (trans), William of Malmesbury, *Chronicle of the Kings of England,* (Bohn, London, 1847/Forgotten Books, 2015)

Giles, J.A. (trans), Roger of Wendover, *Flowers of History,* (Bohn, London, 1849/Forgotten Books, 2012)

Hart, Cyril, 'Athelstan 'Half-King' and his Family' from Peter Clemoes (ed), *Anglo-Saxon England Volume 2,* (Cambridge University Press, Cambridge, 1973)

Hart, C.R., *The Early Charters of Northern England and the North Midlands,* (Leicester University Press, Leicester, 1975)

Hart, William Henry (ed), *Historia et cartularium Monasterii Sancti Petri Gloucestriae: Volume 1*, (Cambridge University Press, Cambridge, 2012)

Herbert, Kathleen, *Peace-Weavers & Shield-Maidens: Women in Early English Society*, (Anglo-Saxon Books, Bury St Edmunds, 1997)

Hill, Paul, *The Age of Athelstan: Britain's Forgotten History,* (Tempus, Stroud, 2004)

Hollis, Stephanie, *Anglo-Saxon Women and the Church,* (Boydell Press, Woodbridge, 1992)

Hough, Carole, 'Women and the Law in Seventh-Century England' from Michael Jones (ed), *Nottingham Medieval Studies Vol LI*, (Nottingham University Press, Nottingham, 2007)

Hoyt, Bill (ed), J.A. Giles (trans), *Ethelwerd's Chronicle: From the Beginning of the World to 975AD by Fabius Ethelwerd*, (Kindle Edition)

Humble, Richard, *The Fall of Saxon England,* (BCA by arrangement with Arthur Barker Ltd, London, 1975)

Insley, Charles, 'The Family of Wulfric Spott: An Anglo-Saxon Mercian Marcher Dynasty?' from David Roffe (ed), *The English and their Legacy 900–1200: Essays in Honour of Ann Williams,* (Boydell Press, Woodbridge, 2012)

John, Eric, 'The End of Anglo-Saxon England' from J. Campbell (ed) *The Anglo-Saxons,* (Penguin Books, London, 1991)

Johnson South, Ted, *Historia de Sancto Cuthberto,* (Boydell & Brewer, Woodbridge, 2002)

Key, Michael John, *Edward the Elder*, (Amberley, Stroud, 2019)

Keynes, S. and Michael Lapidge, *Alfred the Great,* (Penguin Books, London, 1983)

Keynes, Simon, 'Edward, King of the Anglo-Saxons' from N.J. Higham and D.H. Hill (eds), *Edward the Elder*, (Routledge, Abingdon, 2001)

Kirby D.P., *The Earliest English Kings,* (Routledge, Abingdon, 1992)

Klein, Stacy, S., *Ruling Women: Queenship and Gender in Anglo-Saxon Literature*, (Notre Dame Press, Indiana, 2006)

Lancaster, Joan C., *The Coventry Forged Charters: A Reconsideration*, Historical Research Volume 27, Issue 76, pages 113–140, November 1954

Lapidge, Michael and Michael Herren (trans), *Aldhelm: The Prose Works*, (D.S. Brewer, Woodbridge, 1979)

Lapidge, Michael (trans & ed), Byrhtferth of Ramsey, *The Lives of St Oswald and St Ecgwine,* (Oxford University Press, Oxford, 2010)

Lapidge, Michael, John Blaire, Simon Keynes and David Scragg (eds), *The Blackwell Encyclopaedia of Anglo-Saxon England*, (Blackwell Publishing, Maldon & Oxford, 1999, 2001)

Lawson, M.K. *Cnut: England's Viking King,* (Tempus, Stroud, 2004)

Leahy, Kevin, *Anglo-Saxon Crafts,* (Tempus, Stroud, 2003)

Levison, Wilhelm, *England and the Continent in the Eighth Century: The Ford Lectures 1943*, (Clarendon Press, Oxford, 1946)

Love, Rosalind C. (ed & trans), *Three Eleventh-Century Anglo-Latin Saints' Lives: Vita S Birini, Vita et Miracula S Kenelmi, Vita S Rumwoldi,* (Clarendon Press, Oxford, 1996)

Love, Rosalind C. (ed & trans), *Goscelin of Saint-Bertin: The Hagiography of the Female Saints of Ely,* (Clarendon/Oxford University Press, Oxford, 2004)

Lund, Niels, 'King Edgar and the Danelaw' from *Medieval Scandinavian Studies 9*, 1976

Maund, Kari, *The Welsh Kings,* (Tempus, Stroud, 2000)

McClure, Judith and Roger Collins (eds), *Bede: The Ecclesiastical History of the English People,* (Oxford University Press, Oxford, 1994)

Mellows, Charles, and William Thomas Mellows (eds), *The Peterborough Chronicle of Hugh Candidus,* (Peterborough Museum Society, Peterborough, 1980)

Miller, Molly, 'The Dates of Deira' from Clemoes, P. (ed), *Anglo-Saxon England Volume 8,* (Cambridge University Press, Cambridge, 1979)

Morris, Christopher J., *Marriage and Murder in Eleventh-Century Northumbria,* (Borthwick Institute Publications, York, 1992)

Nelson, Janet, 'The First Use of the Second Anglo-Saxon *Ordo*' from Julia Barrow and Andrew Wareham (eds), *Myth, Rulership, Church and Charters: Essays in Honour of Nicholas Brooks,* (Routledge, Abingdon, 2016)

Newark, Tim, *Women Warlords*, (Blandford, London, 1989)

Owen, Gale R., 'Wynflæd's Wardrobe' from Clemoes, Peter (ed), *Anglo-Saxon England Volume 8*, (Cambridge University Press, Cambridge, 1979)

Owen-Crocker, Gale R., *Dress in Anglo-Saxon England,* (Boydell Press, Woodbridge, 2004)

Parker, Eleanor, *Beyond the Warrior Queen*, History Today Magazine, (September, 2018)

Preest, David (trans), William of Malmesbury, *Gesta Pontificum Anglorum,* (Boydell Press, Woodbridge, 2002)

Pretty, Kate, 'Defining the Magonsæte' from Bassett, Steven (ed), *The Origins of the Anglo-Saxon Kingdoms,* (Leicester University Press, Leicester, 1989)

Ridyard, Susan J., *The Royal Saints of Anglo-Saxon England: A Study of West Saxon and East Anglian Cults*, (Cambridge University Press, Cambridge, 1988)

Robertson, A.J., *Anglo-Saxon Charters,* (Cambridge University Press, Cambridge, 1956)

Rollason, D.W., 'The Cults of Murdered Royal Saints in Anglo-Saxon England', from Peter Clemoes (ed), *Anglo-Saxon England Volume 11,* (Cambridge University Press, Cambridge, 1983)

Rollason, D.W., *The Mildrith Legend: A Study in Early Medieval Hagiography in England*, (Leicester University Press, Leicester, 1982)

Ronay, Gabriel, *The Lost King of England,* (Boydell Press, Woodbridge, 1989)

Rowley, Sharon M., *The Old English Version of Bede's Historia Ecclesiastica,* (D.S. Brewer, Cambridge, 2011)

Sawyer, P.H., 'The Charters of Burton Abbey and the Unification of England' from *Northern History 10*, (1975)

Sharp, Sheila, 'The West Saxon Tradition of Dynastic Marriage' from N.J. Higham and D.H. Hill (eds), *Edward the Elder*, (Routledge, Abingdon, 2001)

Sims-Williams, Patrick, *Religion and Literature in Western England 600–800*, (Cambridge University Press, Cambridge, 1990)

Stafford, Pauline, *Queen Emma and Queen Edith,* (Blackwell Publishers, Oxford, 1997)

Stafford, Pauline, 'Political Women in Mercia, Eighth to Early Tenth Centuries' from Michelle P. Brown and Carol Ann Farr (eds), *Mercia: An Anglo-Saxon Kingdom in Europe,* (Leicester University Press, Leicester, 2001)

Stafford, Pauline, 'The Annals of Æthelflæd: Annals, History and Politics in Early Tenth-Century England' from Julia Barrow and Andrew Wareham (eds), *Myth, Rulership, Church and Charters: Essays in Honour of Nicholas Brooks,* (Routledge, Abingdon, 2016)

Stenton, Frank, 'The Historical Bearing of Place-Name Studies: The Place of Women in Anglo-Society' from Doris Mary Stenton (ed), *Preparatory to Anglo-Saxon England: Being the Collected Papers of Frank Merry Stenton,* (Oxford University Press, Oxford, 1970)

Stenton, Frank, *Anglo-Saxon England,* (Oxford University Press, Oxford, 1971/1989))

Stenton, Doris Mary, *The English Woman in History*, (Allen & Unwin, London, 1957)

Stevinson, Jo and John Stevinson, *Qwenfryth, Abbess of Winchcombe*, (Booklet printed by the Friends of St Peter's, Winchcombe, 2015)

Symons, Thomas (trans), *Regularis Concordia,* (Oxford University Press, Oxford, 1983)

Telford, Lynda, *Women in Medieval England*, (Amberley, Stroud, 2018)

Thacker, Alan, 'Kings, Saints and Monasteries in Pre-Viking Mercia' from *Midland History Vol 10, Issue 1* (Phillimore, Felpham, 1985)

Thacker, Alan, 'Dynastic Monasteries and Family Cults: Edward the Elder's Sainted Kindred' from N.J. Higham and D.H. Hill (eds), *Edward the Elder*, (Routledge, Abingdon, 2001)

Thompson, Victoria, *Dying and Death in Later Anglo-Saxon England*, (Boydell Press, Woodbridge, 2004)

Timmer, B.J., *Judith*, (Methuen & Co., London, 1952)

Turner, Andrew and Bernad J. Muir, *Eadmer of Canterbury: The Lives of Saints Oda, Dunstan & Oswald*, (Clarendon Oxford University Press, Oxford, 2006)

Wainwright, F.T., 'Æthelflæd Lady of the Mercians' from Peter Clemoes (ed), *The Anglo-Saxons: Studies in Some Aspects of their History and Culture Presented to Bruce Dickens,* (Bowes & Bowes, London, 1959)

Wallace-Hadrill, J.M., *Early Germanic Kingship in England and on the Continent,* (Oxford University Press, Oxford, 1971)

Ward, Simon, 'Edward the Elder and the Re-establishment of Chester' from N.J. Higham and D.H. Hill (eds), *Edward the Elder*, (Routledge, Abingdon, 2001)

Watt, D.E.R. (ed), *A History Book for Scots: Selections from Scotichronicon by Walter Bower*, (John Donald/Birlinn, Edinburgh, 2017)

Webb, J.F. and D.H. Farmer, 'Eddius Stephanus: Life of Wilfrid' from *The Age of Bede,* (Penguin Books, London, 1983/1998)

Whitehead Annie, 'In Search of Dunmail' from *Cumbria Magazine Vol 66, No 1,* (April, 2016)

Whitehead, Annie, 'Rioting in the Harlot's Embrace: Matrimony and Sanctimony in Anglo-Saxon England' from *Sexuality and its Impact on History: The British Stripped Bare,* (Pen & Sword, Barnsley, 2018)

Whitehead, Annie, *Mercia: The Rise and Fall of a Kingdom*, (Amberley, Stroud, 2018)

Whitelock, Dorothy, *Anglo-Saxon Wills,* (Cambridge University Press, Cambridge, 1930/2011)

Whitelock, Dorothy, *English Historical Documents Volume I c. 500–1042,* (Oxford University Press, Oxford, 1955)

Whitelock, Dorothy, *The Will of Æthelgifu*, (Lord Rennell edition, Oxford, presented to the Roxburghe Club, 1968)

Williams, Ann, A.P. Smyth and D.P. Kirby, *A Biographical Dictionary of Dark Age Britain: England, Scotland and Wales, c.500– c. 1050,* (B.A. Seaby, London, 1991)

Williams, Ann, *Kingship and Government in Pre-Conquest England 500–1066,* (Macmillan Press, Basingstoke, 1999)

Williams, Ann, *Æthelred the Unready: The Ill-Counselled King,* (Hambledon, London, 2003)

Williams, Ann, 'Wills in Pre-Conquest England', from *Foundations (Journal of the Foundation for Medieval Genealogy)* 9 (2017), pp. 3-20 – personal copy

Williams, Ann, 'On the Spindle Side: The Kinswomen of Earl Godwine of Wessex' from David Roffe (ed), *Festschrift for Hirokazu Tsurushima*, (No title for the volume at time of publication – personal pre-publication copy)

Williams, Ann, 'Names, Status and Service in the Will of Wynflæd (S 1539)' from Steven Bassett and Alison Spedding (eds), *Duncan Probert's Memorial Volume* (No title for the volume at time of publication – personal pre-publication copy)

Wood, Michael, 'Wynflaed's Will', *History Today Magazine,* (November, 2018)

Woolf, Alex, 'View from the West: An Irish Perspective on West Saxon Dynastic Practice' from N.J. Higham and D.H. Hill (eds), *Edward the Elder*, (Routledge, Abingdon, 2009)

Wormald, Patrick, 'The Age of Offa and Alcuin' from Campbell J. (ed), *The Anglo-Saxons,* (Penguin Books, London, 1991)

Yorke, Barbara, *Kings and Kingdoms of Early Anglo-Saxon England,* (Routledge, Abingdon, 1990)

Yorke, Barbara, 'Edward as Ætheling' from N.J. Higham and D.H. Hill (eds), *Edward the Elder,* (Routledge, Abingdon, 2001)

Yorke, Barbara, 'The Women in Edgar's Life' from Scragg, Donald, (ed), *Edgar King of the English, 959–975,* (Boydell Press, Woodbridge, 2008)

Online Sources:

Bradshaw, Henry, the Life of St Werburge, archive.org

Bristol University, bris.ac.uk/news/2010/7073.html

British Library, blogs.bl.uk/digitisedmanuscripts/2016/03/coronation-gospels-in-edinburgh.html

British Library, blogs.bl.uk/digitisedmanuscripts/2017/06/making-a-good-impression.html

Chronicon abbatiae de Evesham, ad annum 1418 by Evesham Abbey, Dominic, William Dunn Macray, Thomas de Marleberge, archive.org

Clerk of Oxford, aclerkofoxford.blogspot.com/2018/09/domne-eafes-deer.html

Dig Ventures. Com, digventures.com/2018/02/radiocarbon-dating-confirms-skeletons-found-in-vicarage-garden-are-probably-viking/

Dig Ventures. Com, digventures.com/coldingham-priory/timeline/diary/the-radiocarbon-dates-are-in

Dig Ventures. Com, digventures.com/coldingham-priory/timeline/types/videos/

Dig Ventures. Com, digventures.com/coldingham-priory/timeline/diary/the-radiocarbon-dates-are-in/

Epistolæ, epistolae.ctl.columbia.edu/letters

Forester, Thomas, *The chronicle of Florence of Worcester with the two continuations; comprising annals of English history, from the departure of the Romans to the reign of Edward I* (London: H.G. Bohn 1854), archive.org

Giles, J.A., (trans) Nennius, *Historia Brittonum*, yorku.ca/inpar/nennius_giles.pdf

Greer Fein, Susanna, *Art. 116, De martirio sancti Wistani* University of Rochester, rochester.edu/teams/text/fein-harley2253-volume-3-article-116

Hearne T, *Hemingi chartularium ecclesiæ Wigorniensis, descripsit ediditque Volume 2,* play.google.com/store/books

Irish Archaeological and Celtic Society, Dublin; MacFirbis, Duald, O'Donovan, John, *Annals of Ireland. Three fragments, copied from ancient sources by Dubhaltach MacFirbisigh; and edited, with a translation and notes, from a manuscript preserved in the Burgundian Library at Brussels* (Dublin: Irish Archaeological and Celtic Society, 1860), archive.org

Kessler, Peter, and Dawson, Edward, '*Mercia's British Alliance*', historyfiles.co.uk/FeaturesBritain/EnglandMercia01.htm

King's College London & University of Cambridge, Prosopography of Anglo-Saxon England, http://www.pase.ac.uk/index.html

King's College London & University of Cambridge, The Electronic Sawyer, http://www.esawyer.org.uk/about/index.html

Kornbluth, kornbluthphoto.com/images/Balthild7.jpg

Kylie, Edward, *The English Correspondence of St Boniface,* Microform, archive.org

Liebermann, Felix, *Die Heiligen Englands: Angelsächsisch und Lateinisch* (Hanover: Hahn 1889), archive.org

Miller, Sean, Anglo-Saxon Charters (Anglo-Saxons.net), http://www.anglo-saxons.net/hwaet/

Norwich, City of Stories, cityofstories.co.uk/the-seal-matrix-an-ancient-tale-of-romance

Parry, Blanche/Richardson, Ruth: 'Scandal in the Nunnery', blancheparry.co.uk/articles/ruth_out_about/absolute_hereford/2012/absolute_hereford_october/absolute_hereford_october.pdf

Rabin, Andrew, 'Female Advocacy and Royal Protection in Tenth-Century England: The Legal Career of Queen Ælfthryth' from *Speculum Vol 84 No 2*, (University of Chicago Press, Chicago, 2009), https://www.jstor.org/stable/20466541

Roffe, David, 'Hereward "the Wake" and the Barony of Bourne: a Reassessment of a Fenland Legend' from *Lincolnshire History and Archaeology* 29 (1994) 7-10, http://www.roffe.co.uk/articles/hereward.htm

Royal Irish Academy; Maguire, Cathal MacMaghnusa, O'Cassidy, Rory, Hennessy, W. M. (William Maunsell), MacCarthy, Bartholomew, *Annala Uladh = Annals of Ulster otherwise, Annala Senait, Annals of Senat: A Chronicle of Irish Affairs* (DubliHM Stationery Office, 1897-1902), archive. org

Source Books, sourcebooks.fordham.edu/basis/gregory-hist.asp#book4

Telegraph, telegraph.co.uk/science/2018/11/27/anglo-saxon-burial-site-shows-dark-ages-enlightened-times

Turgot, *Life of Margaret*, archive.org

The Annals of Tigernach, University College Cork Digitised Manuscripts, celt.ucc.ie//published/T100002A/index.html

Wehling, Alice, "Royal Daughters in Anglo-Saxon England." (2017), digitalrepository.unm.edu/hist_etds/206

Whitehead, Annie, *The Attack on Llangorse,* https://englishhistoryauthors.blogspot.co.uk/2016/06/the-attack-on-llangorse-19th-june-ad916.html

Whitehead, Annie, *Anglo-Saxon Attitudes*, anniewhitehead2.blogspot. com/2018/10/anglo-saxon-attitudes-transcript-of.html

Whitehead, Annie, *Captive Nuns*, anniewhitehead2.blogspot. com/2018/08/captive-nuns.html

Whitehead, Annie, *The Æthelflæd Paradox*, anniewhitehead2.blogspot. com/2018/07/the-thelfld-paradox-my-tamworth-litfest.html

Index

Acha of Deira, 1-4, 8-11, 26, 173n70

Adderbury, Oxon, 78

Adomnan, abbot, 27

Æbbe, abbess, 3, 10, 25-7, 29-30, 154, 160, 165, 173n70

Æbbe, daughter of Eormenred of Kent, 38, 176n27

Ælfflæd, abbess, daughter of Oswiu of Northumbria, 12, 15, 18-19, 21-3, 29, 133, 138, 154, 161, 172n59, 173n67

Ælfflæd, daughter of Ceolwulf, wife of Wigmund, abbess, 55-7, 59, 134

Ælfflæd, daughter of Offa of Mercia, 49-50

Ælfflæd, testatrix, wife of Ealdorman Byrhtnoth, 139

Ælfflæd, wife of Edward the Elder, 72-7, 79, 157, 183-4n13

Ælfgar, ealdorman, 79

Ælfgar, earl of Mercia, 109, 118-19, 151

Ælfgar, landholder at Moredon, 145

Ælfgifu, daughter of Edward the Elder, 74-5

Ælfgifu, daughter of Godwine, 120

Ælfgifu of Northampton, xv, 104-06, 108-11, 113, 144-5, 157, 189n21

Ælfgifu of Shaftesbury, wife of Edward the Elder, 79-80, 141, 143, 163

Ælfgifu, wife of Ælfgar of Mercia, 109

Ælfgifu, wife of King Eadwig, 81-5, 91, 95

Ælfgifu, wife of Wulfgeat, 145

Ælfgifu of York, wife of Æthelred II, 97-9, 185n31

Ælfgifu, her daughter, 101, 105

Ælfheah, archbishop of Canterbury, 108, 113

Ælfhelm, earl of Northumbria, 101-04, 145

Ælfhere, ealdorman of Mercia, 88, 94, 101, 119, 146

Ælfswith, foster mother, 99, 143

Ælfthryth, daughter of Alfred the Great, 60-1, 129

Ælfthryth, daughter of Offa of Mercia, 48

Ælfthryth, wife of Cenwulf of Mercia, 52

Ælfthryth, wife of King Edgar, xi, xv, 85-8, 90-100, 113, 138-40,

142-3, 146, 156-7, 188n80, 188-9n6

Ælfweard, son of Edward the Elder, 68, 71-2, 74, 76, 79, 98, 183n5

Ælfwine, son of Oswiu of Northumbria, 16, 21

Ælfwynn, daughter of Æthelflæd, 66-9

Ælfwynn, religious woman, 69, 186n40

Ælfwynn, wife of Athelstan Half-king, 142-3

Ælle of Deira, 2

Æthelbald, king of Mercia, 45, 136

Æthelbald, king of Wessex, 128-9

Æthelberht, brother of Domneva, 39, 41

Æthelberht, ealdorman, 97

Æthelberht, king of East Anglia, 47-8

Æthelberht, king of Kent, ix, 4-6, 33-4, 43, 126-7, 129, 167nn9,12

Æthelburh, abbess of Barking, 174n2

Æthelburh, abbess of Fladbury, 47-8, 178n11, 179n15

Æthelburh, daughter of King Anna, 31-3

Æthelburh, daughter of King Offa, 47-9, 179n15

Æthelburh, queen, xi, 132

Æthelburh, St, 161

Æthelburh 'Tate', wife of Edwin of Northumbria, xv, 4-9, 33-4, 60, 126-7, 155, 168n22

Æthelflæd of Damerham, 79-80, 139

Æthelflæd *Eneda*, 85-7, 90, 186n50

Æthelflæd, Lady of the Mercians, x, xi, xvi, 51, 60-9, 82, 101, 133, 155, 157, 163, 181nn50,52, 182n58

Æthelflæd the White, beneficiary, 85, 186n50

Æthelfrith of Bernicia, 2-5, 8-10, 26, 131, 167n8, 173n75

Æthelfrith, ealdorman, 85

Æthelgifu, beneficiary, 85

Æthelgifu, daughter of Alfred the Great, 60-1, 147, 181n42

Æthelgifu, testatrix, 140-2

Æthelhelm, atheling, 73, 75

Æthelhelm, ealdorman of Wiltshire, 73-5

Æthelhild, daughter of Edward the Elder, 74-5

Æthelhun, son of Æthelburh 'Tate', 7

Æthelred, brother of Domneva, 39-41

Æthelred, king of Mercia, 14-15, 36-9, 42, 133, 166n6, 170n43, 171nn49,50

Æthelred, king of Northumbria, 48-9

Æthelred, king of Wessex, 58-9, 61, 82, 181n40

Æthelred, Lord of Mercia, 55, 62-4, 66-8, 181n50

Æthelred *Mucil*, 59

Æthelred II, the 'Unready', 87-8, 92, 95-107, 109-10, 113, 122, 139-40, 145-6, 151-2, 157, 164, 188-9n6

Æthelric of East Anglia, 18, 24, 171

Æthelswith, seamstress, 142

Æthelswith, wife of Burgred of
    Mercia, 58-9, 138, 180n37,
    181nn40,50

Æthelthryth, daughter of
    Æthelburh 'Tate', 7

Æthelthryth, St, wife of Ecgfrith
    of Northumbria, abbess, 24-7,
    29-37, 131, 146, 155, 160-1,
    172n61, 173n76, 198n1
    and see Tawdry

Æthelwalh, king of the South
    Saxons, 134, 148

Æthelweard, son of Alfred the
    Great, 60-1, 76, 181n47

Æthelweard, chronicler, 82, 85,
    152, 163

Æthelwine, ealdorman of East
    Anglia, 143

Æthelwold, cousin of Edward the
    Elder, 63-4, 73, 82, 146-7, 183n8

Æthelwold, ealdorman of East
    Anglia, 90

Æthelwold, St, 80, 85, 89-90,
    92-4, 96-7, 99, 101, 161, 164
    see also Regularis Concordia

Æthelwulf of the *Gaini*, 55, 60,
    82, 185n37

Æthelwulf, king of Wessex, 82,
    128, 138, 194nn11, 12

Æthilheard of the *Hwicce*, 14-15

Aidan, bishop, 18-19, 172n57

Ailred of Rievaulx, 97, 123

Alcuin of York, 46, 48-9, 178n8

Aldfrith, king of Northumbria, 13,
    16-17, 22-3, 27, 156, 159, 161,
    170n41

Aldhelm, abbot of Malmesbury,
    17, 137, 172n60, 177n46
    see also De Virginitate

Alfred the Great, viii, xv, 50-2, 55,
    57-63, 71-6, 78, 81-2, 100-01,
    128-9, 138, 146-7, 154, 180n39
    Life of, *see* Asser

Alfred, son of Emma and Æthelred
    II, 100, 110-11, 113, 116-17

Alhflæd, daughter of Oswiu of
    Northumbria, 12-14, 167n9,
    170nn41, 44

Alhfrith, son of Oswiu of
    Northumbria, 12-13, 18-19,
    21, 23, 29, 153, 170n41,
    172n61

Anglo-Saxon Chronicle (ASC), viii,
    xi, 3, 13, 17, 32, 39, 48, 50-1, 55,
    60, 62-3, 72, 87, 100, 105-06,
    109-10, 112, 116, 118, 124, 132-3,
    144-8, 150, 163, 170n43, 194n11

Anna, king of East Anglia, 18, 24,
    31-3

Annals of Æthelflæd – *see*
    Mercian Register

Ashingdon, battle of, 105-06

Asser, (*Life* of Alfred), 50-1, 58-62,
    65, 73, 128, 138, 156, 192n11

Athelstan, atheling, 97-100, 102,
    140, 143, 188n6

Athelstan Half-king, 90, 142, 185n37

Athelstan, king, 68, 70-2, 74-7, 79,
    87, 89, 164, 182n64, 183nn4,5

Athelstan Rota, ealdorman, 79-80

Balthard, 137

Balthild, St, queen, xi, 129-31
    194n19

Life of 129-30
and see Seal-matrix
Bamburgh, 2, 12, 105-06, 131
Bardney, abbey, xiii, 15, 67,
  173n67, 181-2n52
Barking, abbey, xiii, 17-18, 22,
  86, 95, 138, 162, 174n2
Bebba, xi, 2-3, 131-2
Bede, viii, 2-10, 12-13, 15-20,
  22, 25-8, 30, 32-3, 35, 39,
  60, 126-7, 130-3, 155-6, 162,
  167nn8,11, 168n19, 169n23,
  170n44, 175nn6,12, 178n8,
  193n8, 198n1
  see also Historia Ecclesiastica
Bedeford, Kent, 47
Beorhtferd, possible son of
  Burgred of Mercia, 58
Beorhtferth, 56-8
Beorhtgyth, 137
Beorhtric, king of West Saxons,
  50-1, 58, 128, 159
Beorhtwulf, 57-8
Berhtwald, possible son of
  Wulfhere of Mercia, 36
Bernicia, 2-4, 8-11, 14, 21-2, 26,
  29, 131, 173nn70,75
Bertha, queen of Kent, 4-5, 37,
  126-9, 131, 167-8nn9, 12,
  193n4
Blinding, 88, 104
  of Ælfgar, 145
  of Alfred, son of Emma, 110
  of Wulfheah and Ufegeat, 101,
    104, 106, 110, 145
  divine:
    of Cwoenthryth, 54
    of Edith, 115

Bolton, Timothy, 105, 190nn27,
  28, 31
Boniface, pope, 7, 168n18
Boniface, St, 17, 42, 134-7
Breguswith, 18
Bretwalda, 4-6, 131, 154, 167n11,
  168n22
Bridgnorth, 64
Bugga – *see* Hæaburh
Burgred, king of Mercia, 57-9, 62,
  138, 180n37, 181n50
Burhs,
  building of, 63-4, 69
  as name element, 133
Byrhtferth of Ramsey, 92, 94-5,
  171n50
Byrhtnoth, ealdorman, 80, 139

Cadwallon of Gwynedd, 8-10,
  41, 119
Cædmon, poet, xiii, 20-1
Canterbury, 120, 176n31
  archdiocese of, xiv, 8, 23, 46-7,
    52-4, 83, 109, 116, 178n9
  Christ Church, 80, 124
Carlisle, 28
Catterick, North Yorks, 49
Cenwalh, king of West Saxons, 132-3
Cenwulf, king of Mercia, 52-6, 60
Ceolred, king of Mercia, 15-16,
  37, 42-3, 45, 136-7
Ceolwulf, king of Mercia, 53, 55-7
Ceolwulf II, king of Mercia, 57,
  59, 62, 180nn34, 37
Charibert, king of the Franks, 126
Charlemagne, emperor, 45, 47,
  49-50
  wife of, 49

Charles the Bald, 128
Charles the Simple, 74
Chelles, 19, 40-1, 130-1
Chester, 63, 66, 150
    abbey, 36-7, 120, 163
Chich, 148-9, 197n79
Childeric, 130
Chippenham, Wilts, 58
Chirbury, 64
Christina, sister of St Margaret, 122
Clofesho, 53, 178n9, 179n28
Cloth – *see* Textiles
Clothar, 130
Clovis II, 130
Cnut, king, ix, xv, 102-11, 113-14,
    116, 118-19, 122, 151, 160,
    164, 190n27, 191n44
Coenred, king of Mercia, 14,
    36, 42
Coinage, 6, 46, 48, 66, 108-09,
    113, 124, 127
Coldingham, abbey, xiii, 25-30, 160
Compiègne, 23
Cookham, monastery, 46-7, 178n9
Corbridge, second battle of, 65
Corfe, 95
Coronations, 72, 74, 86, 92-3, 95,
    107, 121, 128
    see also Ordo
Coventry, 149-51
Crowland, abbey, 48, 143-4
Cudda, monk, 11
Cumbria, 12
Cuthbert, St, xiii, 22, 26, 28, 76
    Life of, xiii, 23, 28
Cuthburh, wife of Aldfrith of
    Northumbria, abbess, 17-18,
    22, 156, 159, 171n52

Cwenburh, wife of Edwin of
    Deira, 4, 167n8
Cwenburh, wife of Mildfrith, 43
Cwoenthryth, abbess, xiv, 52-5,
    60, 159, 179nn27-9
    and see Blinding, divine
Cyneburh, abbess of
    Gloucester, 35
Cyneburh, daughter of Penda, 13,
    45, 153, 170n43
Cyneburh, St, 153
Cyneburh, wife of Oswald of
    Northumbria, 9, 153, 169n30
Cynegyth, wife of Cenwulf of
    Mercia, 52
Cynehelm – *see* Kenelm
Cyneswith, daughter of Penda of
    Mercia, 45, 170n43
Cynethryth, wife of Offa, xiv,
    45-8, 50, 134, 177n3, 178n9
Cynethryth, wife of Wiglaf of
    Mercia, 134, 178n10
Cynewise, wife of Penda of
    Mercia, 12, 45

Danelaw, 61, 98, 103, 105, 110
Deira, 1-3, 8-12, 18, 21-4, 26,
    29, 131, 155, 169nn31, 34,
    172n61, 173n70
Denmark, 105, 107-12, 148
Derby, 64, 182n55
De Virginitate, 17, 42, 137
    see also Aldhelm
Domesday Book, 120, 148,
    195n54
Domne Eafe – *see* Domneva
Domneva, wife of Merewalh,
    abbess, 38-40, 155, 163, 177n38

Double Houses (monasteries), xiii-xiv, 17, 41-2, 47, 53, 147, 154, 159, 162, 172n60

Dover, 116

Dugdale, William, 36

Dunbar, 27

Dunfermline, 123, 125, 165

Dunstan, St, bishop and archbishop, 80-1, 83, 85-6, 88-92, 94, 120, 164, 183n3
Life of, 81, 84, 86

Durham:
cathedral, 72, 76
bishops of, 121, 146

Eadbald, king of Kent, 5-6, 9, 34, 38, 129, 168n15

Eadburh, abbess of Thanet, 42, 134, 136-7, 162-3, 198n1

Eadburh, daughter of Offa, wife of Beorhtric of Wessex, xv, 49-52, 58-9, 128, 154

Eadburh, mother of Ealhswith, 59, 180n39

Eadburh, St, daughter of Edward the Elder, 77-8, 156, 164
Life of, 78, 164

Eadburh, St, daughter of Penda, 149

Eadburh, wife of Wulfhere of Mercia, 35, 135

Eadflæd, daughter of Edward the Elder, 74-6

Eadflæd, noblewoman, 145-6

Eadgifu, abbess of Leominster, 147-8

Eadgifu, daughter of Edward the Elder, 74-5, 183n13

Eadgifu the Fair – *see* Edith Swanneck

Eadgifu, wife of Edward the Elder, 76-83, 91, 94, 157, 184n20, 185nn32, 33, 38
Eadgifu, her daughter, 77

Eadgyth, daughter of Æthelred II, 97, 101, 105

Eadgyth, daughter of Edward the Elder, 74-5

Eadgyth, St, daughter of Penda, 149

Eadmer of Canterbury, 86-7, 94

Eadred, king, 69, 80-1, 89, 143, 185n32

Eadred, son of Æthelred II, 97

Eadric Streona, earl of Mercia, 101-02, 105-06, 149, 152

Eadwig, king, 79, 81-3, 85, 89, 143, 157, 185n36, 186n46, 189n12

Eadwig, son of Æthelred II, 97, 106

Eafe of the *Hwicce*, 133-4, 148, 194n29

Ealdgyth, widow of Morcar, 109

Ealdgyth, widow of Sigeferth, 102

Ealdgyth, wife of Gruffudd of Wales and Harold Godwineson, 119-20

Ealhild, legendary queen, xii

Ealhswith, wife of Alfred the Great, 58-61, 73, 76, 78, 82, 181n41

Ealhswith, wife of Wulfric Spott, 145

Eanflæd, daughter of Edwin, wife of Oswiu of Northumbria, xii, xv, 5, 7-12, 14, 16, 18, 20-1, 23-4, 33, 133, 155-6, 161, 169nn31, 34, 36, 170n41, 173n67

Eanfrith, king of the *Hwicce*, 133, 194n28

Eanfrith, son of Æthelfrith of Bernicia, 3, 8

Eangyth, abbess, 136, 139

Ecgberht, king of Kent, son of Seaxburh, 33-4, 39-40

Ecgberht, king of West Saxons, 50-1, 56, 179n17

Ecgberht, son of Æthelred II, 97

Ecgburh, abbess, 135-6

Ecgburh, East Anglian, 135-6, 195n35

Ecgfrida, wife of Uhtred of Bamburgh, 146

Ecgfrith, king of Mercia, 45-8, 52, 178n8

Ecgfrith, king of Northumbria, 11-12, 15-16, 21-9, 171n49, 172n61, 173n67

Ecgwynn, wife of Edward the Elder, 70-2, 74, 77, 87, 164, 182n1, 183nn3, 4

Eddisbury, 64

Eddius Stephanus, 11, 130

Edgar the atheling, 122-3

Edgar, king, 69, 79, 83-95, 97-100, 142-3, 147, 184n29, 185n38, 186nn42, 50

Edgar, son of Æthelred II, 97-8

Edgar, son of St Margaret, 125

Edith, daughter of Godwine, queen, wife of Edward the Confessor, viii, 100, 114-23, 138, 156-7, 184n21, 192n67
and see Blinding, divine

Edith of Polesworth, St, daughter of Edward the Elder, 72, 164

Edith Swanneck, 120, 192n72

Edith of Wilton, St, daughter of King Edgar, 86-9, 94, 160, 164-5
Life of, 87
and see Seal-matrix

Edmund, infant son of King Edgar, 92, 98, 100

Edmund Ironside, king of Wessex, 97-8, 102-07, 122, 188n6, 189n21

Edmund, his son, 106, 122

Edmund, king of Wessex, 20, 79-81, 89, 139, 141, 143, 161, 184n29, 185nn30, 32

Edmund, son of Harold Godwineson, 120

Education, 19-22, 40-1, 61, 65, 78, 87, 89, 114, 133, 135, 138, 140
and see Literacy

Edward the Confessor, king of England, 100, 103, 107, 110-22, 150-1, 156
Life of, viii, 100, 114-17, 121-2
laws of, 122

Edward the Elder, king of Wessex, 60-1, 63-4, 66-8, 70-9, 82, 90, 146-7, 156-7, 159, 164, 180n39, 182n1, 183n4, 196n73

Edward the Martyr, king of Wessex, 85-9, 91-2, 94-6, 188n82

Edward, son of Edmund Ironside, 106, 122

Edward, son of St Margaret, 125

Edwin of Deira, king of Northumbria, 2-10, 13, 18, 20-1, 33, 126-7, 131, 154-6,

167n8, 168nn15, 22, 169nn31, 34, 173n67

Edwin, earl of Mercia, 118-19, 121, 151

Edwin, priest, 140

Edwin of Wessex, half-brother of Athelstan, 71, 74, 76, 183n5

Elmet, (Leeds) 3, 18, 167n7

Ely, 24, 30

    abbey, xi, xiii, 24-5, 30-7, 84, 95, 107, 110, 142, 160-1, 163, 173n76, 175n12, 198n1

see also Liber Eliensis

Embroidery – *see* Textiles

Emma, queen, viii, 99-103, 105-13, 117, 121-3, 126, 129, 138, 140, 156-7, 164, 189n12, 191n47

    and see Encomium Emmæ Reginæ

Encomium Emmæ Reginæ, viii, 106-07, 109, 111-12, 114, 138, 197n87

    and see Emma

Eorcenberht, king of Kent, 11, 34, 36, 38, 175n12

Eorcongota, daughter of Seaxburh, 31, 33

Eormenburg – *see* Domneva

Eormenhild, wife of Wulfhere of Mercia, 31, 33-9, 155, 160

Eormenred, king of Kent, 38-9

Erchinoald, 129-30

Eustace of Boulogne, 116

Evesham, abbey, 14, 56, 115, 118

Exeter, 63, 101, 120

Faremoutiers-en-Brie, 31, 33

Felix, 143-4

see also Guthlac

Fell, Christine, xi

Fin, Irish princess, 16, 170n41

Finberg H.P.R., 14, 40, 135, 148

Five Boroughs, 64, 182n55, 189n21

Fladbury, abbey, 14-15, 47-9, 133, 178n11, 179nn15, 16

Flanders, 61, 111, 116, 118, 127, 129, 138, 181n42

Florence of Worcester, 10, 20, 25, 38, 71, 150, 167n12

Frankia, (kingdom of the Franks), 4-6, 8, 19, 28, 31, 35, 37, 41, 50, 74, 126-30, 167n9, 168n22, 179n17, 193nn1, 5, 194nn11-2

Frithuwald of Surrey, 148-9

Fulford, battle of, 121

Gaimar, Geoffrey, 90-1

Gainsborough, Lincs, 104

Gilling, 10, 169-70n36

Glastonbury, abbey, 20, 94, 161

Gloucester, 9, 35, 67, 135, 153

Godgifu, daughter of Emma, 100, 113

Godgifu, wife of Leofric of Mercia – See Godiva

Godiva, 149-51

Godwebb, 141

    and see Textiles

Godwine, earl, 109-10, 112, 114, 116-18, 147, 149, 191nn47, 56

Goscelin of St Bertin, 35, 40-1, 86-9, 94-5, 160, 162-5, 175n6

Gospatric, 117

Gregory, pope, 21, 172n59

Gregory of Tours, 126-7

Gruffudd, king of Wales,
119-20, 147
Gunnhild, daughter of Emma,
108-09, 113
Gunnhild, daughter of
Godwine, 114
Gunnhild, daughter of Harold
Godwineson, 120
Gunnhild, wife of Pallig, 152
Guthlac, hermit, 136, 143-4
Life of, 135, 143
and see Felix
Gyrwe, South, 24
Gytha, daughter of Harold
Godwineson, 120
Gytha, wife of Godwine, 109,
114, 116, 120, 147, 191n56

Hackness, xiii, 20, 161
Hæaburh, 136
Hanbury, Staffs, 37
Harald Hardrada, 121
Harold Godwineson, 116-23, 151
Harold, his son by Ealdgyth, 120
Harold Harefoot, 104-05, 108-11, 151
Harthacnut, 108-113
Hartlepool, abbey, xiii, 19, 21
Hastings, battle of, 120-1, 123
Henry I of England, 125
Henry III of Germany, 108
Henry of Huntingdon, 14, 62,
65-6, 95, 125, 132, 150,
152, 167n8
Heptarchy, 1
Hereric, nephew of Edwin of
Deira, 2-3, 18
Hereswith, sister of St Hild,
18-19, 24, 32
Hereward the Wake, 151, 161

Heriot, 139
Hexham, abbey, 27
Hild, St, abbess, xiii, 12, 18-21,
23-4, 29, 54, 133, 154, 161-2,
172nn57, 59
Hildelith, abbess of Barking, 17,
22, 42, 137, 162, 177n46
Hincmar, bishop of Rheims, 128
Historia Brittonum, 7, 131
see also Nennius
Historia Ecclesiastica, 2, 17, 28,
32, 170nn43, 44
see also Bede
Hlothhere, king of Kent, 33-4
Holme, battle of the, 77, 82, 147
Hugh Candidus, 13, 94, 115,
170n43
Hungary, 122-3
Hwicce, 14-15, 35, 45, 52-3,
133-5, 148, 178n11, 181n50

Icanho, 41
Imma, thegn, 33-4
Ine, king of West Saxons, 17, 132,
144, 196n66
Iona, 18, 27, 173n67
Ireland, 118
Iurminburg, wife of Ecgfrith of
Northumbria, 27-8,
154, 176n27

John of Worcester, 48, 56, 85, 97,
101, 105, 116-17, 147
Judith of Flanders, wife of King
Æthelwulf and his son, 59,
127-9, 138, 194n11
Judith of Flanders, wife of Tostig,
116, 118, 129, 131, 194n14
Judith, poem, 65

Kenelm, St, 54-5, 180n31
  Life of, 55
Keynes, Simon, 54
Kirk Hill – *see* St Abbs

Leicester, 64-5, 182n55
Leoba, abbess of
  Tauberbischofsheim, 134-6
Leofgifu, testatrix, 140
Leofric, son of Queen
  Ælfthryth, 90
Leofric, earl of Mercia, 109, 112,
  116-19, 149-51
Leofwine, son of Godwine, 119-20
Leofwine, stepson of Wynflæd,
  146, 196n71
Leominster, 40, 147-8, 177n39
Liber Eliensis, xi, 13, 24, 26, 30,
  32, 34, 36, 79-80, 85, 93,
  142, 160
  see also Ely Abbey
Liber Vitæ
  Lindisfarne, 13
  New Minster, 61, 84, 107
  Reichenau, 51-2
Lindisfarne, 11, 13, 18, 20, 26
  and see Liber Vitæ
Lindsey, 15
Liobsind, abbess, 41
Literacy, xv, 17, 19, 22, 46, 53, 78,
  114, 127, 134-42, 166n11, 172n59
  and see Education
Liudhard, bishop, 127, 193n5
Llanfillo, Brecon, 41
London, 6, 40, 62, 66, 102,
  106-07, 111, 116, 148, 187n67
  bishop of, 174n2
Ludeca, king of Mercia, 56-7
Lyminge, Kent, 9, 169n29

Magnus of Norway, 109, 112-13
Magnus, son of Harold
  Godwineson, 120
Magonsæte, 38, 41-3
Malcolm Canmore, 123-5,
  155, 165
Maldon, battle of, 139
  poem, 80, 139
Margaret, St, queen, xi, 122-6,
  155, 165
Marsworth, land at, 95, 186n44
Matilda, abbess of Essen, 152
Matilda, daughter of St Margaret,
  wife of Henry I, 125
Medeshamstede, 13
  and see Peterborough
Mercian Register (annals of
  Æthelflæd), 62-4, 66-7, 181n52
Merefin, 38
Merewalh of the *Magonsæte*,
  38-9, 40-3, 177n43
Mildburg, St, 38-9, 41-3, 162,
  177n37
  Life of, 37
  Testament of, 38-9, 41-3
Mildfrith, 38-40
Mildgyth, 38, 40
Mildrith, St, 38-42, 136, 162-3
  Legend of, (including *þa
    halgan*), 33-5, 37-41, 162
Milton Regis, abbey, 33
Minster-in-Thanet – *see* Thanet
Monastic Reform (Benedictine),
  xiv, 80, 83-4, 90, 92-4, 139,
  143, 154, 161
Morcar, earl of Northumbria,
  118-19, 121, 151
Morcar, thegn, 102-06, 109
Much Wenlock – *see* Wenlock

Nechtanesmere, battle of, 22
Nennius, 7, 131-2
  see also *Historia Brittonum*
Nest, princess, 119
Nicholas of Worcester, 86
Nidd, River, synod of, 23
Normandy, 100-02, 106-07,
  110-11, 115, 191n47
Northampton, 118
  see also Ælfgifu of
    Northampton
Norway, 108
Nunnaminster, Winchester, 61,
  78, 164, 185n33
  see also Winchester

Œthelwald, son of Oswald of
  Northumbria, 10, 12,
  169nn30, 34
Offa, king of Mercia, xiv, xv,
  45-50, 52-3, 56, 59, 134, 154
Ordgar, ealdorman, 90
Ordo, coronation, 72, 107, 128,
  183n6
  and see Coronations
Ordulf, brother of Queen
  Ælfthryth, 98
Osbern of Canterbury, 86
Osbert de Clare, 78, 164
Osburh, mother of Alfred the
  Great, 61, 138
Osferth, 60-1
Osgyth – *see* Osith
Oshere of the *Hwicce*, 14,
  135, 148
Osith, St, 148-9
Osred, king, son of Aldfrith of
  Northumbria, 22-3, 136, 173n75

Osthryth, daughter of Oswiu &
  Eanflæd, wife of Æthelred of
  Mercia, xv, 14-16, 42, 46, 133,
  135, 171nn49-50
Oswald, *filius regis*, 61
Oswald, king of Northumbria, 3,
  8-10, 12, 15, 24, 26, 29, 67, 153,
  169nn30,34, 173n67, 182n52
Oswald, St, bishop of Worcester,
  archbishop of York, 80, 90, 94,
  187n70
  Life of, 92
Oswine, king of Deira, 2-3, 8-11,
  169nn31, 34, 36
Oswiu, king of Northumbria, xv,
  3, 9-21, 23-4, 26, 33-4, 133,
  153, 155, 169nn31, 34, 36
Osyth – *see* Osith
Otto, emperor, 74-5
Oxford, 66, 109, 118, 162

Pallig, 152
Paulinus, bishop, 5, 8, 20
Pavia, Italy, 51, 59, 180n37
Peada, son of Penda, 13, 38, 155,
  167n9, 170nn43, 44
Pectanege, 47, 178n9
Pega, 143-4
Penda, king of Mercia, 5, 8-9,
  12-16, 24, 34, 38, 41, 45, 52,
  119, 132-3, 153, 169n30,
  193n2, 197n79
Pershore, abbey, 78, 164
Peterborough, 13, 118, 170n43,
  188n80
  and see Medeshamstede
Pfalzel, Germany, 22, 138
Picts, 8, 17, 22, 28, 45

Rædwald, king of East Anglia, 3-6, 131, 154-5, 168n22
and see Sutton Hoo
Ragnall, 65-6
Ramsey, abbey, 111, 143
Reculver, minster, 53, 179n28
Regularis Concordia, 92-4
see also Æthelwold, St
Reichenau – *see Liber Vitæ*
Repton, Derbys, 57, 59, 180n33
Rheged, 12, 18
Rhianfellt, 12-13, 18, 170n41
Rhun, priest, 7, 20, 170n41
Richard of Normandy, count of Rouen, 99-100
Richard II, count of Normandy, 99, 101
Ripon, 23
Robert of Jumièges, 116
Roger of Wendover, 29, 48, 72, 81, 95, 97-8, 119, 132, 150-2, 171n49, 180n31
Rollason, D.W., 38, 43
Rome, 11, 23, 42, 54, 59, 108, 124, 127-8, 132, 168n15, 180n37, 194n34
Runcorn, 64

Sceargeat, 64
Scotichronicon, 123
and see Walter Bower
Seal-matrix:
Balthild, St, 130
Edith, St, 89, 164
Seaxburh, queen of Wessex, xi, 132-3, 187n61
Seaxburh, St, queen of Kent, 30-40, 157, 160-1, 175n12
Life of, 33

Shaftesbury, abbey, 61, 79, 141, 147, 163, 181n42, 188n81
Sigeferth, thegn, 102-06, 109, 189n21
Sigehelm of Kent, 77
Sigehere of East Saxons, 149
Sihtric, 72
Silflæd, testatrix, 139
Simeon of Durham, 49, 173n67
Sims-Williams, Patrick, 38, 41, 135
Siward of Northumbria, 112, 116-17
Southampton, 72, 110
St Abbs, 29-30
Stafford, 64
St Albans, Herts, 130
Stamford Bridge, battle of, 121
St Brice's Day, massacre, 100-01, 113, 152
Stenton, Doris Mary, ix, xi
Stenton, Sir Frank, 40, 109
Stoke-by-Nayland, Suffolk, 139
Stone, Staffs, 36
Streaneshealh, - see Whitby
Sutton Hoo, 3, 131
and see Rædwald
Swegn, son of Godwine, 116, 147-8
Swein Forkbeard, 102-05, 111, 151-2
Swein, nephew of Godwine, 112
Swein, son of Cnut, 104, 108

Tamworth, 64-5, 67-8, 144
Tauberbischofsheim, 134
and see Leoba, abbess
Taunton, Somerset, xi, 132

Tawdry, 30, 161
    see also Æthelthryth, St
Tette, mother of Guthlac, 144
Tette, sister of Ine of Wessex, 144
Tettenhall, battle of, 63
Textiles:
    embroidery, xiv, xv, 76, 78, 114,
        124, 131, 135, 141-2, 152
    cloth, xiv, 107, 124, 131, 135-6,
        141-2
    and see Godwebb
Ða halgan – see Mildrith, St,
    Legend of
Thanet, minster, vi, xiii, 17,
    38-40, 42, 53, 136, 159, 162,
    179n28
    Isle of, 39-40
Thietmar of Merseburg, 106
Theodore, archbishop of
    Canterbury, 23
Thomas of Marlborough, 56-7
Thored, 97, 99
Three Fragments, 63, 65, 67
Threekingham, Lincs, 37
Thunor, servant, 39
Tondberht of the South *Gyrwe*, 24
Tostig, earl, son of Godwine, 116-
    18, 120-1, 129
Trent, battle of the, 15-16, 21, 33,
    171n49
Turgot, bishop, 123-5

Ufegeat, 104
    and see Blinding
Uhtred of Northumbria, 101,
    105-06, 146
Uscfrea, son of Æthelburh
    'Tate', 7-8

Walcher, bishop of
    Durham, 121
Walter Bower, 123-4
    and see Scotichronicon
Waltham Abbey, 120
Waltheof, earl, son of Siward of
    Northumbria, 117
Wantage, 61, 185n33
Wareham, 95, 159
Warwick, 64
Weardbyrig, 64, 68-9, 182n58
Wenlock, minster, xiii, 41-2, 67,
    137, 162
Werburg, St, 36-7, 41, 160, 163,
    176n23
    Life of, 37, 163, 176n23
Werferth, bishop, 67
Wergild, 39
Wherwell, abbey, 95, 99, 116-17,
    156, 185n33, 192n67
Whitby, abbey, xiii, 12, 18-19,
    21-2, 133, 138, 154, 161-2,
    172nn59, 60, 64, 173n67
    Synod of, 12, 18, 21, 23
Whitelock, Dorothy, 139
Widsið, poem, xii
Wight, Isle of, 138
Wiglaf, king of Mercia, 56-7, 134,
    178n10
Wigmund, 56-7
Wigstan, St, 57, 180n33
Wihtburh, daughter of King Anna,
    31-2, 35
Wihtred, king of Kent, 35, 40
Wilburh, daughter of Penda,
    148-9, 197n79
Wilfrid, St, bishop, 11, 20, 23-9,
    130, 134, 154-5, 172n61

Life of, 11, 23, 25, 36, 130, 161, 173n73

William of Jumièges, 152

William of Malmesbury, 17, 20, 23, 28, 34-9, 43, 54, 67-8, 71-2, 74, 77-8, 87-90, 95, 108, 114, 121-2, 132, 148, 152, 161, 163

William of Normandy, 121-2, 151
Life of, 112, 121

William of Poitiers, 112, 121

Wilton, abbey, 75-6, 84, 86, 88-9, 114-15, 117, 122, 156, 164-5, 184n17, 186n40, 192n67

Wimborne, abbey, xiii, 17-18, 23, 144, 147, 159, 171n52, 196n73

Winchcombe, abbey, xiii, 47, 53-5, 57, 60, 134, 178n10, 179n25
annals of, 53

Winchester, 109-10, 112-13, 156
New Minster, 61, 75-8, 83-4, 115, 121, 156, 159
Charter, 83, 91, 94, 98
and see Liber Vitæ
Old Minster, 98
St Mary's – *see* Nunnaminster

Winwæd, battle of, 12-13, 15, 18, 24, 34, 169n30

Wolverhampton, 145

Wormleighton, Warks, 146

Worr, ealdorman, 50-2

Wulfgeat, 145

Wulfgyth, testatrix, 93

Wulfheah, 104
and see Blinding

Wulfhere, king of Mercia, 24, 34-6, 38-9, 42, 134-5, 148, 155, 160, 170n43

Wulfhild, daughter of Æthelred II, 97

Wulfhild, St, abbess of Barking, 86, 95
Life of, 86

Wulfnoth, father of Godwine, 109

Wulfred, archbishop of Canterbury, 53-4, 159, 179nn27, 28

Wulfric Spott, 103, 109, 144

Wulfrun, 14, 144-5

Wulfsige, 145

Wulfthryth, abbess, mother of St Edith, 86-8, 90, 95, 164

Wulfthryth, wife of Æthelred I of Wessex, 59, 73

Wulfwaru, testatrix, 138, 142

Wynflæd, litigant, 98, 146

Wynflæd, mother of Ælfgifu of Shaftesbury, 79, 141, 163

Wynflæd, testatrix, 85, 141-2

Wynfrith – *see* Boniface, St

Ymme, wife of Eadbald of Kent, 34

York, 2, 7, 26, 60, 64, 89, 118, 172n57
archbishopric, 23

Yorke, Barbara, 6

Yorkshire, North, 49, 162